A.Br.

22-12.19

COLLECTOR'S DAUGHTER

Karj's

The Untold Burrell Story

Sue Stephen – was
someone I saw often
and knew all the
Glasgow boys! her
husband was on often
+ Sandy Stalters

A. R=tt.

Kailjui

2015

COLLECTOR'S DAUGHTER

The Untold Burrell Story

SMO Stephen

ISBN: 978-0-9562013-1-7

(First edition published in 2014 by
Glasgow Museums under ISBN: 978-1-908638-05-2)

Reprinted in 2015 by
Susan Mary Orr Stephen

Designed and typeset by Mark Blackadder

Printed in the UK

Contents

Foreword

Sir Peter Hutchison, Bart
First Trustee, Sir William Burrell's Trust

Sir William Burrell was an intensely private person. He shunned the press, relatively few photographs exist, and a sketch for the *Bailie* magazine was the nearest he came to having his portrait painted. It is generally known that the origin of his fortune lay in some extremely shrewd shipping deals, but many visitors to Pollok Park must have wondered about the background and family life of this lifelong passionate collector.

This memoir of his only daughter Marion, later Silvia, tells the story with skill and sympathy. It bears the authentic stamp of personal knowledge and meticulous research. Many novels maintain the tension with the reader through a sense of impending disaster, but this is real life and the denouement in Hutton Castle is as dark and gothic as any of the medieval treasures in the castle rooms. One can only speculate if the relationship between father and daughter had developed differently whether the destination of the collection might have changed.

The publication of this book comes as the thirtieth anniversary of the Burrell Collection's opening is being celebrated, and plans are being laid for a substantial refurbishment of the museum. It is very appropriate that this intimate family story will now give a greater understanding and background to one of the most generous donations of works of art in the history of the United Kingdom.

Kippen, 2013

Acknowledgements

When my godmother died in 1992 I resolved to record her story because I was already aware that she had led a most extraordinary life. I had never attempted to write a book or expected to uncover a fascinating Burrell history, let alone a unique insight into the world of Sir William Burrell. Largely due to my family circumstances, the project dragged on for more than two decades.

Without the help of Janet Bell-Irving I could never have begun. As Marion Burrell's cousin, as well as her Trustee, Janet kindly allowed me to have the vital research material which lay in my godmother's flat. Armed with Marion's address books I was able to contact her numerous friends and relations. Letters sped far and wide while journeys through the UK allowed me to make more than 50 recorded interviews. Suddenly I discovered a host of new friends, and Marion would have been pleased because she loved making introductions. Having basked in their warmth and cherished their memories, I am sad that so few of these good people have lived to read this book because those who deserve my greatest thanks are no longer here to witness the fulfilment of their contributions. Most of all I regret the absence of one of Marion's dearest friends, Caird Wilson, who entrusted me with her personal memoirs.

Invaluable help and archive information has been supplied by my friends at the Burrell Collection/Glasgow Museums as well as by Carol Murphy at the Balfron Library and by librarians here and across the globe. Richard Drew, publisher of Burrell's biography, has given me generous support, while my literary efforts have been greatly enhanced through the guidance of Michael Horniman. Sound advice has also been welcomed from Dr Richard Marks, Rosemary Reid-Kay, Fiona Robertson and the late Bobby Younger. I would have been lost without Susan Miller's expertise in genealogy, Pat Thomson's technical skills and Graham Flett's unfailing attention to the tiresome mysteries of my computer. My whole-hearted thanks are gratefully offered to every one of the kind people who supported my protracted labours.

My gratitude to my husband and family for sustaining me through the interminable process of getting this book completed is more than I could ever express.

Introduction

The city of Glasgow celebrated a long awaited event when Her Majesty Queen Elizabeth II opened the Burrell Collection on 21 October 1983. Unfortunately Sir William Burrell the collector did not live to enjoy his triumph because he had died in 1958 at the age of 96. Twenty years later his daughter had performed a public ceremony by 'cutting the sod' in Pollok Park so that building could begin on the museum which now houses the Collection. In some quarters, Miss Burrell's enthusiasm for this task came as a surprise because she and her parents had been for many years estranged.

The rift had occurred in 1950 when Marion Burrell fled from her home at Hutton Castle, never to return. To the outside world the cause of this disaster remained a mystery, as did her decision, late in life, to change her name to 'Silvia'. Sir William, who guarded his privacy, would not have welcomed revelations which his daughter withheld while she lived, but now their conflicts can safely rest among the pages of history.

The lady who rejected her given name was my very dear godmother. Having been born to a life of privilege, persistent clashes between passion and parental power destroyed her dreams and made her lurch from wealth to poverty. With inborn grit she endured it all, learning to smile through adversity. Those who knew Burrell's daughter found her endearing, captivating, fascinating, dominating and sometimes downright infuriating. Her zest for life was insatiable and unforgettable. My interest was kindly received, and after she died I was allowed to inherit the evidence she had carefully preserved, ensuring that in the end her story could be told. In addition to the bond we shared, family links have allowed me to record an extraordinary saga which would otherwise have been forever lost.

Sue Stephen
Balfron, 2013

Timeline

1692   William Burrell, the *Forefather*, comes to Bassington.

1782   His grandson, George Burrell the *Gambler*, sells out to the Duke of Northumberland.

1880   The *Gambler's* grandson, George Burrell the *Grafter*, is born in Alnwick.

1814   George the *Gambler* dies as a tenant still living at Bassington.

1820s George the *Grafter* comes north and finds employment at the port of Leith, near Edinburgh.

1831   George marries Janet Houston (his 2nd wife) and moves to Port Dundas, Glasgow.

1832   William Burrell the *Entrepreneur* is born.

1856 Burrell and Son is founded by George the *Grafter* and his son, William the *Entrepreneur*, William marries Isabella Guthrie in December.

1861 William Burrell the *Collector* is born in Glasgow (their 3rd child).

1872 The Burrells move to Bowling on the Forth and Clyde Canal.

1873 Mary Burrell (their youngest child) is born at Bowling.

1875 William the *Collector* leaves school and joins Burrell and Son.

1876 Constance Mitchell is born.

1880 Burrell and Son move their Glasgow office from Port Dundas to George Square, Glasgow.

1881 George the *Grafter* dies.

1885 William the *Entrepreneur* dies.

1891 The Burrells move to Devonshire Gardens in Great Western Road, Glasgow.

1901 Mary Burrell marries Ralston Mitchell in January; Queen Victoria dies; William Burrell marries Constance Mitchell in September.

1902 Marion Burrell is born at Great Western Terrace.

1909 Grandma Mitchell dies in September; Marion,
      aged seven, launches the *Strathlorne* in October.

1912 Grandma (Isabella) Burrell dies.

1914 Marion attends Laurel Bank School in Glasgow;
      World War I breaks out.

1916 William Burrell buys Hutton Castle; Marion is sent
      to boarding school at Heathfield near Ascot.

1917 Kilduff in East Lothian is rented.

1919 Rozelle in Ayrshire is rented.

1921 Marion attends a 'finishing' school in Paris; her
      engagement to Captain Leslie Watson is broken off
      and never announced.

1922–3 The Burrells tour India, Burma and Ceylon.

1925 Broxmouth Park in East Lothian is rented;
      Marion's first London Season with Florence, Lady
      Garvagh.

1926 General Strike in Britain.

1927 Marion's second London Season with Lady
      Clodagh Anson; William Burrell is knighted.

1929   Marion's engagement to the Hon. John Benson is broken off.

1931   Marion's engagement to the Hon. Patrick Balfour is broken off.

1932   Marion's love affair with Major Sholto Douglas.

1935   Marion's love affair with the Spanish diplomat Jose Plaza.

1939   Burrell and Son finally closes; World War II breaks out.

1940   Marion serves as a volunteer nurse at Peel Hospital, Selkirk, then at Edenhall Hospital.

1944   Sir William Burrell presents his Collection to the City of Glasgow.

1948   Marion's affair with a mysterious foreigner called 'Matthew'.

1950   Marion escapes from Hutton Castle; for a year she serves as Matron at Newlands School in Sussex.

1951   Marion mostly stays with her Mitchell relations at Perceton.

1952   Ralston Mitchell dies; Marion travels and works in South Africa, Australia and New Zealand.

1954 On returning to Scotland Marion rents rooms in South Queensferry.

1958 William Burrell dies at Hutton Castle, aged 96.

1960 Marion buys a home of her own at Findhorn Place, Edinburgh.

1961 Constance Burrell dies at Hutton Castle, aged 85.

1964 Mary Mitchell dies at Perceton.

1978 Marion changes her name to 'Silvia' and cuts the sod for the Burrell Collection building in Pollok Park, Glasgow.

1983 Her Majesty Queen Elizabeth II opens the Burrell Collection.

1992 Marion Burrell dies at Findhorn Place, aged 89.

1993 The *Silvia Burrell* lifeboat is named at Girvan.

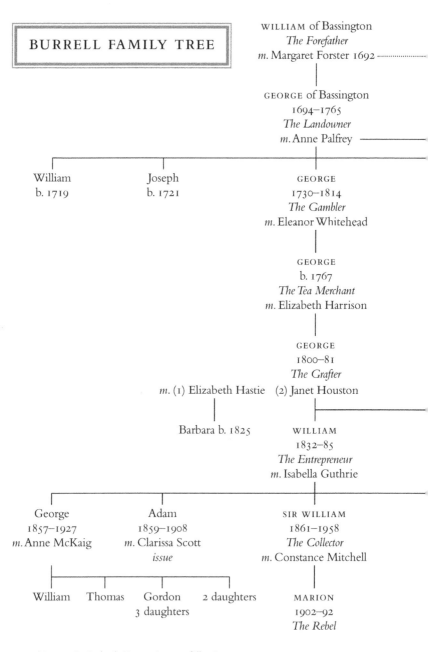

BURRELL FAMILY TREE

WILLIAM of Bassington
The Forefather
m. Margaret Forster 1692 ······················

GEORGE of Bassington
1694–1765
The Landowner
m. Anne Palfrey ──────────

William
b. 1719

Joseph
b. 1721

GEORGE
1730–1814
The Gambler
m. Eleanor Whitehead

GEORGE
b. 1767
The Tea Merchant
m. Elizabeth Harrison

GEORGE
1800–81
The Grafter
m. (1) Elizabeth Hastie   (2) Janet Houston

Barbara b. 1825

WILLIAM
1832–85
The Entrepreneur
m. Isabella Guthrie

George
1857–1927
m. Anne McKaig

Adam
1859–1908
m. Clarissa Scott
issue

SIR WILLIAM
1861–1958
The Collector
m. Constance Mitchell

William   Thomas   Gordon   2 daughters
3 daughters

MARION
1902–92
The Rebel

★Appears in Author's Connections on following page

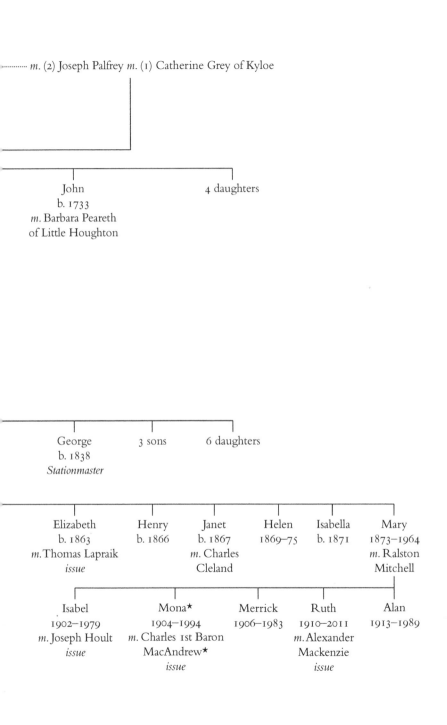

m. (2) Joseph Palfrey   *m.* (1) Catherine Grey of Kyloe

John
b. 1733
m. Barbara Peareth
of Little Houghton

4 daughters

George
b. 1838
Stationmaster

3 sons   6 daughters

Elizabeth
b. 1863
m. Thomas Lapraik
issue

Henry
b. 1866

Janet
b. 1867
m. Charles
Cleland

Helen
1869–75

Isabella
b. 1871

Mary
1873–1964
m. Ralston
Mitchell

Isabel
1902–1979
m. Joseph Hoult
issue

Mona★
1904–1994
m. Charles 1st Baron
MacAndrew★
issue

Merrick
1906–1983

Ruth
1910–2011
m. Alexander
Mackenzie
issue

Alan
1913–1989

THE AUTHOR'S CONNECTIONS

THOMSON

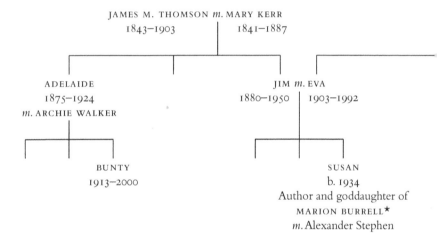

JAMES M. THOMSON *m.* MARY KERR
1843–1903 | 1841–1887

ADELAIDE
1875–1924
m. ARCHIE WALKER

JIM *m.* EVA
1880–1950 | 1903–1992

BUNTY
1913–2000

SUSAN
b. 1934
Author and goddaughter of
MARION BURRELL★
m. Alexander Stephen

Those marked ★ are also on the Burrell Family Tree

Jim Thomson and Eva MacAndrew were second cousins because the
mothers of Mary Glen Kerr and Francis Glen MacAndrew were sisters,
Agnes and Janet Orr, whose brother Sir Andrew Orr also appears in the
text.

MACANDREW

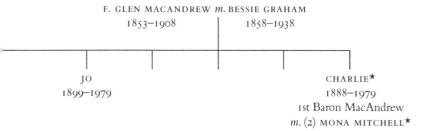

F. GLEN MACANDREW *m.* BESSIE GRAHAM
1853–1908 | 1858–1938

JO
1899–1979

CHARLIE★
1888–1979
1st Baron MacAndrew
m. (2) MONA MITCHELL★

CHAPTER I

Marion

At Hutton Castle in Berwickshire, Sir William Burrell's household had erupted in a burst of activity as everyone became immersed in preparations for a joyful family occasion. Guests had been invited and the celebration planned. Busy days were interrupted by deliveries of costly wedding gifts, and final fittings for the bridal gown had already been completed. The year was 1931, and the great event was rapidly approaching when, 12 days before her smart London wedding was due to take place, the bride opened the morning paper and gazed in disbelief. Her eyes fixed on a devastating announcement:

'The marriage arranged between the Honourable Patrick Balfour and Miss Marion Burrell will not take place.'

Neither Marion nor the man about to claim her hand had authorized this bombshell. Yet, with his wife's full agreement, Sir William had inserted the declaration without the knowledge of bride or groom. With a single stroke this brief printed statement destroyed their daughter's hopes of married happiness. How could her parents treat her in this way?

From the beginning Marion's life was far from common-place. She was the only child of an ambitious man accustomed to success. William Burrell first found fame as a Glasgow ship owner, and having made his fortune in the world of commerce he became a leading collector in the world of fine arts. An autocrat who went his own way, he thought and acted differently from other men. Burrell's daughter was also destined to be different as she would bear the stamp imprinted by her father.

When Marion was seven years old, a significant event took place which was to become permanently etched on her memory. One chilly October morning in 1909 her parents had taken her to Dumbarton, where a new ship was to be launched. On arrival at the shipyard they were welcomed by gentlemen with bowler hats, and joined by others with smartly dressed ladies whose stylish plumes seemed out of place in the drab surroundings. There was an air of anticipation as the party set out through a sprawling labyrinth of workshops and lofty iron cranes.

The child looked eagerly about her. She was neatly buttoned against the cold with cheeks aglow and fair curls escaping beneath her velvet hat. As she trotted to keep pace, her small hand was firmly gripped by a mother who did not encourage childish exuberance. Constance Burrell looked steadily before her, showing no sign of parental warmth. Tightly laced and superbly tailored, Burrell's wife presented an elegant figure discreetly enhanced by her matchless jewels and furs.

The visitors trod warily, avoiding muddy puddles as workers with cloth caps and grimy faces watched them going by. The shipyard clangour was dying away as most of the men had already downed tools – tradition allowed them to take a break when a ship was being launched. Men who laboured through the seasons would see the hull that they created instantly transformed upon entering the element where ships can voyage to the ends of the earth. During the reign of King Robert the Bruce his galleys were built here on the Leven, and by the twentieth century shipyards had been established in the basin where the waters of Loch Lomond flow into the River Clyde.

Shipbuilding had long been a family affair while men worked together in close knit squads. The shipyard of Archibald McMillan and Son had been owned by their family for three generations, and the vessel they were about to launch – a new cargo ship for Burrell and Son – would be family-owned as well. As the launch party neared the slipway the crowd had grown so dense that space had to be made for the guests to pass. The platform gathering was dominated by a tall silver-haired man with a bristling moustache and an unmistakable aura of authority. Beneath heavy brows the penetrating eyes of William Burrell observed the scene where Dumbarton's ruined castle looks down from the rock. In boyhood he had roamed among the ancient walls and crags, but today his mind was fixed on the matter in hand.

Tugs were standing by to take charge of the new ship. The tide was slowly rising and launching conditions were good; the recent gales were over and no strong gusts were threatening to swing the ship. William Burrell watched intently, not missing a thing though he had witnessed many launches. His competitors were floored by his phenomenal success. 'They watch me making money like slate stones' he once said, for his scheme was to sell the entire Burrell fleet during a boom and invest the proceeds until there was a slump. Then, when shipyards were crying out for work, he would take advantage of rock bottom prices and order large numbers of ships to be ready for trade when business recovered. The strategy was simple, though one that few would dare to emulate. There had been a slump during the previous year, and while others cut back to sit out the recession, Burrell had ordered eight ships. Four had already been launched.

Now another was about to join her sisters, but this launch would be a special one because the sponsor who would name the ship was William Burrell's daughter. That morning, at their home in Glasgow, Marion's day had begun in a flurry of excitement when her lessons were abandoned to prepare for the event. She was already aware of her father's position and intensely proud of the Burrell fleet, but when they set out on the train for Dumbarton she had no idea that she would be asked to launch the ship. The news came as a shock. When her parents explained that the invited sponsor was indisposed, Marion quickly asked why her mother did not perform the ceremony. 'It would not be the done thing', she was told; Constance was in mourning for her mother who had died four weeks before.

As Marion tried to prepare herself for her unexpected task the suspense seemed almost unbearable. Standing there in her button boots the child felt breathless and dwarfed among the grown ups. Time seemed to have stopped while everyone stood about waiting. Seagulls were squealing overhead when a gentleman pulled out his pocket watch and quietly checked the time. It was almost midday, but still the waiting dragged on as the launching of a ship is not governed by the clock, but by the never-ending rhythm of the tide. Slack water is vital for the safety of a launch and the critical moment had not yet come.

The young sponsor gazed aloft and wondered if that towering mass of steel could really move. The hull was longer than a football pitch and as high as a two-storey house. Where the narrow bow loomed above the platform a bottle of champagne was hanging on a cord. Almost before she had time to blink it was thrust into her hands. Grasping the precious missile Marion squared for action. Without hesitation she took a deep breath and called out the words she had rehearsed: 'I name this ship *Strathlorne*. May God bless her and all who sail in her'.

Many years later she recorded her experience:

> In those far off days, there was no nonsense about pressing a button. On the contrary, you had to throw the bottle of champagne with all your might. It was reinforced with red, white and blue ribbons thus making it harder to break, and the whole operation had to be accomplished as the ship had started to move out. After an interminable wait to the sound of hammering as the blocks supporting her were loosened, a shout went up, she started to move, and I flung the bottle with all my strength. But it was not enough, and the bottle swung back unbroken. For a ship to go out unchristened is regarded by seamen and owners alike, as bad luck. Foreseeing this, a great giant had been stationed behind me, and as the bottle swung back he grasped it and flung it at the retreating bow. It crashed and broke and as the champagne trickled down a cheer went up.

'Three cheers for the *Strathlorne*!' With a pounding heart the little girl watched her ship depart. Hardly moving at first, the vessel seemed reluctant to leave, then almost imperceptibly she gathered momentum sliding farther and faster till the monstrous wall of steel was charging with the force of an avalanche. *Strathlorne* entered the water and bobbed a graceful curtsey which sent her wash splashing about the Leven. When the tumult was over, the dark hull of the new merchant ship lay silhouetted in the basin. Suddenly the tension broke as the platform party converged in a chorus of chatter. Grown ups were paying compliments and fussing over Marion. Lost for words, she gave them all her most beguiling smile, while feeling as if her heart might burst from this unfamiliar deluge of happiness.

William Burrell's daughter rose to the occasion just as he knew that she would. During her journey in the train she had hung on his words while he explained to her the whole exciting process of the launch. She longed to please him, and that day Marion had indeed fulfilled her father's expectations. The hitch with the bottle was by no means unusual and did nothing to mar her success. In that long forgotten era when children were 'seen and not heard', it was a new experience to find herself publicly fêted. The launch was followed by a formal luncheon with the sponsor seated in a place of honour next to the company chairman. When the meal ended with speeches and toasts Marion was delighted to find herself being treated like a grown up. Constance was, however, somewhat disapproving of excessive attention being lavished on her daughter.

Tradition dictates that the builders present the sponsor of a launch with a gift to mark the occasion. As the lady who withdrew had requested a brooch, Marion was thrilled when Mr McMillan invited her to come and choose one. The child was almost overwhelmed when confronted by the gorgeous items of jewellery displayed in a row of silk-lined boxes. In the end she picked an elegant crescent exquisitely set with rubies. But it seemed a little elderly for a very small girl, so afterwards her father asked the jeweller to exchange it. It was typical of Burrell's sense of fun that he chose for his daughter a charming brooch in the form of a turtle made with diamonds surrounding a huge baroque pearl. Marion was enchanted, and thus began her lifelong love of jewellery.

Two other Clyde launches shared the same tide, and next day the morning papers gave news of the *Gloucester* which had been launched at Dalmuir by the Duchess of Montrose. Though details of the Burrell ship were also reported there was no mention of Marion. William Burrell did not encourage publicity, but he was content for the *Glasgow Herald* to announce that the vessel she had launched was fully equipped with the modern benefit of electric light.

Strathlorne was destined to be a lucky ship with a life at sea which would span three decades. When back in her schoolroom at Great Western Terrace Marion made herself a special album with photos of 'her' ship and on the cover she painted the company flag, a blue swallowtail with a white circle emblazoned by a red cross.

Today, *Strathlorne's* birthplace is greatly changed. The shipyards have gone and the Leven is a quieter place. Warehouses have replaced the busy slipways and the basin seems so narrow it is hard to imagine the big launches that once took place. By the time *Strathlorne's* sponsor reached the end of her life, Dumbarton Castle was overlooking a peaceful waterway with swans gliding between moored motor boats and trim white yachts, while on the riverside cherry trees flowered by a pub where old hands still met and remembered the famous shipyards.

CHAPTER 2

From Bassington to Bowling

The Burrells lived in the west end of Glasgow where Marion's childhood home formed part of a massive terrace designed by Alexander 'Greek' Thomson. It was a treasure house filled with rare and beautiful objets d'art collected by her father. In 1901, the year before his child was born, Glasgow had held an International Exhibition to celebrate Scotland's achievements and William Burrell had been publicly acclaimed for lending generously from his collection. As he watched the visitors marvel at his works of art the collector glowed inwardly with silent satisfaction.

Like those of all ambitious men, Burrell's plans were expansive. While urban industrialists were buying country houses he contemplated nothing less than a castle, and it would have to be a capacious one. Though castellated houses were in favour at the time, a genuine Scottish castle seemed the ideal home for his family and even more so for his rapidly increasing collection. For years he had nurtured this romantic dream because his medieval tapestries, stained glass and oak coffers were crying out for a baronial setting, and having fixed his goal he had no doubt that the castle he yearned for would one day be found.

William Burrell's ancestors had come a long way and now he intended to leave his own mark. Many centuries ago Burrells had migrated from France and settled in various parts of England. William was descended from a landed family who once owned Bassington, near Alnwick in Northumberland (Burrell family tree p.xviii). In 1692 the first William Burrell of Bassington had received this residence with over 200 acres of farmland as a wedding gift from his father, George Burrell of Chibburn in the chapelry of Widdrington.

William Burrell of Bassington fathered a dynasty of Georges. His own son, George, succeeded to the property, but when his grandson followed, this George disgraced them all and gambled away his inheritance. Gambler George's family fell on hard times and because no property remained to inherit, his son had to go off to Alnwick and earn his living as a tea merchant. This was a come down, even though the tea trade was considered a gentlemanly profession. The tea merchant's daughter continued the business, but the trade at Alnwick offered little to sustain his sons.

Stage coaches rumbled down the Great North Road bringing news of prospects in Scotland, where a canal now spanned the Lowlands, linking the Firths of Forth and Clyde. New factories and warehouses were springing up and business there was thriving. The tea merchant's eldest son took note and saw his opportunity to make good. This young George Burrell was a grafter who left his home in Northumberland and travelled north to seek his fortune.

Grafter George was the Collector's grandfather. Hordes of manual workers were clamouring for a share of the new prosperity, but George came from an educated family and was able to find employment as a clerk. His first place of work was at the port of Leith near Edinburgh. He married there and sired a daughter, but his wife died, probably in childbirth. With a young child to support, George badly needed a wife and before long married again. His second wife was Janet Houston, a strong and hardy young woman, and the daughter of a carpet manufacturer from the Renfrewshire village of Houston. George and Janet made their home in Glasgow and 11 more children were born.

The Burrells could not have chosen a worse time or place to raise their family. Because of the great industrial boom a population explosion had caused hardship and overcrowding of such magnitude that Glasgow was said to have become the unhealthiest city in Europe. The hazards of urban life were a nightmare, and while slum conditions continued to spread, crime was rife with people struggling for survival among the city streets. In areas without sanitation or clean water lanes ran with sewage, and heaps of excrement were cleared by night to be used as fertilizer. The poor were half starved and sparsely clad, most of them barefoot. Foul air invaded every home, and due to this prevalent filth and disease at least five of the Burrells' offspring fell sick and died in childhood.

With grim determination George and Janet somehow managed to nurture and educate their surviving children. They lived in a tenement in New City Road, near Port Dundas, where barges came laden with iron, coal, cotton and foodstuffs as well as passengers. The noisy terminal on the canal clamoured with shouting men and heavy horses. Folk called the place 'the Harbour on the Hill'. Though the city buzzed with activity, times were hard for the Burrells so George put in long hours of work while Janet scrimped and saved. As soon as their sons were old enough they too were put to work. The eldest was called William, a big brawny lad with a strong sense of purpose and a cheerful outlook on life.

As the Burrell family forged ahead, their prospects started to improve and George's painful years of grafting at last began to reward him. Fortune had smiled on them because young William was not only remarkably bright, he was fired with the will to succeed. George recognized his son's ability, and when he reached 24, father and son made a masterly decision. They set up a shipping business together on the Forth and Clyde Canal, and so, in 1856, the famous company of Burrell and Son was founded. From the start, William Burrell was recorded as 'ship owner' and his father as 'shipping clerk'. Their fleet began humbly with two canal boats, one of them named the *Janet Houston* after William's mother.

William had ambitions in more than one direction; as he also had an eye for the girls, he had been courting. The object of his love was Isabella Guthrie, a fine-looking Glasgow lass, tall and capable with a lively brain to match his own, and it was not long before the young couple became engaged. However, their wedding had to be delayed because William was made to wait for months while his lovely Isabella accompanied her father on a long sea voyage by sailing ship to New Zealand. She was no ordinary girl. The marriage of William and Isabella took place on 31 December 1856 and so the year of Burrell and Son's inauguration ended with a family celebration.

The birth of George and Janet's youngest child had taken place during that triumphant year and after William and Isabella came to live in nearby Scotia Street, there was another birth – Janet and George's first grandchild. William fathered yet another George, who was then followed by

Adam, and in 1861 a third son arrived when a new William Burrell joined his brothers. As this tiny infant made his entry in a three-room tenement flat, nobody guessed that one day he would become a great man and bring fame to his native city.

By this time, the world in which the Burrells lived had undergone more change because industries were burgeoning and products were being shipped to the farthest outposts of the world. Prosperity had brought railways, gas light and clean water. With new schools and hospitals, theatres and banks, Glasgow had been transformed and become Britain's Second City. After all the struggles of his forebears, wee Willie Burrell had timed his entrance well.

As his ambitious parents forged ahead they followed the trend by moving to the west of the city where fresh winds could waft away the acrid sooty smoke. A larger flat was found in Willowbank Street, near the new West End Park surrounding Kelvingrove House, and as their progeny increased Isabella applied her skills in managing her household. It was the first home Willie Burrell would remember. Tenement life was primitive then, with meals cooked on an open fire and laundering done in the communal washhouse. When tap water first reached tenement sinks it had to be heated in kettles, and bath time was a weekly affair with turns in the tub after father. At least it was cosy in front of the kitchen fire, because the first tenement bathrooms were like prison cells. Earth privies were 'out the back', and when indoor sanitation was introduced, neighbours had to share a dingy closet on the landing. Having suffered these early discomforts Willie developed a lifelong fetish which drove him to install modern bathrooms with all the latest fittings in every house that he owned.

From an early age the boy asked questions. He wanted to know about his mother's travels when he came upon green stone trinkets made by Maoris or scrimshaw work that sailors carved on the bones of whales. Home industries still flourished in Glasgow, with weavers working on their looms and women making lace and beadwork. Every kind of craft intrigued him. Though most children want to be one of the crowd, young Burrell was happy to be different and showed his independence from the start. While his siblings were playing games in the yard other things intrigued him. When visiting neighbours he would contemplate the candlesticks, musical boxes and china 'wally' dogs displayed in their parlours, and when he was permitted, handling these objects may have prompted his observation that the quality of an item can often be guessed from its weight.

While Glasgow prospered, overcrowding continued and Willie often witnessed hardship. Knowing that members of his family had striven to survive had made him learn the merit of economy – 'Waste not, want not' was a lesson he would never forget. As soon as he was old enough, Willie Burrell began his own career in commerce as a newspaper boy, delivering papers each morning before school.

Meanwhile Burrell and Son forged ahead but, with the advent of railways, activity on the canal had begun to decline. While the Burrells continued to own canal boats and handle inland cargoes, they extended their interests to the coastal trade, and then began conveying cargoes to the Mediterranean. When Willie was ten years old the company ships were voyaging as far as India, via the new Suez Canal. As Burrell and Son became established in world shipping George continued to hold shares in the canal boats while the new ships were held in the name of his son.

As they continued to prosper the Burrell family left Glasgow and moved to Bowling, conveniently situated on the Forth and Clyde Canal. The village of Bowling was at the canal's western terminus and in 1872 Willie's father bought a villa there called Elmbank. Like other villas which were springing up around the Firth of Clyde, Elmbank stood in its own garden. It was to be their family home for almost two decades. The unpretentious two-storey house was built in stone with a gabled roof. It had a gleaming kitchen range, modern bathroom fittings and all the desirable attributes of a Victorian ideal home where two domestic servants were employed. The following year, on a stormy Christmas Day, the Burrells' youngest child was born. Mary's arrival completed their family of nine. Isabella was inspired to launch into verse to commemorate this happy occasion:

> Mary, thou art my youngest
> And well-beloved child
> You came when snow was on the Earth
> And winds blew fierce and wild.
> It was the day when Christ was born
> That day the angels sang
> Peace and goodwill. Goodwill and peace
> Far out their voices rang.
> Peace and goodwill to thee my child
> And love both full and free.
> Dear God who gave his Son for us
> Did send you unto me.

While Isabella ruled her roost with an iron rod she was a warm-hearted mother who encouraged her daughters as much as her sons but, in the course of time, Willie became her most favoured son and Mary her dearest daughter. While discipline was firmly administered young Willie was lucky to be born to outstandingly able and ambitious parents. With a lively and jovial father and a creative, adventurous mother there was no shortage of humour and fun in the Burrell family. But Willie hungered for stories and listened with rapt attention to the tales of former times told by his hard grafting grandfather, George.

From the hill above Bowling the children could see Dumbarton Rock and explore the remains of the Antonine Wall. His father often wondered why Willie liked to prowl around ruins instead of joining in family games, but the tales of Sir Walter Scott had fired the boy's imagination with scenes of pageantry and battles from the past. As Burrell and Son prospered, William and Isabella could afford to send their sons off to boarding school at St Andrews in Fife. The Abbey Park Preparatory School took about 70 boys. Willie was 12 when Mary was born and had already joined his brothers. During his school days in the old cathedral town an alarming incident occurred which Marion later recorded.

As a little boy my father had a strange experience when he was at school at St Andrews. There was a holiday and it was put to the vote what the boys would like best to do. The vote was for the shore and a swim. Uncle Adam was at the school too and was a strong swimmer. My father was swimming with a bigger boy when the latter apparently got cramp. Involuntarily he clutched at the nearest thing which was my father and dragged him down. Together they sat on the sandy bottom and my father distinctly remembered incidents of his short life pass before him.

The bigger boy's brain also seems to have been ticking over as he argued coolly he was drowning but there was no necessity to drown Burrell too! With that he let go and Burrell shot to the surface like a cork shouting out that the big boy was drowning. When he surfaced it was Uncle Adam who grabbed hold of him. No master seems to have been present and the boys didn't know what to do, so resorted to the rather primitive method of holding him upside down to get rid of the sea water and this kill or cure treatment was successful. But it left a deep impression on a sensitive young mind.

Young Burrell had had a narrow escape, and his brush with death became even more poignant a short time later when his six-year-old sister Helen (Nellie) died tragically from tubercular meningitis at Millburn House, Largs, where the Burrell family spent seaside holidays. Knowing that the child had been taken from them when his own life had been spared may have intensified the urge for success which seemed to drive his life. But Willie's schooldays did not continue for long.

At 14 he entered Burrell and Son as office boy and the thing that struck his mind at this period, was rushing across the square to the GPO with telegrams. These telegrams were to form an enduring part of him. He was throughout his long life a great sender of 'telewackies' as he called them and infinitely preferred this mode of communication to either writing letters or the telephone which he rather disliked.

His father spotted him helping the ledger clerks and reckoned it a waste of time to send the lad back to school, so Willie was taken on at a clerk's salary. At Hamiltonhill, near Port Dundas, a Burrell shipyard was established on the canal to build the coastal cargo boats which became known as 'Clyde puffers'. Because the canal was narrow puffers had to be launched sideways. Burrell and Son were by then operating tramp steamers throughout the world and the firm's revenue was further increased through managing ships for other companies. In 1877 when 'Young Mr Willie' was still learning the ropes, one of the Burrell ships became involved in an extraordinary incident at sea.

> While in the Bay of Biscay, the *Fitzmaurice* encountered a great storm. One of the crew reported to the captain a large whale had been sighted. On the captain examining the object with binoculars, he announced it to be, not a whale, but the cylinder containing Cleopatra's Needle which was being towed to England and had broken loose in the storm. The question was, how to rescue it? The seas being what they were? A volunteer was called for to swim over and board her. This was duly performed by a courageous seaman. A hawser was then passed but broke. This was repeated but not till the 3rd attempt did a hawser hold. The cylinder was then towed back by the *Fitzmaurice* to Ferrol.

When Cleopatra's famous Needle finally reached its place of honour on the Thames Embankment, Willie's father received £2,000 salvage (about £154,000 today) and distributed it among the crew. The Pasha of Egypt had presented the obelisk as a gift to George IV before anyone paused to consider the problem of transporting it. Marion Burrell was always proud of the part her family firm had played.

While Willie was still in his teens he began his first forays into the world of art, and various accounts of this survive. Marion said, 'It was one of the worst garbled stories about my father' and wrote down the version he had told her.

He used to frequent the auction rooms during his brief hour off for lunch, and on one occasion was much impressed by the beauty of a portrait. This was a lady and was of Kit-kat size [three feet by two feet]. He described her as having a curl of hair hanging over one shoulder, and he decided to bid for her. The portrait fell to him at 18/-. When he went round to see his new purchase he appears to have realised for the first time that it had no frame, and as he had no more money for a frame, he told the auctioneer to put it up again. The second time it only fetched 15/-. He therefore dropped 3/- on the deal, and in the light of later knowledge always maintained it was a Raeburn.

It was about this time his love of collecting really took hold, and in his little room at Bowling, where they lived, he had a collection of landscapes by an artist called Brown. There were invariably cattle grazing and it was inevitable that the artist should become known as 'Coo Broon'. Grandfather was very out of sympathy with this trait in his offspring, and took him to task, saying he was wasting his money on such things, and would be far better to buy a cricket bat. The Coo Broons were eventually scrapped, along with a still later collection as his taste evolved.

Willie was unperturbed when his family poked fun as he always enjoyed a good laugh. With his sharp wit, infallible memory and ear for amusing stories, he became an entertaining raconteur. When telling stories in the Glasgow vernacular he always excelled. Young Burrell took stock of everything he saw and heard and from an early age he possessed remarkable perception. According to Marion, her father could walk into Woolworths and come out having picked the one item of genuine value. Value always interested him, but his penetrating curiosity was sometimes disconcerting. When visiting friends in later years, he would examine an object which caught his eye and embarrass his host by suddenly asking how much he had paid for a possession which had belonged to the family for generations.

Though Elmbank was a pleasant house Willie Burrell was becoming aware of dwellings that were even more desirable. The local castles were mostly ruined, but fine mansion houses could be seen on the banks of the Clyde. His home by the terminus of the Forth and Clyde Canal overlooked a small and busy port where traffic passed by land and sea. The railway to Glasgow served the village and Clyde steamers called there as well, so the Glasgow office of Burrell and Son was less than an hour away whether travelling by steam train or sailing up river by steamer.

Sometimes Willie chose to voyage on the Clyde as he liked to walk on deck and look around. Cruising up river gave him food for thought. Woods and parkland surrounded the gracious country houses which could be seen at Erskine, Auchentoshan and Mountblow. Since the Act of Union in 1707, Glasgow merchants had been able to prosper from transatlantic trade. The new found wealth of 'sugar barons' and 'tobacco lords' had enabled them to buy land and build grand houses where they could live in style. Willie studied their elegant mansions and wondered who was living behind the tall windows with pale linen blinds.

Abruptly the countryside became scarred by new industry on the north bank of the river where the Glasgow shipbuilders J & G Thomson had moved their company down river to a green field site. Blocks of tenements had been built to house the workforce, and the new town was to be known as 'Clydebank', a name taken from the riverside property in Glasgow where the Thomson brothers had started their company with an engine works in 1847. (James Thomson, the co-founder, was my great grandfather.) In 1899 the new Clydebank shipyard would become John Brown's, and give birth to the world's most famous liners.

Young Willie's lively sense of humour would have been tickled when Garscadden House loomed on the hill above Yoker, as tales were rife about the drunken roistering which once took place there. When the laird sank to oblivion at his own dinner table a guest was said to have enquired 'Whit gars Garscadden nae gash the nicht?' and received the reply 'Wheesht mon, he's been deid thae twa oors but I didna like tae disturb the conviviality.' (Translation for non-Scots speakers: 'Why does the laird of Garscadden not display his usual sagacity this evening?' Reply: 'Kindly lower your voice sir, our host passed away two hours ago but I refrained from mentioning it lest the company be needlessly disquieted.')

At Elderslie, Scotstoun and Blythswood more estates had been created from the wealth of the previous century, but the scene changed again as commuters neared the city. Sunny woods and parkland were replaced by dreary sheds and cranes while the skies became darkened by the spreading pall of industrial smoke. On arrival at the Broomielaw, paddle steamers churned through murky water where passengers disembarked amid a forest of masts and funnels. While the gracious homes of a former age were being engulfed by progress, Willie couldn't help yearning for the life style they had once enjoyed.

Meanwhile Burrell and Son expanded to form a business alliance with Schenker and Co. in Vienna. When the Adria Steamship Company was formed, the arrangement was a successful one which would give Willie opportunities to travel. Fourteen ships were built with Hungarian names and young Mary Burrell launched one when she was seven. Due to Burrell and Son's enormous output, the ladies of the family had numerous opportunities to become adept in the art of naming ships.

When Willie was 19 he was appointed head cashier for the company in Glasgow to handle the finances of Burrell and Son while his brother George took charge of the technical side. The company office moved to George Square in the city centre. Willie's grandfather retired knowing the firm that he and his son had founded was secure and thriving in the hands of William and his sons. George and Janet Burrell had made their home in Byres Road, in the West End of Glasgow, where the grafting George Burrell eventually died in 1881.

Burrell and Son continued to prosper under the skilled management of William Burrell, assisted by his sons, George and Willie. Then four years after their grandfather died the Burrell family suffered a loss which was totally unexpected. In June 1885, when Willie's father was only 53 and still at the height of his business career, he became ill with liver disease and died two months later. A much loved father had been taken from his family, and the guiding light of Burrell and Son suddenly extinguished.

CHAPTER 3

Great Western Road

William Burrell's untimely death was deeply mourned by his family firm as well as by those he had loved. In every way he had been a big man and his loss created a gaping void. As a young man blessed with energy and a charismatic personality, he had co-founded Burrell and Son and then steered the company with ability and sound judgement. The remarkable success of this enterprising man had provided the roots from which the achievements of his famous son would ultimately grow. Marion in later years recorded her father's comments.

> Grandfather was an extrovert. My father used to say he had such a hearty laugh that even though they didn't hear the joke the clerks in the office were all in fits at the sound of bubbling joy.

Isabella adored him, and about six weeks before her own death in 1912 she believed he had appeared to her vividly, comforting her with his presence. At the time of William's death their close-knit brood was becoming dispersed and now that the mainstay had gone from Burrell and Son, young

George and Willie would have to take over. While still a bachelor Willie continued to live at home with his mother. In 1883 his brother George had married Ann Jane McKaig; then Adam wed Clarissa Jane Scott, from Ireland, in 1886. Having served the company as a marine engineer, Adam abandoned the shipping world to study medicine and became a doctor. He departed with his family to live abroad, finally settling in New Zealand. Henry (Harry), the fourth Burrell son, had also served the company as an accountant, but died of tuberculosis while still a young man.

George was already a partner in Burrell and Son, and Willie now joined him. No senior Burrell remained to provide guidance for William's sons; a Burrell uncle, also named George, had served in the shipping office but changed his allegiance to the railways and became the Station Master at Cumbernauld, outside Glasgow. Young George and Willie were catapulted into managing the company aged 28 and 24. The brothers had inherited an onerous responsibility – when their father died the firm was managing a large fleet which included several ships owned by other companies. Many people wondered how they would cope, but the young Burrells showed themselves more than equal to the demands which had been suddenly thrust upon them.

George continued to manage the fleet while Willie handled the company finances. A recession had set in during the mid 1880s, biting hard at the time when their father died, so Burrell and Son had avoided placing orders, and launched no ships between 1882 and 1888. Meanwhile Willie devised another source of revenue, inviting his father's friends to invest in individual ships which were then managed as separate financial units. Before long the backers were rewarded with handsome dividends.

After her elder sons had departed, Isabella continued to manage her household at Bowling with three daughters still at home, while young William emerged as head of her family. Being financially independent and already a wealthy man, he was well equipped to handle the family affairs. Isabella was confident in his judgement, and together they formed a close and trusting alliance. These two strong characters got on well although William's mother was a force to be reckoned with. When travelling in Ceylon (Sri Lanka) Isabella had wished to purchase some sapphire rings and found herself short of cash. Without hesitation the jeweller insisted 'Madam, you can take away anything in my shop'. It seems she had become a 'grande dame' whose presence demanded obsequious service. (Her granddaughter Marion was to inherit this trait.) On another occasion, Isabella was voyaging on a Greek ship which encountered a violent storm. While passengers were prostrate with seasickness, the terrified crewmen cowered below decks, praying for deliverance. Isabella was so enraged that she castigated the sailors for abandoning their posts and ordered them to return and man their ship. Flailed by a fury worse than the storm the crew obeyed, the ship survived and everyone lived to tell the tale.

When operations at Burrell and Son were scaled down during the recession, Willie saw a chance to travel and consider his prospects abroad. Leaving his brother George in charge, he arranged a passage to Australia and New Zealand and invited his mother to join him. It was a bold decision for a new widow to make, but having made provision at home, Isabella gladly set out on another long sea voyage. Instead of boarding a sailing ship this time she travelled in a steam-powered passenger liner though the advance in technology did not always bring comfort. While his mother remained unperturbed Willie was often seasick. In spite of this setback the expedition was a success, and Marion recorded her father's account of a memorable visit to Rotorua in New Zealand.

> The great volcanic eruption of 1886 had only taken place a few years before and was still very fresh in living memory. They went, among other places, to the buried village of Te Wairoa. Buried because when the great eruption occurred, the whole side of Mount Tarawera was blown out and the huge missing gap [is] still to be seen today. Lava covered the whole of Te Wairoa and engulfed many people. There was an old hermit who foretold this disaster and was disbelieved. However when he proved to be only too true [sic], the villagers turned against him and he was found dead 3 days later.

Willie and his mother were deeply affected by the devastation as well as the ancient Maori culture. The 'hermit' was an aged *tohunga* who prophesied doom when a phantom war canoe was said to have appeared and then suddenly vanished on the waters of Lake Tarawera. When he survived after being buried for days in ash the Maoris were frightened because they believed he had cast evil spells and caused the catastrophe. According to an official report, despite his protests he was taken to hospital where they cut off his ash-matted hair. This offence against the *tohunga's* religion was believed to have caused his death.

Back in 1856, when the young Isabella voyaged to New Zealand with her father, their sailing ship had taken a course near Milford Sound in South Island and Isabella had longed to return to that remote mountainous haven. Her hopes had been raised in 1882 when the S.S. *Tarawera* was launched on the Clyde at Greenock for the Union Steamship Company. The vessel was designed to serve in New Zealand as a pleasure steamer for conveying tourists to places of interest. Though no opportunity to make the journey with her husband seems to have arisen, her tour with Willie allowed her to realize her dream.

Grandma Burrell had told of the voyage that she and her father had made when she was a young girl and Marion recorded the story in her memoirs:

> Isabella Guthrie was tall and handsome with a good brain. At 23 she became engaged to William Burrell. In the same year her father Adam Guthrie became ill and was ordered 'a long sea voyage', long indeed. Grandma went as his companion as it was a matter of a sailing ship that took them to New Zealand. My father told me that with her handsome good looks, there was not an unmarried man on board who did not propose marriage to her. However she stuck loyally to William Burrell and married him on her return.

This is the kind of story Victorians liked to tell, and Marion was happy to accept it, but the vision of an elderly gentleman reclining on a deckchair while his dutiful daughter tenderly wrapped him in rugs is nothing but a myth. William Burrell knew full well there were no pleasure cruises for convalescents in 1856. To tell the truth, Grandma Burrell was not always as 'grand' as her descendants may have believed, but they have even more reason to be proud of her.

Isabella's story is a mystery still to be unwound. The Guthries' home in Glasgow was not far from the Burrells. Adam, her father, being a younger son of an Ayrshire tenant farmer, had left and become a marine pilot, a coal agent and then a contractor. He had married Elizabeth Duncan, the daughter of a shoemaker who was also a Burgess of Glasgow. Isabella and two of her sisters were dressmakers, and her brother George was a potter who learned his trade at the Port Dundas Pottery. Adam Guthrie was 63 when he and Isabella left British shores. His wife had recently died and, with Isabella, their youngest child still living at home, it may have seemed a good time for father and daughter to seek a change. But travel to New Zealand was no vacation because global sea journeys were for emigration or for trade. The voyage would have lasted about three months. Conditions were rough on a heaving ship with banks of sails as high as a five-storey house, and some vulnerable passengers failed to survive the journey.

In her memoir Marion seemed unaware that Isabella and her father had actually sailed to Australia the previous year in 1855, when the *Glenroy* delivered them to Victoria after Isabella's brother George had already arrived in 1852. As the Gold Rush was in full cry George had gone to Bendigo and joined in. He must have struck lucky, because the following year he married one of his mother's relations out there, and by the time Adam and Isabella arrived he was operating an inter colonial shipping business out of Melbourne. This might explain how Isabella and her father made their trip to New Zealand, but by 1856 George's luck had ran out and he was said to be insolvent.

Isabella's sister Mary had emigrated too, and that year she married Hugh McColl who also came from Glasgow. But

Isabella missed their September wedding in Melbourne because she had left Australia in August to sail home on the *James Baines* and marry William Burrell at Hogmanay. Surprisingly, she was not accompanied by her father as he had chosen to stay in Australia and lived there until he died in 1874.

As a young Victorian girl in her early twenties Isabella was an amazing traveller, although her journeys raise some speculation. Was her solo departure pre-planned? Few voyagers took the return journey to Britain, but some first-class passengers employed servants to tend them and the capable Isabella may have worked her passage. With the narrow tiered bunks in the women's quarters measuring approximately 56 by 18 inches, shipboard life would have offered her few comforts, but the intrepid Miss Guthrie seemed undaunted. Whatever proposals came her way on the long voyage home, a lively young lady midst a crew of lusty sailors would not have been short of attention.

The comely dressmaker possessed great charm for she had learned the manners of her clients. Before the invention of sewing machines, when hand-made garments were fitted in the homes of Glasgow gentry, Isabella had been able to study their ways. Fired with ambition, this determined lass had set her heart on William Burrell. The year 1856 ended in a riotous New Year celebration, when she and William were toasted by family and friends who probably knew them by more homely names like 'Billy and Isa' or 'Will and Bel'.

Isabella's sea adventure galvanized her resolution. When she became Mrs William Burrell her sights were set high as she and her young husband were fired with ambition, and there is strong evidence of the influence extended to their famously successful son. When the Burrells arrived in Glasgow society their neighbours would have been horrified to learn of Mrs Burrell's unchaperoned girlhood adventure, so contact with her relations would seem to have been suppressed lest the terrible truth leaked out. Isabella's grandchildren were kept in the dark, and only recently has the fuller picture come to light.

When Willie Burrell and his mother returned to Scotland after their tour, Burrell and Son sprang into life with ten new ships, and with business booming the ship-owning brothers quickly established their reputation. Due to the link with the Adria Steamship Company Willie was appointed Austro-Hungarian Vice-Consul in Glasgow, and later Consul-General. On visiting the offices of Schenker in Vienna he was welcomed by the Austrian family and highly amused when they all called him 'Villie'. He was captivated by the courtly Viennese and learned to emulate the gracious manners of his hosts. His visits to Vienna were memorable times and his friendship with the Schenkers continued for many years. In the elegant music-loving capital there were palaces, museums and galleries as well as tempting opportunities for collecting. On continental visits he was sometimes accompanied by his mother who was his steadfast ally, advising him always to seek items of the finest quality. While Isabella was supporting Willie she also encouraged her daughters to travel abroad and learn foreign languages. Although young ladies were rarely given opportunities of this kind, she took pains to seek out respectable establishments where her daughters could be chaperoned while broadening their education. Elizabeth, the eldest girl, went to study in Germany, and later on Bella and Mary were sent to Paris and Lausanne. Willie was called upon to escort his young sisters to their destinations and, having warned them against the dangers of accepting gifts from gentlemen and forming undesirable attachments, he set out on an adventure of his own.

On an expedition to Morocco he hired a guide called Mustapha in Tangier. Having noted his client's keen eye for works of art the guide told him of some fine embroidered curtains in Tétouan. The collector was agog, so horses were hired for a ride which would take them all day. Tétouan lay beyond a wooded valley known to be frequented by robbers and darkness was falling as they approached. Marion clearly enjoyed this parental yarn:

> Mustapha appeared nervous and made a series of sharp whistles under his breath, which my father used to copy. Tetuan [sic] in those days was a walled town and at last they reached it in safety, only to find the gates shut for the night. Mustapha made a great din to announce their arrival. But the inhabitants mistook it for a trick of the robbers, and refused to let them in. They were now in the unenviable position of not only being refused the safety of the town, but of being shut out beside the robbers.
>
> Mustapha however held a trump card. All day he had been carrying a murderous looking musket and now said if he were to fire this off it would convince the inhabitants that the travellers were honest men. This was his big moment. He raised the weapon to his shoulder, fired, and exactly nothing happened. After renewed shoutings and cajolings however, the gates were at last opened. The weary travellers entered, and next day the curtains were procured.

These desirable hangings may still be conserved among the

treasures of the Burrell Collection. Although the artist Joseph Crawhall, whose work Burrell came to admire, was in Tangier, no record survives of a meeting in Morocco. At that time, the politician, writer and adventurer Robert Bontine Cunninghame-Graham was there, and Marion preserved a story of his friend 'Creeps' Crawhall which he recorded in a collection of essays entitled *Writ in Sand*. When Crawhall's leisure hours were not spent riding to hounds with the Tangier hunt, he sometimes took to heavy drinking. Once he disappeared for a week till his friends tracked him down in a brothel. While enjoying the facilities the artist had been paying his way by painting pictures on the walls of that house of ill repute. If travellers keep a sharp look out those rare Crawhall murals may be rediscovered one day in a red-light quarter of old Tangier!

Many years later Crawhall was invited to dine with the Burrells in Glasgow, but after enjoying his dinner he dropped off to sleep and they had to send him home in a taxi. The artist's habits did not change.

By the 1890s William Burrell had amassed a wide range of artefacts, though many were later discarded as his taste changed and progressed. In Scotland he became aware of fellow collectors. Among them were Thomas Glen Arthur, whose father had founded a warehouse firm, his business partner Arthur Kay, and the Paisley thread manufacturer William Coats, who had a fine collection of paintings. John Holms the stockbroker shared Burrell's pleasure in medieval works of art.

Family weddings took place when Janet Burrell married Charles Cleland, stationer and paper manufacturer, in 1888, and Elizabeth wed Thomas Lapraik, ship owner of the Douglas Steamship Company of Hong Kong, in 1891.

Glasgow was ablaze with new prosperity, and at night the streets were bright with theatres, music halls and circuses. The city entered a dynamic era of culture and gaiety while the West End thronged with the beau monde of successful industry. William Burrell celebrated the new decade by buying his mother an elegant terraced house in Great Western Road which far outshone the homely villa she had occupied at Bowling. Desirably sited on the edge of town where cattle grazed in fields nearby, No. 4 Devonshire Gardens was fully staffed and equipped with a laundry, as well as a coach house and stables in the mews at the rear. The Burrells' arrival in town was soon followed by afternoon calls, introductions and invitations and it was not long before the family became caught up in receptions, evening parties and soirées. Glasgow was humming with new wealth and commerce. Here the elite began to merge with the would-be elite, as merchant families who had made their fortunes during the previous century, were joined by industrialists. The progeny of landed gentry who had risen as sugar barons and tobacco lords now started to jostle with the sons and daughters of coalmasters, shipbuilders, thread manufacturers, provision merchants and sanitary engineers. Neighbours in Great Western Road would have been interested to meet the stately widow who had arrived in Devonshire Gardens with two unmarried daughters, Bella and Mary and an eligible bachelor son. A prosperous young ship owner would have seemed quite a catch, especially one with elegant manners, discerning taste and a fund of entertaining stories.

My own grandfather lived with his offspring across the road at No. 1000 Great Western Road in a mansion he had named Glentower. James MacIntyre Thomson came from the shipbuilding family who established the yard at Clydebank. Before the untimely death of his wife he had built the biggest house on the street and designed it for entertaining. West End parties were lavish affairs, where carriages disgorged gentlemen in swallow-tail coats and elegant ladies in rustling silks. But for all their outer grandeur these Glaswegians were not stuffy. Their dancing was so lively that starched collars collapsed in perspiration and it was even claimed that when dancing the 'Lancers' the ladies' feet were sometimes seen to brush the chandeliers! At Glentower there were gala evenings when music resounded from two grand pianos and the young Burrells came over to join the guests among the aspidistras and imposing potted palms.

There were three young Thomsons, including my Aunt Adelaide. She was said to have been a good-looking girl, and when she was old enough to put her hair up Willie Burrell began to take notice. His interest in castles may have been whetted as Adelaide's great-uncle owned two in Clackmannan. He was Sir Andrew Orr, a publisher who became Lord Provost of Glasgow, but soon after he bought the two properties his wife and only child died. After these sad bereavements he had no heir, so his married sister Agnes Kerr brought her family to join him at Harviestoun while her son was groomed to inherit the estates (author's connections p.xx). Sir Andrew's sister was Adelaide's grandmother, and when a Glasgow friend asked, 'Agnes dear, don't you feel isolated out at Harviestoun?' she replied, 'Oh but it's so central! We're half way between Dollar and Tillicoultry!' Harviestoun was conveniently connected with an avenue to each village. According to Marion, her father had fallen for Agnes' granddaughter, the beautiful Adelaide Thomson, but the romance did not last. The cooling off was probably mutual, unless, perhaps, the socially ambitious James

Thomson had reservations about his daughter forming an alliance with newcomers from Bowling.

In a period when fortunes could be made almost overnight, lifestyles could rapidly change. Those who considered themselves established did not always welcome those who were not, and even within families barriers could spring up. Willie Burrell gleefully described an incident in Glasgow when he and his mother were lunching one day in the North British Hotel. It was a handy place for them to meet, being near to the company office. That day Willie was taken by surprise when Isabella suddenly leaned across the table and hissed 'Don't look round, Willie dear. I think that's my sister!'

Glasgow's new wealth made the 1890s a golden age for collectors. Dealers who imported works from the Continent were also glad to interest their clients in art from nearer home and Burrell wasted no time in getting to know them. Alexander Reid was one who influenced him, and having had the forethought to offer Burrell special rates, the dealer became a particular friend. Reid championed the group of talented artists who became known as the Glasgow Boys. He opened a new Glasgow gallery early in 1894 and Burrell was delighted to attend a celebratory dinner where these artists were out in force. During that year, Burrell had supported George Henry and EA Hornel on their painting excursion in Japan, sending them £100 when they ran out of funds for the passage home. That year he commissioned John Lavery to paint a portrait of his sister Mary. The result is enchanting – she stands in youthful elegance, with dark ribbons from her feather fan falling against her pale taffeta dress. The portrait was not intended to be a gift as it remained in her brother's possession and thus became part of the Burrell Collection.

William was in buoyant form when Burrell and Son took advantage of another slump in world trade. When shipyard orders were short and prices had plummeted he and George promptly ordered a dozen new steamers for the Strath Line. The brothers spied another opportunity to profit by also buying nine second-hand ships. During 1894 company ships were launched from yards both north and south of the border and on 5 June that year the *Strathord* was launched at West Hartlepool by Mary Burrell.

Although she was 12 years younger than Willie, the two were very close. Mary had a keen eye for objets d'art and her judgement came to be greatly valued. Their sister Bella accompanied them on an expedition to Earlshall Castle in Fife, which had been restored for RW MacKenzie by Robert Lorimer. It was there that Burrell and the architect became acquainted. As Lorimer had a talent for the medieval style Burrell became a potential client. Both were bachelors in their thirties and their mutual interests prompted a friendship which may also have been influenced by Robert's liking for Willie's 'rather engaging sisters.'

The two men were drawn together, although their origins seemed poles apart. Lorimer came from Edinburgh, and his father was a professor of law. Early in their marriage Lorimer's parents had discovered Kellie Castle in Fife in a state of disrepair and faithfully restored this ancient seat of the Earls of Mar and Kellie while Robert was being educated in Edinburgh. During the restoration of Kellie Castle he acquired an understanding of Scottish architecture and learned the art of arranging paintings, furniture and objects of beauty to complement their surroundings.

Aware of their different backgrounds, the architect was impressed by Burrell's knowledge and taste while Burrell was intrigued by Lorimer's concepts and the ingenuity of his designs. Having enthused over the collector's brass alms dishes Lorimer introduced him to finely worked mother-of-pearl. When his wealthy friend lost no time in acquiring a collection of exquisite pearl boxes and card cases Lorimer could not help envying his financial resources. With the benefit of Burrell funds, the pair made forays to the Continent in search of treasures to enhance the Burrell home. Lorimer was amazed to see Willie track down dealers in foreign towns and bargain as if he were in an eastern bazaar. Observing the business man's commercial acumen he was dumbfounded by the methods he used to outstrip competitors. The cut and thrust of Burrell's world were totally new to Lorimer.

Fostering the Arts and Crafts movement, Lorimer employed the finest craftsmen. His interior designs were much admired but working in an earlier style sometimes created problems when installing modern lighting and plumbing. Burrell helped him by drawing his attention to Gothic candelabra which he had seen on the Continent. The architect adapted traditional designs with remarkable success and even applied his skill to bathroom fittings, which were made for him by Shanks of Barrhead. A particularly elegant lavatory pedestal became a feature in Lorimer houses. The model was marked with the name 'Remirol', which is Lorimer spelt backwards. The designer was treated to a good deal of ribaldry in the New Club where a fellow member quipped 'Now you'll go down in posteriority'.

In his zeal for craftsmanship Lorimer employed the Clow brothers, a pair of couthie Scotsmen who were skilled wood-carvers. Because they always spoke together, they became known as Tweedledum and Tweedledee. Some of their finest work was executed for William Burrell, and Lorimer sent them abroad to study examples of medieval craftsmanship in Paris. To solve the language problem the Scotsmen bought a phrasebook. When one of the brothers was nearly knocked off the pavement by a passing wheelbarrow he protested in fluent French 'I thocht it wus defence to hurl them things doon the trottoir'. The pair enjoyed themselves so much they missed the boat-train home and sent their employer a telegram saying 'Gauche derrière' (left behind).

In 1898 Robert Lorimer was invited to join the Burrell family on a tour of the Netherlands. Willie's repartee with the Amsterdam dealers was highly entertaining and when he made them knock down prices for his friend, Robert was delighted. There were six in the party, including Bella, Mary and another young bachelor named Ralston Mitchell. Willie took charge and acted as guide, while Isabella presided. When Robert joined another Burrell holiday the following year he became attracted to Willie's sister Mary. She was a captivating girl who shared his love of form and harmony in architecture and in art, but when her interest diverted to Ralston Mitchell, Robert had to stand down. He may have been a little peeved, as he later told a friend that Mary's accent had put him off, but I remember no trace when I knew her later. William Burrell, on the other hand, made no attempt to disguise his place of origin or appear to be other than a Glasgow businessman. He spoke with a kind of rasping lisp and, rather than lose his distinctive Scottish burr, he would apply it more broadly whenever he considered it advantageous.

Though Mary's affections had turned elsewhere, the bond between Willie and Robert grew stronger. Burrell's ambition to reside in baronial splendour had increased as his collection grew larger, but an ideal castle to house it all was not easy to find. Nonetheless, he succeeded in interesting Robert in a boyish dream of his to restore a cliff top ruin he coveted in Fife – Newark Castle near St Monans. Lorimer obliged by drawing up plans, but as it was not available for purchase it could only be a fanciful exercise; the dream would have to wait.

In 1899 George and William Burrell responded to a major boom in trade by selling off the entire Burrell fleet. Three years later their shipyard at Hamiltonhill closed, after having built Clyde puffers for three decades. Burrell and Son continued to operate as shipping agents but ordered no ships for the next nine years. Still in his thirties, William had made a fortune while running their fleet on a shoestring. In spite of his romantic inclinations where castles were concerned, he was totally dispassionate in business life and more than a little ruthless. To him Burrell and Son was simply a means of making money, and he showed no inclination to take high office and serve the shipping industry at national level.

Having secured prominence among the collectors of Scotland, Burrell was glad to devote more energy to the art world and to lend works from his collection to galleries and exhibitions. During the following years he moved into public life and in November 1899 he was elected to the Council of Glasgow Corporation, representing the Exchange Ward. As Convener of a subcommittee on health he threw himself into addressing Glasgow's housing problems. Three years later he was elected to serve the city as a magistrate. Having witnessed years of urban poverty William Burrell began to tackle Glasgow's notorious slums. Marion wrote:

With his usual wholeheartedness [he was] taking a

great interest in the slums and dreadful housing conditions in the 'back lands' where to get in more tenants
the Rachmans of those days had built tenements in
what should have been breathing space between house
and house. With the same object [sic] there were few
if any passages and the only way of getting from room
to room was to pass through other people's already
over crowded dwellings. This led to prostitution and
much vice of many sorts and to the spread of disease.
He therefore advocated the destruction of these 'back
lands' and was consequently extremely unpopular with
the grasping landlords. His inspection of premises
became positively dangerous and he had to be accompanied by a policeman. On one occasion they were
standing together at the bottom of a flight of stairs in
one of the tenements when a brick came hurtling
down but luckily missed them both.

Meanwhile, Willie's collecting continued and in September
1900 Lorimer joined the Burrells on their annual tour. In
Germany the romance between Mary and Ralston Mitchell
blossomed, and on a balcony at Heidelberg Castle they
became engaged. Though Ralston's family came from
Lanarkshire they had probably met in Glasgow where the
Mitchells had a town house. Their family firm was Edmiston
and Mitchell, a Glasgow-based company engaged in shipping
and the importation of timber.

Another romance was in the air; one of Ralston's young
sisters had appeared on the scene. Constance Mitchell was
25 and Willie found her enchanting. Before long he had
fallen under her spell, and later that year a second engagement was announced. The Burrells and Mitchells were

delighted because of this double alliance; it was not unusual for two or more siblings to marry into the same family when sharing a household carriage required most social outings to be taken 'en famille'.

William's private life centred on Great Western Road, and when he came to choose a wife he found no need to look further. Constance Mitchell was a fine-looking girl, charming, dignified and elegant. Robert said he thoroughly approved and reckoned it was time that his friend settled down because Willie was now over 40. When asked to be best man he was delighted and complimented William on his chosen bride, commending her 'angelic temper'. The comment suggests that Constance was compliant, a virtue her husband would have considered most desirable, for in that era of male supremacy few could have been more domin-ant than William Burrell. He welcomed Constance as a matchless wife, and resolved that she would be upheld as his most precious treasure; she in turn was entranced by the mature William Burrell and his commanding aura of success.

Ralston and Mary were married on 9 January in Hillhead Parish Church, Glasgow. Burrell lavished generous gifts on his sister, including a diamond necklace, silver dishes and a mother-of-pearl fan. Two weeks later, a shadow descended upon the city, when Queen Victoria died on 22 January. Royal mourning was proclaimed, and for a time, weddings looked like funerals as loyal subjects swathed themselves in inky black crepe. But Glasgow did not mourn for long, and Edward VII had come to the throne by the autumn when William and Constance made their vows on 13 September at Westbourne Free Church. The honeymoon was spent in Spain and Gibraltar while Robert prepared the marital home for their triumphant arrival. William had left detailed instructions to ensure that everything would be perfect to welcome his bride.

When the couple returned from their nuptial journey it was not to the echoing vaults of a baronial hall. Instead Constance found herself in Glasgow amid the splendour of No. 8 Great Western Terrace, recently purchased by her husband. To complement William's collection the staircase had been built of oak, employing the Clow brothers to create a series of finials and newel posts surmounted by heraldic beasts. They had also been commissioned to carve the marital bed, and like the staircase it was constructed to Lorimer's design. The bridal chamber was furnished with a 'Gothic' bedstead conceived in the Flemish style.

The interiors had been mostly left devoid of embellishment, so while the happy couple were abroad Robert had taken infinite trouble to prepare a welcome by thoughtfully arranging each room. The bride's reaction is unknown, but William was far from delighted. In no way could he admire Lorimer's efforts to harmonize objects with their surroundings; Burrell considered his works of art far too important to be treated as mere adjuncts to a scheme of decor. Fortunately for all concerned this conflict of opinion was short lived, and soon the two men were busily engaged in furbishing the Burrell nest while Constance settled into her role as William Burrell's consort. She was now married to one of Glasgow's public figures and the world seemed filled with exciting prospects. Before many months had passed, William and Constance were happily anticipating the birth of their child.

CHAPTER 4

A Solitary Childhood

Privileged people rarely enjoy the carefree lives that others suppose. The birth of Marion Burrell on 6 August 1902 did not turn out to be the joyous event that might have been expected, and despite her parents' well-laid plans, her destiny was not to be the one for which they hoped.

Few fathers could have anticipated the birth of their first-born child more eagerly than William Burrell. With 40 years behind him the prospect of fatherhood was entirely new and, as in other matters, he took command. Constance was tended with every care while William's mind became focused on future developments. Being used to large families, it seemed natural to contemplate a dynasty. Though his own start had been a humble one, his child must have the best. At once he thought of the baby's cradle. No ordinary bassinet would do. Unlike other Edwardian fathers, William gave this matter considerable thought, and commissioned Robert Lorimer to design a cradle fit to receive the awaited Burrell child.

Robert was intrigued. Though no input from Constance was recorded, the two men started planning and Robert spent a wet Sunday afternoon drawing up the design. With the skills of the Clow brothers, a piece of exquisite 'French Gothic' carving was created. The Burrell cradle seemed fit for a prince, panelled in oak with an angel guarding each corner and the watchful pelican in her piety standing at the head. According to Christian tradition the bird was revered as the epitome of motherhood because she was said to pierce her breast with her beak so that her young might feed on her blood.

William insisted that his wife must have the best medical care, and Professor Murdoch Cameron led the field as the celebrated pioneer of Caesarean operations. In those days, when a doctor's equipment could fit into one small leather bag, it was normal for births to take place in the home. The Royal Maternity Hospital where Cameron presided was then a charitable institution supported by an Ayrshire distiller, Archibald Walker who had recently married Adelaide Thomson, my aunt. But in spite of William Burrell's careful preparations, the birth did not go well. Constance did not present her husband with the son and heir that he would have welcomed, but with a baby girl. For his wife, the symbol of the mother pelican was almost prophetic because her experience of giving birth turned out to be complicated and excruciatingly painful. This cruel stroke of fate seemed ironic, and William was deeply concerned because after the birth she continued to suffer while struggling to regain her strength. Postnatal depression may have contributed to the problems which continued to distress her.

According to custom, their daughter was baptized in a simple ceremony at their home, and being the first-born daughter, was named after her maternal grandmother. Marion was a healthy child, and though her welcome may have been subdued, she arrived at No. 8 Great Western

Terrace to find herself surrounded by relations. Grandma Mitchell presided at No. 10, with her sister, 'Aunt Shaw with the sequinned ear trumpet', next door in No. 9, and after Grandma's daughter was established at No. 8, a niece brought her family to live at No. 7. A hundred yards westward Grandma Burrell's home was in Devonshire Gardens; and turning the other way, Aunt Mary and Uncle Ralston were almost as near in Belhaven Terrace. Each house could be reached in minutes without even crossing the road. In May that year Mary Mitchell had also given birth to a daughter, named Isabella after her maternal grandmother, although everyone called her Isabel.

With the prospect of numerous cousins nearby Marion seemed guaranteed a happy childhood. But fate had decreed there would be no more little Burrells in Marion's home, and this was a continuing sadness. William and Constance had looked forward to raising a family, and neither would have wished her to be an only child. William longed for a male heir because, in matters of inheritance and in business, the succession of sons was paramount. While daughters might be dearly loved, male children commanded a superior status among families of substance. It was a disaster that poor Marion had been born a girl.

A cloud had descended on their lives because Constance's health and happiness never fully recovered. William could not have been more concerned for his wife when they realized she would not bear another child. The cause remains uncertain, but the problems of childbirth were often hard to treat. Constance may have developed an aversion to sex through continued pain, or been petrified by the fear of another agonizing confinement. The situation could have been even more serious, as after a traumatic delivery it was not unusual then for doctors to warn that a subsequent pregnancy would endanger the mother's life. Modern birth control was not available, so total abstinence would have been the only safe option – with a life at risk there could be no margin for error. Whatever the reason, the physical side of the Burrells' marriage seems to have ended, but even if this was the case, their unspoken tragedy united them more strongly. William never ceased to cherish his wife, while Constance supported him devotedly in everything he did.

Meanwhile the infant Marion was unaware of the heartache she had caused, and being a stalwart little character fared well enough. Edwardian babies were coddled and parcelled in layers of complicated clothes, and all small children were kept in their place, which was of course the nursery. The nanny entrusted to rule this domain was often adored by her charges, and as she was an expert in her field, mothers rarely interfered. A daily visit was enough, and perhaps a bedtime story in the drawing room after the tea trays had been cleared away. Constance accepted her lot and consoled herself by making sure that her daughter was dressed in the prettiest frills and ribbons to be seen in Great Western Road.

Having given the baby a brief inspection, William's relationship with Marion became little more than a nodding acquaintance. Gentlemen avoided nurseries like the plague and 'parental bonding' had not been heard of. While Constance was convalescing in her quiet drawing room, he addressed himself to the works of the Glasgow Corporation, called regularly at the Burrell office, and attended to the completion of their still unfinished home. Lorimer was getting worried by the lack of progress. He thought the place still looked dreadfully bare, but William had a passion for tapestry and so the pair of them went off to hunt them down in Paris. Before long the Burrell dining room was enveloped from wall to wall in a world of medieval pageantry and William was immensely pleased by the effect. As the tapestries needed a lot of wall space this may help to explain why he suddenly sold off 40 paintings the following year. The loss to his collection of fine works by Manet, Whistler, Monticelli and Daumier was regrettable, but other purchases were soon to follow: Chinese ceramics and bronzes had become a recent interest.

In 1903 he commissioned Glasgow Boy George Henry to paint a portrait of his mother. Although Henry's works were widely acclaimed, this one gave him problems, and his first attempt was not well received. The next was even less successful but, when his earlier effort could no longer be retrieved, the Burrells said they had preferred it. The result is rather a fearsome portrait. Unlike the disarming damsel described in her youth, the mature Isabella confronts the viewer with the look of a school marm about to administer corporal punishment, and this must surely be how the hapless artist saw her.

From her childhood Marion remembered the street vendors who cried their wares in Kelvinside. Behind the tall houses knife grinders trundled down the lanes while others mended cane chairs and an old woman came calling for 'Old rags and rabbit skins'. Telephones and electric lights were among the latest innovations. Electric tram-cars had arrived in Great Western Road and they clanged along on metal rails, but most of the traffic was still horse drawn and motor cars were rare. At dusk the 'leerie' would pass by, lighting the gas lamps on the terrace. In winter the whole street could disappear in a blanket of fog which was cold and clammy and smelled like pea soup. During the summer months the Burrells escaped from the city, following the trend of Glasgow gentry in renting houses out of town.

One of Marion's earliest memories was of walking with her nanny at a house they had taken in Dunblane when she was surprised to see a mischievous housemaid tipping a slop pail out of a bedroom window. The child was clearly impressed. From an early age Marion had a mind of her own and often rebelled against authority, but Constance was unprepared for insubordination. As a young Edwardian mother she had expected to reign in a gracious world filled with orderly calm where her little daughter would be proffered from time to time like a pretty doll to amuse her. Marion had come as a terrible shock, and despite, or because of, the endless attention Constance had received, ill health continued to tax her patience and leave little energy for dealing with tantrums. To an inexperienced mother the nanny's day off could give rise to unpleasant situations. There were ugly scenes and Marion told of a ghastly incident when her mother completely lost control. There must have been a major row, because Constance became so desperate to stifle her daughter's screams that she seized a cushion, forced it over the child's face and used all her strength to smother her infantile protests. Somehow disaster was averted and normality returned. In later life Marion told this story without a hint of emotion, even though her own mother had brought her to the verge of suffocation.

A deep psychological problem had begun to manifest itself. Having been noted for her placid and submissive disposition, Constance's violent rage may have been due to a hidden resentment towards the child whom she blamed for causing her pain. Her vicious burst of fury was not an isolated incident and most sadly, as time would tell, all was not well with Constance Burrell.

While Marion was still a small girl, her mother had to undergo a major operation. The problem was said to have been caused by a defective kidney, and in those days the prospect of surgery was both risky and frightening. Nurses were employed to attend the surgeon who operated in the home. As usual William spared no expense in providing the best care available, but his wife endured another devastating experience. After the operation, Constance became distressed whenever the nurses changed her dressings so William insisted on taking over and tenderly changed them himself. During her mother's convalescence Marion remembered how he had tried to protect his wife from being disturbed by ordering straw to be spread over the cobbles in front of their house to deaden the sound of horses' hooves. The trauma some patients were made to suffer is now hard to believe. One of Marion's cousins recalled a ghastly childhood experience when she underwent an operation in the house next door. Chloroform was applied on a piece of cotton wool as she sat in a chair, drifting in and out of consciousness while the doctor slowly snipped away her tonsils. The horrors Constance had to face have never been disclosed, but the after-effects of her painful ordeals were to be long lasting.

While Constance was convalescing, Mary Mitchell produced a second daughter and, following tradition she was also named Marion, after her paternal grandmother, but confusion was avoided as this child was known as Mona. Eventually, five young cousins were born along the road, which made it hard for Constance to reflect on the empty cradle at Great Western Terrace. Instead she sought solace in William. Though family members showed concern about her maladies, awkward subjects were avoided. Only William seemed to understand, and he continued to protect her.

While supporting his wife through this difficult period, Burrell was tackling slum clearance and addressing the housing conditions in Glasgow. But advancement through public works was not for him, and he did not find local government fulfilling. Committee work was not his style because he was used to giving orders and did not welcome opposing views. Instead he preferred to focus his energy in fields where he excelled. In the aftermath of the South African War, he had patiently watched a brief boom and then another slump. When it had bottomed out Burrell and Son went into action and in 1905 William and George took the shipping industry by storm as they sprang back into operation. That year an entirely new fleet came into being when they placed orders for no less than 20 ships. The following year William retired from Glasgow Corporation.

Burrell's courtship with public life had been a testing ground. Even as a ship owner he was disinclined to be involved at public level. His interest did not lie with the industry but in managing ships for profit. And he played hard. Two of his kinsmen were employed by Burrell and Son and served on a company ship, but when they tried to offer suggestions he promptly gave them their books. Though his methods were not popular he was unrelenting.

The secret of his success was often attributed to 'Burrell's luck', but he was a shrewd opportunist who knew how luck can be created. When he learned that the Royal Navy was sending ships to serve in a distant part of the globe, he would calculate the quantity of fuel that the navy might require and reap handsome rewards by dispatching steamers to supply them. After the San Francisco earthquake of 1906 he was said to have gained a monopoly in shipping building materials to the stricken city, so when Burrell and Son ordered 20 ships in 1905, his plan had been made with scrupulous deliberation. William Burrell grasped every opportunity to make money because collecting was his ultimate objective. When she was older, Marion asked her father to what quality he owed his success; without hesitation he replied with one word 'Application'.

While great works were afoot, young Marion was making progress in a different sphere. Her own 'application' was being directed towards Mr Webster's dancing class in the Burgh Hall, where pupils were enlisted from the age of three. With nannies watching on the sidelines, Mr Webster presided in tails and spotless white gloves. The boys and girls learned to stand and sit correctly with hands politely clasped on laps and ankles neatly crossed. Before attempting the waltz and the polka it was necessary to distinguish the right foot from the left, and those who were unduly challenged received extra tuition from Miss March, in the boot room. But Marion soon became an enthusiastic dancer.

When she was five, Sir Frederick and Lady Henderson moved into No. 7. Although her new neighbour was Grandma Mitchell's niece, Marion was told to address her cousin as 'Lady Henderson'. The Hendersons had four sons and one daughter, Vera, who was just a year older than Marion. Sir Frederick owned one of the new motor cars but he also kept a landau. Carriages were part of everyday life. Grandma Mitchell enjoyed 'carriage exercise', so quite a lot of time was spent exercising Grandma. Along at Belhaven Terrace, the Mitchells had a victoria and a carriage horse called Glencoe, but the suburb of Milngavie was the furthest he could manage. As the victoria was low slung and open sided, young Mona fell out in Byres Road but being rather a bouncy child she was retrieved without damage.

Marion was pleased when Vera came to live next door, but things did not turn out as she expected. William Burrell had by this time seen just enough of his daughter to make him want to take a serious interest in her upbringing. Marion was a bright little girl and he had begun to assess her potential. If he and Constance were to be granted this single child, albeit female, he would make sure that she became an heiress worthy of the Burrell name.

His first move was to banish the nanny. With scarcely a word of warning Marion's cosy nursery life ended and her formal education began. There were to be no half measures, and Constance was content to go along with everything suggested. William's sisters, having studied abroad, could converse in foreign languages while he could not. This irked him greatly, and so he resolved that Marion should become a linguist. When the child was five years old, a French governess was engaged with strict instructions that her charge should speak no other language. This rigid regime allowed no fun with cousins or friends, so while the others went off to learn their three Rs at Mrs Mac's School in Roslyn Terrace, Marion was closeted with her governess in the schoolroom at No. 8. It was a miserable existence for them both. Unlike a nanny, a governess was rarely loved and the rebellious Marion caused many headaches for the unfortunate Mademoiselle.

The child's life was carefully regulated. While Mary Mitchell treated her small daughters with the sensible liberality she had enjoyed at Elmbank, William could remember leaner times in the Glasgow tenement, and frowned on indulgence. A walk-in cupboard was filled with toys but

Marion was allowed only one plaything at a time. The little Mitchells were incredulous when they learned of this restriction, but Marion discovered amusements elsewhere. The woodcarvings made by the Clow brothers were a constant fascination. All kinds of beasts could be found on the stairs, and she loved the baby monkey on the newel post, being fondly embraced in its mother's arms. Marion used to reach up and stroke it, imagining cuddles she would have enjoyed.

Downstairs she would contemplate the tapestries where knights and ladies roamed among strange birds and beasts in landscapes turreted with castles and carpeted with stylized flowers. When these works began to suffer from the permeating Glasgow fog Marion was able to study them closely while she watched them being cleaned by 'dear Mary Brodie', the lady restorer whose cheerful company she never forgot. Perceiving the pleasure enjoyed by his child may have influenced Burrell, in later years, to seek tapestries which delight every age. One displays the Bible like a comic strip. In another, a rural scene shows peasants busy setting rabbit traps while cheeky bunnies are popping in and out of burrows. At a medieval picnic a carafe of wine is cooling in a pond where a large hound is stalking a very small frog. And what fun it is to spot a smartly dressed gentleman having his palm read by a gypsy while her accomplice is slyly stealing his purse. For Marion, the stained glass windows at Great Western Terrace revealed more stories, and her father's collection of paintings became like childhood friends. Though Burrell's ideas on upbringing may seem strange, his methods were not unrewarded because his child was imbued with a love of art which might almost have stemmed from those early awakenings in her 'medieval' cradle.

When she was young, Marion's father introduced her to

the tales of Reynard the Fox. These comic animal stories were a thinly disguised satire, lampooning the nobility and clergy of France who held sway during the Middle Ages. When visiting churches and cathedrals, Marion learned to look out for carvings of the impudent fox, lurking among choir stalls or covertly eyeing cherubs from the shadowy end of a pew. Thomas Glen Arthur, clothing merchant and textile manufacturer, commissioned Joseph Crawhall to make illustrations of the stories. These were later bought by William Coats who sold a limited edition of prints, and when Marion was still in her nursery her father acquired a set.

While the child was learning to appreciate her father's works of art, her widowed Grandma Mitchell presided over her family in Great Western Terrace. Grandma had been born Marion Miller and descended from a threshing miller in seventeenth-century Airdrie in Lanarkshire where her father, Robert Miller, was a coal and iron master. His family lived at Belvedere House in Lanarkshire, which later became a hospital. At 18 Marion Miller had married James Mitchell, a timber importer of Edmiston and Mitchell; her sister married one of the Edmistons. The Mitchells came from Hamilton, not far from Belvedere, and James pursued a career in the West Indian sugar trade before joining his family company. On the Board of the Clyde Navigation Trust, he became Chairman of the Ferries Committee while in private life he was Chairman of the Western Club, Captain of Prestwick Golf Club and a flag officer of the Royal Northern Yacht Club. The Mitchell family was already well established when the Burrells arrived in Great Western Road.

Marion never knew her grandfathers, but her two widowed grandmothers left a strong impression. Grandma Mitchell was regarded as a kind old lady but Marion held a different view. On a childhood visit to No. 10 she had spied an interesting object on Grandma's mantelpiece and was told it was a piggy bank. The child was delighted when her grandmother lifted it down and gave her a bright new penny to drop inside, but as soon as the coin had disappeared Marion wanted it back. To this little girl pennies were as novel as piggy banks because she was never allowed any pocket money. Grandma Mitchell refused to oblige and Marion never forgave her.

William Burrell's cash policy would dog poor Marion throughout her life. Having achieved enormous wealth he was determined that no child of his should take it for granted. He wanted his daughter to appreciate value and quality, and also learn the merit of thrift, just as he had done. She must never be allowed to squander money on worthless trivia, and so no purchase would ever be made without parental supervision. Because William wanted only the best for his daughter, he would not put her at risk by allowing her to spend money of her own. Pocket money was therefore out of the question; when Grandma Burrell gave each of her grandchildren a ten-shilling note at Christmas, Marion's was put straight into the bank and she never even saw it.

As motor cars began to appear in Glasgow the Burrells were not slow to follow the trend. Grandma Burrell was the first member of her family to possess one when William presented her with a dark green Daimler and a uniformed chauffeur to match. One day Grandma arranged to take Marion out in her car for a treat and there was a bustle at No. 8 as the child was summoned and told to get ready. But for reasons unknown, Marion turned bolshie and hid herself in a cupboard. When she refused to come out, Isabella departed without her and her headstrong granddaughter was not invited to drive out with her again. Though Grandma Burrell was intractable, an apology was made and no animosity remained. Grandma Mitchell was reputedly 'good with children' while Grandma Burrell was not, but Marion said she always preferred Grandma Burrell.

Despite her banishment from the green Daimler, she was not for long denied the pleasures of motor travel, because William Burrell also became the owner of a car. Marion recalled that:

Motor cars, as we called them then, were few and far between. If you had a car it went without saying you had a chauffeur whose livery matched the colour of the car. It was unheard of for an owner to drive himself. There was some sense in this, because breakdowns were fairly frequent and a working knowledge of how to get the car restarted was essential. You had a starting handle which was inserted at the lower part of the bonnet and this had to be swung hard to start the engine. If you held the handle the wrong way you would assuredly dislocate your thumb, as at the end of the swing it shot back with great force. There was no heating and no antifreeze. The passengers therefore had carriage rugs, sometimes of fur, and foot warmers. These were copper pans, rather flat, and covered with carpet. The ladies wore motoring veils to tie over their large Edwardian hats, and these tied firmly under the chin in a large bow. Altogether it was quite an undertaking to set out for a drive.

My father used to take us to the country on Saturdays. Lunch at the Dreadnought at Callander was a favourite thing. The Bailie Nichol Jarvie at Aberfoyle another highlight, with the Bailie's murderous looking weapon hanging from a tree, still kept daubed with red paint to signify the blood of the MacGregors. But the lovely road along Loch Lubnaig was my favourite. [Bailie Nichol Jarvie is a character in Sir Walter Scott's novel *Rob Roy*, based on the eighteenth-century outlaw well known in Scottish history.]

Outings to the Trossachs prompted entertaining stories. Whatever the subject, her father was so enthused that Marion found his historical yarns immensely exciting and quickly developed an insatiable thirst for sightseeing. When her parents went on expeditions to the Continent they sent her postcards with interesting pictures and even gave her special albums to contain them. Postcards were a novelty then and Marion collected several series with views of churches, tulip fields, peasant girls, Old Master paintings and a fearsome gallery of gargoyles from Notre Dame. While she was still very young she was taken abroad to see these things for herself. The education of Burrell's daughter had begun in earnest.

I must have been about 8 years of age, when my father and I were walking in the Rue St Honoré, in Paris – with our backs to the Rue de la Paix. There was on the right hand side a small shop. This consisted of an unobtrusive doorway and one not very large window and in the window one picture - but what a picture!! My father stopped as one transfixed which indeed he was. It was as if an electric shock had passed through him and there was a look on his face which I never saw before or since. The picture was none other than

Boudin's *L'Impératrice Eugenie et sa suite à Trouville*. We went into the shop and he told me to ask the price, as he didn't speak French. The Frenchman quoted in 'mille francs' and my French though fluent was purely nursery French and to me it sounded like millions. I translated wrongly, and my father said with an amused smile 'Get him to write it down', and this he did.

Much to Marion's delight her father bought the picture. Against a blue, cloud-streaked sky, the painting shows a troupe of ladies with swaying crinolines and parasols, setting out on a breezy promenade by the sea. The scene conveys an added charm by allowing us the fun of trying to identify the Empress among her elegant attendants. Marion always felt a great attachment for this painting, although it was never in her possession. Her childhood memory of the purchase is remarkably vivid, yet there is a discrepancy. In 1911, Burrell began to record his acquisitions in a succession of purchase books, and this particular Boudin painting is not recorded as being bought until 1923. Boudin was a prolific artist and Burrell bought several of his paintings; the similarity between seaside views could be confusing to a child, especially to one who lived in a house where pictures were frequently appearing and being rearranged. Although a childhood purchase clearly took place, Marion took pleasure in accompanying her father on many similar occasions while she was growing up.

Another mystery is the curious ending to her early recollection of that day in Paris:

My mother thought he was spending too much on works of art and had got him to promise to hold his hand in this respect. We therefore had to double back to the hotel and get her to release him from his promise before the deal could be concluded.

The influence Constance exerted was steadily increasing. She had learned many ways of gaining attention, but could she hold sway over Burrell's transactions? Or had he forgotten his cheque book? Marion never suspected that a demonstration of parental thrift might have been enacted for her benefit. Her hindsight seemed unquestioning and sometimes naive.

Burrell traded in paintings to make room for others. His lack of sentiment on relinquishing works was consistent with his ruthlessness when disposing of ships. Burrell has been described as 'the Millionaire Magpie' but what magpie would discard acquisitions as he did? Despite his enthusiasm for works he acquired, Burrell's collection was always more important to him than any piece that it contained. His ability to detach himself from the desire to possess may have been one of his greatest strengths. Although he was a rich man, his resources did not reach the extent of American collectors such as Henry Frick and William Randolph Hearst. Burrell spent cautiously, always seeking a good bargain. He has sometimes been criticized for a reluctance to purchase and for the loss of works which he sold, but William Burrell's deliberate restraint allowed him to expand his collection far more widely than would otherwise have been possible.

Marion's youthful efforts to speak French appeared to satisfy her father and it was not long before he was seeking to advance her education in another direction.

My father had felt the need of languages very much during his travels and was determined I should speak

Vessels in the Burrell Fleet

PLATE 1. Between 1875 and 1903 Burrell and Son built and repaired coastal steamers popularly known as 'Puffers' at Hamilton-hill on the Forth and Clyde Canal.

PLATE 2. SS *Strathleven* built in 1875 was a refrigerated ship and in 1879 the first to transport meat from Australia to London.

PLATE 3. The SS *Strathlorne*, built in 1909, was launched by Marion Burrell aged seven.

PLATE 4. William Burrell, Sir William's father, lived 1832–87.

PLATE 5. Three young Burrells, left to right: William, George and Adam.

PLATE 6. George Burrell, Sir William's brother. Detail from a portrait which belonged to his grandson, the late George Burrell McKean.

PLATE 7. William Burrell aged 39. From an illustration in *The Bailie*, 5 November 1902.

PLATE 8. William Burrell leaving on a carriage drive with his mother.

PLATE 9. James Thomson with his daughter Adelaide, who later married Archie Walker and lived at Newark Castle in Ayrshire.

PLATE 10. William Burrell and Robert Lorimer (centre) with Isabella Burrell (right) touring the Netherlands in 1898.

PLATE 11. The architect Sir Robert Lorimer as a young man. Portrait by John Henry Lorimer, 1906.

PLATE 12. The cradle designed by Robert Lorimer for Burrell's only child.

PLATE 13. *Above left*: Constance Burrell with the infant Marion who was born in 1902.

PLATE 14. *Above right*: Mother and daughter with Marion aged about four.

PLATE 15. *Right*: Marion aged nine, with spectacles.

PLATE 16. *Left*: Mother and daughter at Kilduff House in East Lothian with Letham the dog.

PLATE 17. *Below left*: Troon, Marion at the seaside aged about 12.

PLATE 18. *Right*: Visiting her Mitchell cousins at Flatfield, Symington in Ayrshire.

PLATE 19. Parents watching the Heathfield school play.

PLATE 20. Marion, second left, as an Amazon in *A Midsummer's Night's Dream*, 1920.

PLATE 21. Marion took this photograph of her father with friends on the Ayrshire coast.

PLATE 22. The three Burrells at the Hotel Metropole, Cannes, 1921.

PLATE 23. Marion at sea on a passage to India 1922–3.

PLATE 24. 'Mother, Daddy and I at Clairmont' Bombay.

PLATE 25. 'Mother in a rickshaw'.

PLATE 26. The Burrells were entertained by the Viceroy at Viceregal Lodge, Calcutta during the Christmas season of 1922.

PLATE 27. 'Daddy and I at Amber Palace', Jaipur.

PLATE 28. *Left and right*: Jim Thomson and his wife Eva (née MacAndrew).

PLATE 29. *Above*: Wedding group at South Park, Ayr in June 1923. Marion Burrell (next the bride) was maid of honour at Eva's marriage to Jim Thomson.

PLATE 30. *Right*: Bessie MacAndrew, Eva's mother.

PLATE 31. Marion in court dress for her presentation at Buckingham Palace in 1925. Two years later she was given a second London Season.

Marion's noble chaperones

PLATE 32. *Right*: London Season 1925.
Florence, Lady Garvagh, the daughter
of Baron Joseph de Bretton of
Copenhagen and widow of Lord
Garvagh of Garvagh, County
Londonderry. Marion was
introduced as her 'goddaughter'.

PLATE 33. *Below*: London Season 1927.
Lady Clodagh Anson, daughter of the
Marquess of Waterford and grand-
daughter of the Duke of Beaufort.

Marion Rawll from her Godmother Florence Garvagh

Compton *Mackenzie* Finds...
A LIVELY PORTRAIT
of the
GAY
'Nineties

FROM time to time we may
read attempts to pro-
phesy what writers of
to-day will be read by posterity.

I have a collection of these in
my scissors-and-paste menagerie of
human *bêtises*, and it is amusing to
read claims for immortality made
twenty years ago on behalf of
writers whose ability to attract the
public has withered even before the
writers themselves are dead.

*LADY CLODAGH ANSON correcting the proofs of
her book of "Discreet Memories," which, says Compton
Mackenzie, is a "precious social document."*

PLATE 34. *Right*: During her London Seasons William Burrell's daughter received press attention.

PLATE 35. *Below*: At a charity sale in the Royal School of Needlework Miss Burrell is seen purchasing an embroidered cushion from the Duchess of York who later became Queen.

Hay Wrightson.

MISS C. M. BURRELL,

The pretty daughter of Mr. and Mrs. William Burrell, and god-daughter of Florence Lady Garvagh. Mrs. William Burrell has a beautiful home in Scotland, Broxmouth Park, Dunbar, where Miss Burrell spends a great part of her time.

French and German. At five my nanny left me and was succeeded by a French governess, so that I became bi-lingual at an early age. The next was a German and a real prison warder of a woman. I hated her and her language.

When the fierce Fräulein joined the Burrell household Marion was nine, so this governess probably encountered even more defiance than her predecessor. Another language had been added to the schoolroom curriculum so when William and Constance went abroad that year they sent their daughter postcards from Karlsbad in Germany. Constance was taking a health cure and seemed to be listless and poorly. She sent her child a postcard of the Stephanienwarte – the picture showed a gruesome tower reminiscent of the one in which the legendary Rapunzel was imprisoned and let down her long hair to be rescued. Perhaps it expressed her mother's feelings at the time because her doleful message read:

> My dearest little Pet, I am still in bed but the doctor is letting me get up tomorrow. I have been wondering what you are doing today. The weather here has become colder. I often wonder what you are doing …

Constance had become adept at appealing for sympathy. The postcards from Marion's father were more enlightening and packed with interesting information. He sent her a picture of two Karlsbad Jews taking the waters at the spa.

> This is a photo of the gentlemen I told you about. You see their long gabardines that cover everything and the one who is bending down you can see the

corkscrew curl on the side of his ear. He has in his hand a cup for drinking the water. It is called in German a Becker.

Another postcard which he sent to Marion showed the Hotel Hermann with two windows marked to indicate her parents' rooms. As they occupied separate bedrooms at home this was their normal arrangement, and with gentry who lived in large houses it would not have been unusual. When travelling away from home, William jokingly blamed the added expense on his snoring. And Constance needed space of her own. Though most of William's purchases would be separately despatched she would hardly have wished to share a bedroom with precious and often dusty acquisitions or have fragile packages cluttering her wardrobe.

While Marion remained in Glasgow her upbringing allowed her few opportunities to meet her young cousins. When they became aware of her monastic routine they thought she must be spineless, though they were to learn otherwise. Unexpectedly a happy interlude took place when Mary Mitchell's fifth child was born. This time it was Mary who suffered a difficult confinement, and while she was convalescing with her new baby her older children were invited to stay with their Uncle Willie and Aunt Connie at Great Western Terrace.

Suddenly the sombre household at No. 8 burst into life with the cheerful babble of young voices. Marion was enchanted to have four cousins staying under her own roof. Constance read stories to the younger ones while Marion showed Isabel and Mona her favourite things. Games and laughter broke the ice and brought them all together. Undaunted by her enforced solitude Marion had an impish sense of fun and plenty of amusing ideas to entertain them. The young Mitchells enjoyed getting to know their cousin and never forgot their visit to the mysterious house up the road. But their Uncle Willie was seldom at ease with free-range children among his treasures, and the metal tacks on their shoes made him fear for his marble floors.

Marion had another stroke of luck when the hated German governess departed – by 1913 signs of international unrest may have hastened the prison warder's withdrawal. The change made Marion's parents decide on a new approach, and their daughter, at the age of 11, finally went to school. Laurel Bank School for Girls was within walking distance of her home. Due to her enforced seclusion she had rarely met other children and she suddenly arrived in a world which resounded with female chatter and summoning bells. In a classroom filled with girls she began to learn school discipline and the unfamiliar necessities of taking turns and sharing. For the first time she encountered competition, organized games, badges and prizes.

Though Marion felt out of step she learned quickly and, in spite of the shock of her new environment, coped well with her lessons and began making friends. She was a lively enthusiast with a natural warmth which craved to be returned. Being kept apart had made her yearn to belong, and so it felt good to wear a green uniform and play 'Kick the Can', 'Peever' and 'Grandmother's Footsteps' while joining in crazes for skipping ropes and 'Cat's cradle', not to mention the interminable process of French knitting. Yet the child's extraordinary upbringing was leaving its stamp. She had the manners of a grown up, the mischief of a monkey and a mind which overflowed with surprising information. Though she wanted so much to be one of the crowd Marion often made her mark by being different.

As her life began to change, Great Western Terrace was changing too. The family conclave began to fall apart after the two grandmas died. Without the mortar which had bound them all together family interests were turning to pursuits out of town. The Mitchells and Hendersons were spending time in Ayrshire where they could ride and play golf. The Burrells were frequently away from home, with Constance joining William on collecting tours in Britain and on the Continent. They met the Mitchells rarely now, and as they had adopted conflicting approaches when rearing their young, the two mothers were not always in accord. Mary was becoming aware that the whims of her pampered sister-in-law were often to blame for the harsh regime that her brother inflicted on Marion. Meanwhile, Constance was becoming isolated. While Mary was busy with her family of five, Great Western Terrace seemed an empty place with Marion at school. Feeling miserably deprived, Constance turned once again to her loving husband for comfort and when Willie perceived that the beautiful Gothic cradle was causing her distress it was quietly spirited away.

Mary Mitchell regretted the lack of harmony between their families. Despite the affection she had for her brother they were no longer close, and she was sad that a rift had developed. As bachelors, William and Ralston had been good friends with many interests in common. Ralston Mitchell was extremely able, and like William Burrell he had a strong sense of family duty. As ladies were not expected to take part in financial affairs Ralston had assumed this responsibility on his wife's behalf, but her brother had long been in charge of the Burrell finances and had no wish to relinquish authority.

Trouble arose over Mary's Burrell shares. Early in their

marriage, Ralston had decided to alter her financial arrangements. In 1905 the Burrell brothers had embarked upon another major shipbuilding programme on a scale which eclipsed their previous efforts. Ralston, being a cautious man, was ill at ease with their boldness, and sought to stabilize his wife's position by investing her assets more widely. This meant withdrawing Mary's holdings from the family enterprise, so William would have been forced to buy them in. He took it badly. Though details have not survived, the subsequent acrimony endured. Afterwards Mary had misgivings, but though her shares would have yielded substantial profits she suffered a deeper regret. Ralston's concern for her interests had wounded her brother in a way which William could not forgive. This Burrell trait was deeply embedded in his character. Though Mary tried every way she knew to heal the rift, the two men would never be reconciled.

William felt his responsibilities deeply, and never more than with his wife. Being 15 years older than Constance he was used to taking charge. He hated to see her unhappy and while ill health persisted he lovingly tended her. Having vowed to cherish 'for better, for worse' the trauma which followed Marion's birth had made him feel guilty. Constance was often dispirited and he could not stop blaming himself for the afflictions which had blighted her life. If his wife was to be denied the fulfilment for which they both had hoped, he would never cease to seek other ways of providing consolation. Constance would always be protected and revered, while Marion, his rising star, would be guided, controlled and restrained. The die was cast.

CHAPTER 5

Rolling Stones

Beyond the Burrells' gracious home in Great Western Terrace the world began changing in unexpected ways when war was declared in 1914 and Britain took up arms against Germany and Austria. As usual Burrell was alert and, as the City of Glasgow prepared to play her part, his company was quick to respond because every ship in the Strath Line fleet was urgently needed to keep Great Britain supplied. Glaswegians from all walks of life volunteered to serve their country and soon thousands of able-bodied men were leaving to join the forces. Among them was Marion's cousin, another William Burrell.

Her Uncle George's eldest son was known as 'Young William'. He had joined the family firm as an extremely able aspirant, having inherited an ample share of the Burrell brains. In his twenties William had already shown himself to be a promising successor to manage Burrell and Son. When Marion was a schoolgirl her grownup cousin had escorted her round the company office in George Square. She felt privileged to be admitted to that glass-panelled labyrinth where clerks at tall desks beamed at her over their spectacles. The walls were hung with pictures of ships and the models in glass cases seemed even more intriguing when William told her stories about them. In the 'Private Room' he showed her a large revolving globe and when he pointed out the destinations of Strath Line ships Marion was trans-fixed, picturing steamers with smoking funnels ploughing through the oceans to far-flung ports. Teasingly, he talked to her of 'charter parties' and they laughed when she imagined businessmen enjoying celebrations.

With his seafaring connections, it seemed appropriate that 'Young' William should join the Royal Navy, and Marion was immensely proud when he appeared in uniform. But his departure to the war would always be recalled with sadness, for he was destined to give his life out on the cold grey sea. Had this bright young man survived, the history of Burrell and Son might have taken a different course. As neither of William's brothers was destined to manage the company, the partners would never see their achievements followed by another generation.

Grim telegrams conveyed the losses of fathers, husbands and sons, till hardly a family had escaped. Burrell and Son continued to support members of their office staff who served in the Forces and when an orphaned office boy joined the army William Burrell promised that the firm would provide half his normal salary to augment his army wages if he attained the rank of an officer. In due course the soldier was commissioned and, having survived the war, he returned to express gratitude for his employer's generosity. His early training at Burrell and Son had served him well and he went on to a successful career. Kindly acts cemented loyalty among the staff and William was praised for befriending the office boys who served the firm as he himself had done.

During the unsettled decade which preceded World War

I, the Burrell brothers had outdone the success of their previous building cycles by ordering no less than 32 new ships, and business was booming when hostilities broke out. As the ships were urgently needed for war service the company reaped enormous profits by selling off the Burrell fleet.

In Glasgow the cry was 'business as usual', but many young men had enlisted and even working horses went to war. Industries diversified and life styles changed. Shipyards were busier than ever and some even constructed aeroplanes while Templeton's carpet factory turned to weaving blankets. Women began to play different roles when domestic servants and shop assistants took over from their menfolk to serve as tram conductors and work in factories. There were shortages, delays and queues, and everyone was faced with the need to make do and economize.

At Laurel Bank the redoubtable Miss Hannah Watson rallied her girls to support the war effort. Marion had an aptitude for handcrafts and readily joined her classmates in knitting scarves, socks and blanket squares for the Forces. As fuel was scarce they defied the winter chills by wearing flannel petticoats and liberty bodices over their woollen combinations. One resourceful member of staff was said to combat the cold by insulating her stays with copies of the *Glasgow Herald*! The girls performed at concert parties for the wounded, and gave dancing displays for the Blue Cross animal charity. Being a passionate animal lover Marion was fervent in her efforts to support war horses serving overseas.

Her father was also making changes. During the first year of conflict Burrell's collecting was all but abandoned, but his interest began to rekindle when the slump in trade made prices extremely favourable and the profitable sales of Strath Line ships released substantial funds for making new purchases. In September 1915 a castle in the Scottish Borders came on the market. Hutton Castle, in Berwickshire, was offered for sale by Lord Tweedmouth. The property came with a fine agricultural and sporting estate which extended to almost 2,000 acres. Burrell's years of dreaming were over at last when he decided that this was the castle which was going to be his home.

The purchase of Hutton Castle was concluded early in 1916. It was conveniently placed within easy reach of Berwick-upon-Tweed, on the main railway line between London and Edinburgh and, unlike the ruin in Fife, this castle was not only available, it was also fit for occupation.

Hutton means 'the dwelling on the Hoo', or promontory, because the castle stands on a spur above the River White-adder. William's passion for Scottish history was instantly ignited when he was told that King Edward I had actually slept there. The hated 'Hammer of the Scots' had made a puni-tive visit in 1296 on his way to subdue John Balliol. Before laying siege to Berwick, the invading monarch had made a detour and spent a night at Hutton Castle while his troops camped near by. It would have delighted Burrell to boast of a royal chamber within his walls, but the battered fortress had been rebuilt so that the fifteenth-century keep was now the oldest part still standing. When years of conflict ended, the castle had passed to the first Baron Tweedmouth who turned this former stronghold of the Earls of March and of Home into a gentleman's residence, known for a time as Hutton Hall.

Once Burrell had purchased the property he began to record more items in his purchase books, though most of these acquisitions had to go into store. He made no plans to move in, but asked Robert Lorimer to come and discuss alterations. Lorimer was now married, and had made his name as an architect specializing in designing and altering Scottish houses; he was knighted in 1911. His finest achievements included the restoration of Rowallan Castle in Ayrshire and the building of Ardkinglas House in Argyll, a massive project which had been completed within the astonishing span of only 18 months. Lorimer was presently engaged on a new house near Bishopton in Renfrewshire, which was being built for his own best man, John Augustus Holms.

Holms was a bachelor and the son of a Paisley textile manufacturer. Having made his fortune as a stockbroker he had employed Lorimer to create for him a 'medieval mansion' which he named Formakin. There were paved courts, heraldic carvings, romantic pepper pot towers and a great stone fireplace gleefully inscribed 'God bless the rich for the poor can beg', words which the joker would live to regret.

Like Burrell, Holms was a collector and connoisseur of medieval furniture, tapestries and oriental carpets. He was an engaging character and a man of many parts; an entertaining host and dedicated gardener as well as a keen amateur jockey. Marion would gleefully recall the famous occasion when Johnnie Holms won a point-to-point race and was awarded an ornate silver chalice of unsurpassed vulgarity. My uncle Charlie MacAndrew had also taken part, and when he ribbed Johnnie for acquiring such a hideous trophy the winner agreed, 'It's a vomit of a cup!'

With Formakin still under construction, Robert Lorimer arrived at Hutton Castle ready to tackle another interesting project. He was sadly disappointed. Burrell's castle seemed bleak and featureless because much of its early character had been destroyed by Lord Tweedmouth's alterations. At once Lorimer suggested that Burrell should start afresh and rebuild, firmly maintaining that no other solution would provide a worthy setting for the collection. Burrell would not hear of it; even when Lorimer drew up plans for an entirely new house nothing would persuade him.

The project at Formakin was anathema to Burrell, and he considered Holms to be wildly extravagant. Though the two collectors shared similar tastes they often adopted different views. Both of them were guests of Archie and Adelaide Walker when an awkward situation arose. The Walkers had bought a set of Chippendale chairs for their home at Newark Castle in Ayrshire. Having experts on hand, they consulted the two connoisseurs as to whether the chairs were 'genuine' – actually manufactured in Thomas Chippendale's London workshop – or period furniture made in accordance with the master's design. Burrell and Holms disagreed with such ferocity they continued to quarrel throughout their visit and the authenticity of the chairs was never resolved.

Burrell was right to have doubts about Formakin. Though Johnnie Holms was famed for the midsummer masque which he held among the half-finished buildings, he never saw his mansion house completed. In the newly planted gardens a stone fountain was prophetically inscribed:

Yesterday returneth not,
Tomorrow perchance cometh not,
Today is thine
Misuse it not.

Work on Formakin was abandoned when, due to the misdeeds of his business partner, Holms lost his fortune and fell into debt. In desperation, he approached his friends in turn to borrow money. To each one he pledged as security his prized possession, the seventeenth-century Wagner Garden Carpet. It was named after a previous owner, and many years after Holms died Burrell bought this famous Persian carpet at auction and added it to his collection.

Having observed the Holms' road to ruin William Burrell was determined that nothing of the kind would happen at Hutton. When Lorimer produced innovative plans Burrell rejected them; Formakin's 'medieval' charm was merely an illusion, whereas Hutton was a genuine castle with a genuine Scottish history. In exasperation, Lorimer suggested that his client should whitewash the rooms, move in and postpone the project until after the war. Needless to say his suggestion met with refusal. More plans were produced and at once the two men were at loggerheads over details. Although Burrell felt the need of alterations, he queried structural change and resented the expense.

While their disputes wore on, hostilities continued overseas and life in Glasgow became increasingly difficult. Supplies were short and services were undermanned. The reduction in staff at Great Western Terrace was becoming a burden to Constance; as she struggled to cope with the changing situation, her health suffered so the Burrells spent the summer of 1916 living in hotels. Continental visits were no longer possible, but British hotels could relieve Constance of domestic worries. May and June were spent at the Marine Hotel in Troon on the Ayrshire coast; in July they went south to the Oatlands Park Hotel in Weybridge, and after that, August was spent in Scotland, at the Tinto Hotel in Symington, Lanarkshire. Hotels would continue to feature in the Burrells' lives, both in wartime and in peace.

As Constance clung to William and travelled with him whenever she could, their links with family and friends grew weaker. By exploiting her maladies she had learned how to get her own way, and lived for William's loving attention. Marion was expected to tend her too, but the girl was resentful and harder to manipulate. Wherever they went, it was impossible to escape the war and Constance was rarely at ease. The purchase of Hutton Castle only added to her despondency, as William's new project seemed to have brought nothing but trouble.

As they progressed from hotel to hotel the Burrells hoped each change of scene might be beneficial. Marion's schooling at Laurel Bank had ended when they moved out of town. Her father had no compunction about rescheduling arrangements, and that summer an Italian governess was employed so that another language could be added to Marion's accomplishments. The Italians were allies and Marion made no adverse comments.

The Burrells spent a miserable year while the Battle of Hutton continued with terse communications passing back and forth. Being at the top of his profession Lorimer had expected to take charge and dictate with authority. Unfortunately his client adopted the same approach and a clash was inevitable. The architect recommended an airlock at the main entrance with inner and outer doors placed at right angles to prevent a howling draught. He suggested a cloakroom nearby for waterproofs and muddy boots. Then he warned of the problems confronting elderly people when climbing spiral stairs, but Burrell wanted turnpike stairs and would not be dissuaded. He wanted windows made for his stained glass panels, rooms to display his tapestries and a new wing to house his staff. He also demanded that the massive walls of the keep were thinned so that the rooms inside could be larger.

When Lorimer came up with an estimate of £40,000 (well over three million pounds today), Burrell would not countenance the expense and insisted the castle exterior must remain intact. The spiral stairs continued to be a bone of contention, and when the architect suggested installing a lift his client flatly refused. Though time would prove Lorimer right, William insisted that only spiral stairs would be allowed in his castle. Needless to say, Constance staunchly supported her husband while the disputes raged on.

Having endured her parents' agitation Marion yearned to escape, so she was thankful when autumn came and they packed her off to boarding school. Choosing a school created another headache. Had the Burrells been blessed with a son they would probably have put his name down for Eton. Though Marion's girl cousins went to Bentley Priory and Abbotshill, her parents favoured Heathfield, a school near Ascot and founded by Miss Eleanor Wyatt. Miss Wyatt's father was headmaster of a boys' school, where she had learned to revere Christianity and wield a cricket bat. Having begun by teaching in London's East End, Miss Wyatt hoped that her privileged pupils would learn to benefit others. Heathfield was rather grand, but since the outbreak of war ladies' maids had been discontinued, except for foreign royalty and one or two aristocrats who couldn't survive without personal servants. The rest of the girls were expected to make their own beds and darn their own stockings.

Heathfield came as a shock to Marion. Her father delivered her on 3 October 1916, several days after term had begun – being out of step was going to plague her young life. Having got to know the 'gurls' at Laurel Bank she was now surrounded by 'gels'. Like her compatriots at English schools, she met with the usual reactions to Scottish intonations and words, but Marion learned fast and was soon talking like all the other 'gels'.

The austerity diet was said to include horse meat and jellied cod supplemented by healthy home produce, but in spite of wartime restrictions standards were upheld. 'Swedish' drilling promoted good deportment and it was said that 'a Heathfield girl can be spotted anywhere in the world because of the way she walks'. In due course Marion would prove herself worthy of the claim. To imbue a social conscience, any pupil who broke a school rule was required to inflict herself with an Order Mark and publicly report it. New girls had a lot to learn, but the honour system was nothing to the hazards faced by a young Presbyterian confronted by the mysterious rituals of Anglican worship. Miss Wyatt considered that girls reared by governesses were sadly devoid of religion. Twice daily services were held in the school chapel where the headmistress appeared in a black mantilla while the girls wore little lace caps. Carefully following their lead, Marion learned to genuflect, chant responses and repeat the Apostles' Creed.

In spite of these complications boarding school made a welcome change because home, in any real sense, had almost ceased to exist. The Burrell family never returned to Glasgow; their house in Great Western Terrace was destined to become a repository for her father's collection. Many years would pass before they lived at Hutton Castle so they moved from place to place. While the alterations and altercations continued they needed to be within reach of Hutton, and in 1917 Burrell rented Kilduff House near Haddington, a rambling old house with stables and a home farm.

Furnishings in rented houses were seldom of the best. Aware of her father's taste, Marion once asked him how he could bear to live with such hideous furniture. She was amazed when he told her that it didn't bother him a bit. Constance, however, did not share his attitude. She appreciated quality and was accustomed to the best. William understood her feelings towards alien surroundings and sensed her isolation with Marion at school, so knowing his precious carpets were safely stowed away, he allowed his wife the companionship of a small and hairy border terrier called Letham.

During her summer holidays Marion remembered an expedition to Stirlingshire when they visited Lettre Cottage, close to the Campsie Fells.

I must have been about 14 or 15 when my father took me to see Alexander Reid. Reid was acknowledged to have the most unerring taste and to be the best judge of a picture outside of France. He and my father had a great deal in common and got on famously together. He made a great reputation as a picture dealer and Alexander Reid and Lefevre are a firm who are direct descendants of his taste and knowledge. He had a charming house on the hillside near Killearn to which we went. It was a lovely day and the view over to Loch Lomond and Ben Lomond was superb. A little stream, straight out of the hillside ran through the garden, the borders of which had been cleverly utilised with many different sorts of water-loving plants, and the effect was enchanting. We sat on a bench near this while he and my father conversed. He was not very tall and had a little beard as in his portrait by Van Gogh which was bought in his memory by the Glasgow Corporation.

In his youth he had shared a studio in Paris with

Van Gogh. Both artists were at that time very poor and selling nothing. In despair Van Gogh sweeping his hand round the studio, said to a visitor: 'You can have any of my pictures here for 10 francs'.

As his daughter grew up, Burrell noted her keen interest and perception, though Marion recorded wistfully:

'My father was very absorbed in his business and his collecting and my childhood passed without seeing him hardly at all. Though later when I went to school at Ascot, he always came south with me and fetched me again at the end of term'.

These times spent together were enjoyed by them both because in many ways father and daughter had been cast alike and they had much to share. Constance rarely featured in Marion's school life.

Burrell continued his collecting while he struggled with the endless problems which arose at Hutton Castle, but during Marion's vacations from Heathfield there were picnics by the sea. Faded photos show the Burrells paddling, the ladies with their skirts hitched up and Willie resplendent in his tweed suit with trousers rolled above his knees. When a foreign girl came to stay he took the young ones to the swimming pool at North Berwick and encouraged them to dive by throwing in sovereigns for the girls to retrieve. Afterwards, the visitor was invited to pocket her loot, but Marion was made to give hers back. Burrell's daughter was not to be indulged. He stuck to his guns and still refused to give her pocket money; he and Constance maintained a united front and on shopping expeditions always held the purse strings, William encouraging Constance to take their daughter in hand and provide her with maternal guidance. Had the needs of his wife been less demanding, Marion's need for independence might have received more understanding. But Constance was always accorded first place, and her growing fear of being usurped invariably caused trouble. Accustomed to her husband's attentions, she expected equal consideration from her daughter so Marion's refusal to submit fuelled a cauldron of festering grudges.

By this time the Mitchells were living in Ayrshire. Having rented Flatfield in Symington, Ralston and Mary eventually bought Perceton, a country estate near Irvine. As Marion's cousins were also at English boarding schools, sharing this mode of life created a new bond between them and visits to Perceton became a highlight of her school holidays. She loved to join in the Mitchells' family life while her Aunt Mary made sure she was able to enjoy some of the fun that she lacked at home.

In 1917 Berwickshire did not seem a happy place because progress on Hutton Castle was fraught with disputes and visits to the building site had become an ordeal. Messy reconstruction held no appeal for Marion, and the place had begun to look like a war zone. While masons forged ahead, hostilities between her father and his architect were more intense than ever. By the end of Marion's summer holiday, caustic letters were flying back and forth and the close friendship the two men had once shared was strained to breaking point. Yet again William Burrell fulminated against what he considered to be unnecessary expense, and he wrote:

> Had I known that it would have cost more I would never have allowed the work to go on.

When Lorimer protested that Burrell himself had been responsible for the increase, the latter exploded in fury over the work which had been done and told his architect:

> The result is so unsatisfactory and annoying that I shall not require further professional assistance from you.

Poor Marion was thankful when the Michaelmas term began. At the end of October Lorimer wrote sadly:

> If I cease to act for you professionally, the loss will not be all on my own side. You will not easily find anyone who understands your stuff and the architectural setting it requires as I do. I shall regret, however, if a friendship of nearly twenty years standing, which included some of the pleasantest experiences I have ever had, was to be brought to an equally abrupt conclusion.

William Burrell remained intransigent, with an inability to forgive which was destined to bring misery to them all. There was to be no reconciliation with Robert Lorimer, and the architect's prediction was all too true. After Lorimer had been despatched Burrell abandoned the project and Hutton Castle was closed up and left to languish in its half-completed state before his grand design could be promoted once again.

While her parents contemplated the dismal situation at Hutton, Marion's school life provided a welcome diversion. She joined the Girl Guides and acquired a collection of badges as she became adept at bandaging, signalling and tying complicated knots. As her copperplate handwriting changed to a cursive style more like the angular script of her father, Marion wrote essays about 'The factors which make Britain Great'. She had plenty to say about 'Maritime Power' and 'The Importance of Shipyards and Coalfields' while condemning the injustice of the Glencoe Massacre and extolling the bravery of Captain Scott on his ill-fated Polar Expedition. Like her father she was carried away by historic romance. She was a hero worshipper who viewed life with intensity and conveyed her feelings with passion: 'Have you ever found yourself lying in some dim lonely pine forest with the sun glimmering through the thick Scotch firs? On the gentle breeze the sweet scent of pine needles is wafted towards you.'

Marion was sympathetic and ready with comfort when needed. A Heathfield Roll of Honour recorded the names of fathers and brothers who were lost in the war, and she sadly remembered her cousin William, but when her home life was unhappy she learned to smile and keep her troubles to herself. The gangling girl was becoming tall and lissom when, during the school holidays, her parents took her to visit the artist Sir James Guthrie at Rowmore, his home in Dunbartonshire.

During the war artists sold 'Empty Frames' for the Red Cross, etc. The idea being you chose your artist, size of picture, and finally your own subject. My father bought an empty frame of Sir James Guthrie's with a view to having my mother painted and we all went to lunch with Sir James to discuss the details. He had a delightful house in Rhu amid the trees above Gair-loch [sic] and we were in one of our ghastly furnished houses in East Lothian. The sittings would therefore have entailed staying at Helensburgh. I was 17 at the time and was wearing a large shady hat. His artist's eye appeared to have been caught by the hat, and he announced he wanted to paint me. Sad to say nothing came of the empty frame.

Although Burrell had commissioned John Lavery to portray his sister Mary no painting exists of his wife or his daughter. Constance liked to be admired, and had just turned 40 when her expectation of being portrayed was destroyed by her winsome teenage daughter. The wound was one she never forgot and Marion was never forgiven. Nevertheless, the incident made William even more aware of their daughter's potential.

When the Great War ended in November 1918 Marion was back at school. As Britain recovered from four years of conflict she wrote an essay on the prospect of building a Channel Tunnel. Having considered Britain's security as an island she rejected the idea on strategic grounds, maintaining that the faster travel a tunnel might provide would not justify increasing the risk of a foreign invasion. In the Lent term of 1919 she attended confirmation classes. Joining the Church of England was a serious step, requiring days of silent meditation before being veiled and dressed in white for the solemn ceremony performed by the Bishop of Buckingham. Parents were present but, unlike the English girls, Marion had no godparents to share her celebration because the Kirk into which she was baptized did not provide them.

When peace returned Heathfield soon lost its regime of austerity, but during Royal Ascot week Miss Wyatt was particularly vigilant. The girls were forbidden to walk near the boundary walls and the school gates were kept firmly closed, although it was not clear whether these precautions were intended to keep intruders out or prevent the girls from bolting to the race course. On one memorable occasion when the outside world seemed to revolve round the race meeting, the Prince of Wales turned up with Mrs Dudley Ward. They were hoping to visit her young sister, who was one of the Heathfield pupils, but Miss Wyatt promptly sent the royal entourage packing. No visitors were admitted on a weekday; not even royalty.

But when it came to winning over this determined headmistress Willie Burrell was more successful than the Prince. Repeated gaps in Marion's attendance record could hardly be attributed to illness in a girl who was said to have enjoyed the best of health. At first her absences lasted only for a week or two, but after the war they became more frequent and sometimes continued for over a month. Burrell believed foreign travel to be an ideal form of education, and his extraordinary powers of persuasion worked their charm because Miss Wyatt agreed to his scheme. Marion's photograph albums of this time record carefully annotated visits to the ancient sites of Rome, Naples, Florence and Sicily. To witness the history and geography of Europe made a delightful change from school, and this interest shared by father and daughter gave infinite pleasure to both. Having listened to his tales of the eruption in New Zealand, it was thrilling for Marion to accompany her father on expeditions to Vesuvius, Etna and Stromboli. But while all three Burrells enjoyed the Grand Tours, Marion's school routine was being disrupted and again she was out of step.

During her last term at Heathfield in the summer of 1920 parents were entertained by an open-air performance of *A Midsummer Night's Dream*. The Queen of the Fairies was played by Marion's contemporary, Jean Forbes-Robertson, who was destined to immortalize the role of Barrie's Peter Pan on the London stage. Though Marion also had talent, and welcomed opportunities to perform, her absence at rehearsal times meant that she had to make the most of a walk-on part, having been cast, with three other tall girls, as one of Hippolyta's Amazon attendants. The Fairy Queen received rapturous applause while Marion took her bow with the extras. But her father was gratified to observe her youthful blossoming and, feeling well satisfied with the schooling he had provided, he began to turn his mind to her future prospects.

Burrell commissioned a family tree which traced his Northumbrian ancestry from the first William Burrell who had acquired Bassington in 1692 (Burrell family tree p.xviii). When Marion was still in her teens her father took her on an expedition to visit their ancestral home. The old stone house stands square and symmetrical like one drawn by a child. It was built as a gentleman's farm and remains a desirable property with a substantial stone steading and good land on a sunny hillside above the River Aln. Today Bassington forms part of Hulne Park which belongs to the Duke of Northumberland.

Willie Burrell's family had been reared on a cautionary tale concerning Gambler George who fell into debt and squandered his inheritance. According to Burrell family tradition, the reprobate had taken to high living, spending his time racing and gambling with the 1st Duke of Northumberland, whose eighteenth-century gaming table can still be seen at Alnwick Castle. When George's luck ran out, he paid off his debts by selling his property to the Duke. The story goes that after the Gambler had made his family destitute, his equally profligate wife ignored the pressing need of economy and flatly refused to give up wearing silk stockings. The fate of their improvident ancestor loomed large in the Burrell family.

Although Gambler George let his family down, his other relations continued to prosper. After the founder William of Bassington died, his wife had married a wealthy widower, Joseph Palfrey of Acklington and Morwick. Her eldest son George then wed the widower's daughter Anne; they were the Gambler's parents. The Gambler's two elder brothers inherited Palfrey estates while he and his younger brother John jointly inherited Bassington. George married Eleanor Whitehead and lived there with his family while John married an heiress, Barbara Peareth, and went to live on her nearby estate at Little Houghton. Fortune smiled as John's sons pursued successful careers and one became the first British Governer of Hong Kong. After the Duke purchased George's share of Bassington in 1782 John's share was added in 1807.

The Duke would have had his eye on Bassington for quite a long time. Northumberland Archives name the estate a residual part of his ancestral lands seized during the sixteenth century by Henry VIII, most of which had already been reclaimed. After his transaction with the Gambler was successfully concluded, the Duke allowed George to become a tenant on the property he had formerly owned and remain there until he died in his eighties, in 1814.

The Gambler's son was less fortunate, because the George who became a tea merchant and now lived in Alnwick found his family humiliated and cast as 'poor relations' in the eyes of their well-heeled kinsmen. But country outings could still be enjoyed and Bassington was near enough for family visits.

Young Grafter George was 14 when his improvident grand-father died, so when the Grafter went north to Glasgow and struggled to rear ailing children in the disease-ridden city, he could still remember the green fields in Northumberland where his family might otherwise have lived.

As Grafter George lived on for many years, Sir William Burrell's hunger for family history would have been amply rewarded by the tales told by his grandfather when, reflecting the Duke's desire to reclaim his lost lands, Burrell set out to regain the status his own ancestors had lost. His fortune having been amassed, he was determined that the heiress of Hutton Castle should bring honour to their family name by contracting a prestigious marriage. A glorious future could lie ahead for young Marion Burrell.

The collector's sharp eye for historical connections had noted how other Burrells had achieved distinction. During the eighteenth century a William Burrell in Kent had acquired Knepp Castle and a baronetcy by forming a prodig-ious alliance. In Sussex, a Peter Burrell who wed a daughter of the 3rd Duke of Ancaster became Lord Chamberlain as well as Baron Gwydyr of Gwydyr. In Northumberland, another illustrious family of Burrells held their family seat at Broome Park. As the collector's ancestors had lived in that county they might have been related, but, despite approaches from members of Sir William's family, no connections with any of these Burrells have been found.

Meanwhile Burrell's career in the world of commerce was drawing to a close. After a major building boom the company had entered the war with a fleet of 30 ships which were chartered or sold for war service. When 10 changed hands for treble their cost Burrell gained another fortune. Six ships were lost through enemy action and when hostilities ended only two of the fleet remained. The *Strathearn* was sold in 1919, leaving only the *Strathlorne* to fly the Strath Line flag. The ship which Marion had launched would serve the company until 1930, while Burrell and Son was scaled down to continue in business as brokers and agents until 1939. Since the company was founded, Burrell and Son had owned a total of 95 ships. Because William Burrell chose to profit by trading in ships, few remained in company owner-ship for long. More than 60 quickly changed hands and were renamed. The formidable casualty rate suffered by shipping, both in war and in peace, is shown by the fact that only 20 of the vessels recorded on the Burrell Fleet List survived to reach the breaker's yard.

Marion seemed to have few regrets when her schooldays ended. Although her photographs abound with smiling faces, few lasting bonds were formed and a feeling of alienation seems to have endured. Having spent so much of her youth alone, or in the company of adults, it had been hard for her to join a crowd. Now she was glad to move on. In the absence of a Channel Tunnel she was taken to France by sea. With their daughter's schooling complete, William and Constance Burrell had decided that the next move should be for Marion to be 'finished' in Paris.

CHAPTER 6
First Love

Marion Burrell was 18 years old when she arrived in Paris. She had known the city from childhood visits with her parents, but this time she would be with companions of her own age. After the rigid routine at Heathfield, the prospect of a finishing school in a foreign capital beckoned like a gateway to freedom. Now she could live without the restraint of parental supervision, even though the girls were chaperoned. Being protected from wicked Frenchmen began to seem rather enticing!

Mlle Ozanne's School near the Champs de Mars had become a popular destination for former Heathfield girls who followed a quest for further education. In 1909 Miss Wyatt had bought the property intending to open a finishing school, but she withdrew from the venture and her colleague, Alice Ozanne, had taken over with considerable success. As well as receiving tuition at the school, the girls attended the Cours des Etrangers at the University of the Sorbonne, and Les Cours d'Etterlin near the Place de l'Etoile.

The girls' chaperones were mostly French war widows whose pensions were too meagre to support them. As some of them were not much older than their charges, the girls enjoyed their company and had quite a good time. There were outings to historic sites, galleries and museums. If Marion had seen them already, further acquaintance added to her pleasure as she was interested in everything she heard and saw. She felt at ease in Paris. When the girls talked among themselves they were supposed to speak only in French, but that was no problem to Marion who had been fluent from her nursery. Having mastered the language of the English upper classes she learned to speak the Gallic tongue like a French aristocrat. Mademoiselle Burrell was shaping up well.

To be living in Paris seemed incredibly romantic. On tree-lined boulevards gentlemen sat at café tables puffing their cigars. Shoppers in the Rue de Rivoli looked far more elegant than their counterparts at home. Lovers strolled on the embankments where artists and flower sellers plied their wares by the Seine while barges passed slowly beneath the bridges. Marion feasted on it all as she walked the cobbled lanes of Montmartre, prowled round galleries in the Louvre and toured the Palace of Versailles, picturing the youthful Marie Antoinette absconding from the gilded halls to masquerade as a milkmaid with porcelain pails manufactured by Sèvres.

The finishing course lasted nearly a year and during the Easter holiday her parents took her off to Cannes. While staying at the Metropole, they enjoyed a boat trip to picnic on the Iles des Lérins, and when the Carnival of Flowers took place, they watched in style from a grandstand. Constance Burrell enjoyed foreign travel and her ailments seemed to be forgotten in the Mediterranean sun. She and William were delighted to see how well their daughter had developed. When Marion's course ended in June, they came to Paris to celebrate her entry to adulthood with another family holiday. This vacation marked a turning point; having gazed wistfully at gorgeous gowns in shop windows, Marion was finally allowed to go shopping. Her father had brought his wallet and her mother had come to have her fitted out with a range of new clothes worthy of a young lady entering society. Financial restraint was thrown to the wind as Marion found herself propelled into the most delightful spending spree she could ever have imagined.

Being a dedicated shopper, Constance conducted their expeditions with aplomb. They toured the fashion houses, browsed among the boutiques in the Rue St Honoré and lingered over trays of jewels in the Place Vendôme. Purchases were made for them both and the venture proved a dazzling success. Though Burrell's tastes were generally restrained, he understood his wife's penchant for finery and was happy to indulge her. Here at last was an interest which mother and daughter could share. Marion came home with a wardrobe fit for a princess, and William was proud to see his wife and daughter display their acquisitions. Though Constance liked to be admired, it was always Marion who turned heads for she had the stature of a mannequin and every style made her look like a fashion plate.

While his two ladies were busily spending his money William Burrell also went shopping and added to his collection. Marion was with him on the day when he visited George Bernheim's gallery and purchased from him a beautiful little portrait by Manet. The subject was believed to be the artist's model Elisa. Shortly before Manet died in 1883, he had snatched the opportunity to make a pastel drawing of her to celebrate the occasion when she came to visit him bearing an Easter gift. Burrell paid £360 (over £30,000 today) for this sensitive portrayal of the young girl. Marion greatly admired it and always remembered Bernheim's comment, 'It seems as if the artist breathed her onto the paper'.

Marion was acquiring her father's eye for art along with her mother's eye for fine merchandise. Travel had enhanced her education so that she was articulate and able to converse on a wide range of subjects. Just as her father had done, she had learned to cultivate manners which others found disarming. William's regret that their only child had not been a son was forgotten when she displayed qualities worthy of his aspirations. The child's early promise had been realized, for here was a daughter of whom he and Constance could be inordinately proud. A prestigious marriage for Marion would now be their aim, and Constance welcomed the possibility of acquiring a noble son-in-law. They had no doubt that this child of theirs was worthy of the best. While other parents gave their daughters sets of silver-backed brushes to display on their dressing tables, Marion's were plated with gold.

In 1919 the Burrells had left Kilduff and taken a five-year lease of Rozelle, a country house near Alloway in Ayrshire, surrounded by parkland and woods. When Marion came waltzing back from Paris she was glad to be fully fledged and living within reach of her Mitchell cousins at Perceton. Growing up had brought her closer to her father and the pleasure they shared in his collection became a lasting bond; but though William was determined that she should excel, he continued to restrain her. Marion was permitted to shop on her own provided every purchase was made through a Burrell account. Each item was monitored, and ready cash continued to be as elusive as ever. There were problems with her mother too: Marion enjoyed being treated as an adult now that they had more interests in common, but restrictive policies persisted and harmony did not prevail. While her daughter continued to flourish, Constance continued to wilt and require attention, fearing that her own exalted position might soon be under threat.

Meanwhile Marion began to make new friends and one of the first was my mother, Eva MacAndrew. She was Marion's age and the youngest of a family of six who had grown up at Knock Castle near Largs. Her father, Glen MacAndrew, was a stockbroker whose family had inherited his passions for riding, golf, yacht racing and amateur theatricals. Two yachts had been built for him at William Fife's yard in Fairlie, and his daughter Eva was named after the cutter. She never liked the name but she might have fared worse – his schooner was called *Sunshine*. Her father died when she was four, and before the Great War broke out, his widow, Bessie, moved her family to Ayr which was in the hunting country and more central to county social life. The MacAndrews were a lively lot, though unlike Marion, Eva had never been abroad or even attended a school. To her disgust, she had been raised at home by governesses and later claimed that one had gone mad and the other committed suicide. In spite of these setbacks, Eva was a multi-talented lass who could even swing a lariat.

The two girls first met when Mrs Burrell drove out from Rozelle with her daughter to call on Mrs MacAndrew of Stewartlea. When the latter discovered that Marion had been left in the car with the chauffeur Eva was told to go and welcome her in. At once the pair became friends. Both were tall and willowy and Eva, who had an eye for style was captivated by Marion's exquisite clothes. Her tales of Paris held Eva spellbound, and her brother Jo found their new friend enchanting. Before long Marion was joining in their family activities.

In September, Ayrshire society assembled for the Western Meeting. It was a week when everyone went to the races, and the evenings were merry with parties and balls. After three days of flat racing at Ayr, there was a meeting at Bogside, and that day Willie Burrell escorted Eva and Marion to the races. He was in good spirits, and the girls were delighted when he gave each of them a new pound note so that they could bet on the horses. Jostling with the Saturday crowds the young ones studied their race cards and watched the tic-tac men, hoping to pick up tips. The world and his wife were there, as peers and priests rubbed shoulders on the paddock rails. Familiar faces emerged and gentlemen raised their hats. From the stand they cheered and groaned alternately as winners thundered past. Miss Burrell became a centre of attention, but whether she was in funds at the end of the day, history doesn't relate.

At the dances that week Eva felt shy at first when revellers took to the floor, but her friend was totally at ease as admirers circled about her like moths drawn to a lamp. She seemed to captivate everyone, though she was not a classic beauty. Marion reached almost six feet in her stocking soles and her feet were simply enormous. Her features lacked star quality and her face was overlong. But her heavy jaw was eclipsed by a dazzling smile while her vivid blue eyes seemed to sparkle with an irresistible charm. Marion's ability to enchant could only come from within, and when her parents observed her extraordinary magnetism, they began to worry.

A dance invitation for Marion arrived from Mrs Claude Allan of Kilmahew. The hostess was Constance Burrell's sister Adeline, known to Marion as 'Aunt Ada'. There were four young people in the Allan family, and the event in Dunbartonshire promised to be a lively one as naval officers had been invited. But Marion's parents were becoming concerned about the suitability of her dancing partners and they began to fear that an adventurer might carry her off and try to get his hands on the Burrell fortune. Marion never went to the dance because Constance destroyed her daughter's invitation before she even saw it. When the truth came out there was a monumental row. Being cheated by her mother was an act that Marion would never forgive. Parental efforts to vet her companions continued while her circle of friends continued to increase. She was popular with both sexes because she was good company and did not try to outshine other girls.

While the Burrells were living at Rozelle, she enjoyed playing 'pit-pat' tennis at Newark Castle with the Walkers' young daughter Bunty. Marion remembered watching their fathers walking together one day and, being aware of the early romance between Willie and Adelaide, was struck by the powerful resemblance between those tall, commanding men with distinctive white hair and moustaches. And meanwhile Bunty's mother was having more trouble with those controversial Chippendale chairs. When their friends dined at Newark before Hunt Balls the mahogany was getting scratched by the metal rear buttons on the 'pink' tail coats, and so the inventive Adelaide had cushion pads made to protect the chair backs of her male guests. Alas, her strategy proved a failure when each gentleman picked up his cushion and politely transferred it to the lady seated next to him.

During the summer, Constance Burrell opened a garden fête which was held at Rozelle in aid of the YMCA, and Marion, who never failed to look enchanting in a summer frock and a picture hat, was as usual, in demand. As her diary filled up with even more engagements her parents continued to worry. How could they arrange a propitious marriage when uninvited suitors kept pursuing their daughter? It was just a case of time before one of them would steal her heart and, almost at once, things turned out exactly as they had feared.

Marion Burrell was 19 when Leslie Watson swung into her life and, before anyone had time to draw breath, the pair had fallen in love. Leslie's family home was Neisland in neighbouring Lanarkshire, and the county social round had brought them together. Few of Marion's friends were aware of the romance until she invited Eva to come and watch Leslie take part in a polo gymkhana at Troon. It was organized by the Ayrshire Yeomanry, and although most of the men Eva knew were members of the regiment she had not met Marion's beau. He was already mounted and preparing for action when Marion greeted her with the thrilling news that she and Leslie were engaged. Eva gasped with excitement as she admired the ruby ring that her friend was proudly wearing. Then when the chukka was under way, Marion pointed out her champion among the riders as they pounded past, polo sticks flailing and clashing. Whatever the outcome of the match, Watson's side was loyally supported.

At the age of 27 Captain Leslie Watson was ready to settle down. After Rugby and Sandhurst he had gained a commission in the 7th Dragoon Guards and given war service in Belgium and France as well as Mesopotamia. Coming from a well-regarded county family Leslie had charged like a shining knight to rescue Marion from Burrell bondage. He was tall like her, and a fine-looking man, but it was his warm personality and infectious sense of fun that endeared him to her. Suddenly the prospect of marrying Leslie and sharing the joyful freedom of his world eclipsed the years of parental repression which had fettered Marion's youth. Yet despite their vows of undying love the future she and Leslie planned to share could only be a dream.

Marion's engagement was never announced. Burrell's permission was withheld and Captain Watson was ignominiously banished – he could never be the match that the Burrells were seeking for their daughter. Leslie had no title to inherit. Further to that, a girl of 19 seemed hopelessly inexperienced to a father who had not entered the marriage stakes until he was over 40. If Marion was to marry well she would have to be protected from foolish indiscretions. Some parents might have allowed their daughter time to reconsider, but with Marion's future at stake Burrell was savage, and Leslie's expulsion was final.

William Burrell's attitude seems ironic now because Leslie's forebears had started on their road to success in a similar way to the Burrells; like Grafter George, Leslie's grandfather had worked barges at Port Dundas on the Forth and Clyde Canal. John Watson had then bought a coalfield and acquired a landholding in Lanarkshire surpassed only by that of the Duke of Hamilton. These achievements had brought Watson a baronetcy. Though Leslie was not in line, one day his son would be the 6th Baronet of Earnock. But being socially eligible was not enough to satisfy Burrell's ambitious requirements, and Leslie was not alone, for many good men were rejected. When my kind Uncle Jo dared to show an interest in Marion, he was repulsed with such venom it made him confide to his friend Jack Maclay, 'I used to think that Willie Burrell was a nice man'.

Marion was inconsolable when her engagement was

broken. She shunned her friends and resigned herself to misery. Then she became consumed with wrath and exploded at her parents. Constance was worn out by these outbursts, and when her nerves began to suffer William was burdened with two women in crisis. Anxiety was making his wife unwell while their daughter exhausted her fury and drifted into a sad grey world of her own. Seeing her so dispirited worried her parents even more than her storms of rage. They were genuinely disturbed. Patent remedies were prescribed while William sought ways to revive Marion and reawaken her zest for life.

A healthy diet and fresh air were tried without success. Then her father suggested she might take up riding and would gladly have provided her with the best mounts and tuition. Ayrshire society revolved round the Yeomanry and the Eglinton Hunt, but the Burrells had never been horsey. While Marion's young contemporaries had been galloping ponies about the countryside, her early childhood had been spent in Glasgow. Unlike Eva, who would overcome her trepidation on the hunting field to become a Master of Hounds, Marion showed no desire to be a mature candidate in the art of horsemanship and resolved to support equestrian events with both feet firmly on the ground.

Her father's collection held more appeal for Marion than horses. She was keen to learn and their shared enthusiasm gave pleasure to them both. Together they studied paintings, silver, stained glass, and ceramics. He showed her books with his own pencilled notes neatly entered on the margins, and drew charts for her to learn the dates of Chinese dynasties. Then he recommended she begin a collection of her own, starting with Chinese pottery and porcelain, and wrote down his instructions:

You should gradually get a specimen of each so that they would be a guide to you and you would have a bird's eye view of the whole field and roughly know where you were when a price was offered either by a shop or at auction. But there are such a vast number of frauds, especially in the case of prices prior to Kanghai [the Emperor Kangxi and his reign 1661–1722] that the only thing is to avoid all shops except one or two whom you find you can depend on e.g. Partridge and Hancock and they will vet the prices and keep you right. Bleratt [possibly Bluett] also Sparks are dependable. Besides being dependable a man who knows you spend your money with him will always be careful not to sell you a wrong article – your custom being too valuable. People think they get bargains in small shops but they don't. It is the small shop that gets the mug.

Since Marion was allowed no money of her own it is not known how her collecting was to be financed, though her father contributed items to encourage her and she came to possess some interesting pieces, including a small pottery vessel from the Han dynasty, about 2,000 years old. Burrell's policy of being in charge was again in evidence when he suggested that he and his daughter might set up a small business together, dealing in antiques. It never happened, but Marion was enthused by the idea and flattered by the compliment he paid her. When exercising his extraordinary charm Burrell could captivate young people by suggesting whimsical schemes; one of Marion's girl friends was entranced when he assured her that she would be perfectly capable of taking over and managing a local enterprise known as the Buttercup Dairies. His line of strategy seemed so plausible that she was very nearly convinced.

In spite of William's efforts to divert his daughter it seemed that nothing would repair her aching heart. As the problem continued to trouble both Marion and her parents decisive action would have to be taken. A change of scene seemed the only solution, but assuaging Marion's grief for Leslie Watson was going to take more than a trip down the Clyde. The Burrell parents pondered long and hard before coming up with the answer. Marion must be taken right away in order to 'forget', so William and Constance finally decided on 'A Passage to India'.

This great idea was almost certainly prompted by Lord and Lady Inchcape whose home was at Glenapp Castle near Ballantrae. While the Burrells were living in Ayrshire they met at social gatherings and, apart from being friends, Inchcape and Burrell also made contact in the shipping world. Eight years senior to Burrell, Lord Inchcape was a supremely successful man. Born James Mackay in 1852, he was a ship owner whose ascendancy had sprung from humble roots. After starting out as a clerk he rose to become chairman of both the Peninsular and Orient and the British India Steam Navigation Companies and, through establishing an uncontested line of transport to India and Australia, he achieved a position of prime influence in the Indian subcontinent. Inchcape was a charismatic man and, having been created Baron Inchcape of Strathnaver, he was still an active man at 70, and destined to be honoured with an earldom. That year, he and his wife were planning a voyage to India, taking a daughter of their own who also needed to 'forget'. Elsie was their third child, a pretty girl just a few years older than Marion. During the war Elsie had embarked on an unhappy marriage which had recently been annulled. To make a fresh start she had resumed her maiden name and was known once more as the Hon. Elsie Mackay.

With Lord Inchcape's help and guidance, plans were made for an extensive Burrell tour. The preparations kept everybody busy for weeks while tropical clothing, sunshades, sola topis (pith helmets) and a vast assortment of medical supplies were ordered and packed into a range of leather suitcases, hat boxes and enormous cabin trunks. It was a relief to leave Rozelle at last in the autumn of 1922 when the two families boarded the P&O steamship *Naldera* to begin their voyage to India.

The scheme turned out to be a good one. As soon as Marion stepped on board her life was transformed. She walked the decks in the salty air and watched the sea birds skim the waves. In spite of herself she began to make acquaintances, and after she and Elsie had exchanged their sad tales they quickly became firm friends. But Leslie Watson was not forgotten as miles of ocean slowly tore the lovers apart. Marion had come away with a heavy heart and brought with her an exercise book in which she had copied out a succession of poems which expressed her feelings of misery and desolation. Her anthology of woe contained lines from *The Rubáiyát* by Omar Khayyam:

> The Moving Finger writes; and having writ
> Moves on: nor all thy Piety nor Wit
> Shall lure it back to cancel half a line,
> Nor all thy Tears wash out a Word of it.

From Thomas Hood's 'To an Absentee' she wrote this anguished verse:

O'er hill and dale, and distant sea,
Through all the miles that stretch between
My thought must fly to rest on thee,
And would, though worlds should intervene.
Alas for pleasure on the sea,
And sorrow on the shore.
[The last two lines are from 'Fair Ines'.]

Worst of all came this dismal stanza from 'Second Best',
penned by Rupert Brooke:

Through laughter, through roses as of old
Comes Death, on shadowy and relentless feet.
Death, unappeasable by prayer or gold;
Death is the end, the end.
Proud then – clear-eyed and laughing go
To greet Death as a friend.

But the grieving girl resisted her temptation to take a
running jump into the wake of the ship. The days grew warm
as *Naldera* voyaged through the Mediterranean Sea and then
sailed southward through the Suez Canal. Everything
changed when they reached Port Said. Marion was stirred
by a breath of the Orient when Arab dhows came into view.
Double awnings were erected on board and the ship's officers
appeared in tropical white. At Aden *Naldera* docked to take
on coal and during the long and grimy process the Burrells
were rowed ashore by dark-skinned lascars so that they could
pay a visit to the camel market.

As the voyage continued fellow passengers invited Marion
to join their games on deck, and when a shipboard gymkhana
was held she found herself taking part. There was an obstacle

race for children and gentlemen stripped to their shirt sleeves to belabour each other in the 'spar-fighting' competition and compete in a nautical sprint. Dressed in floating voile and a broad-brimmed hat, Miss Burrell cantered in to win the Ladies' Race, with undisguised delight.

Little by little the parental plan was taking effect and each stage of Marion's recovery was a relief to them all. Even in the depths of an abyss the urge to survive is strong, and Marion was a born survivor. When *Naldera* berthed at Bombay (now Mumbai), the great welcoming archway known as 'The Gateway of India' had not been completed, but Marion's arrival was in no way diminished when all the sounds and smells of the East bombarded her at once. There were horse-drawn gharries and rattling rickshaws, hawkers, beggars, sacred cattle, mangy pi-dogs and dark-eyed ladies in graceful saris of every imaginable hue.

At Bombay the Burrells stayed at Clairmont, a single-storey residence amid shady gardens, where bowing servants attended to their needs. In Rajasthan, Marion rode on an elephant to visit the Amber Palace and inspected the Maharajah's cheetahs in Jaipur. Delhi was not yet the seat of government, though King George V and Queen Mary had laid foundations for the new capital of British India in 1911. The New Delhi building project dragged on for 18 years. After Edward Lutyens was appointed to design the government buildings Herbert Baker had been co-opted, but the two architects fell out and the massive scheme was not completed till 1929. When the Burrells arrived construction was still underway, and on viewing this monumental building site William Burrell could recognize a situation not unlike his own at Hutton Castle. But Marion was fascinated by ancient Delhi where she could trace the history of the Great

Moguls at the Qutab Minar and the Tomb of Humayun. At Agra they visited the Taj Mahal by moonlight:

> It must (like Venice) be one of the places which doesn't disappoint. There was a moon and mist on the river beyond it so that it appeared completely ethereal, floating on the mist and floodlit by the moon. Next day we went back to see it by daylight and it was almost equally beautiful.
>
> Lord Curzon, that great appreciator of beauty, found it in a sad state and it was he who had the foreground not only tidied up but had the inspiration of water channels. [According to Islamic tradition these channels represent the waters in the gardens of Paradise.]

The Burrells visited crowded bazaars and watched artisans weaving fabrics and carving exquisite objects in ivory and jade. Constance and Marion could browse over silks and embroideries while William watched craftsmen at work and studied their methods. Indian merchandise was tempting and purchases were made. William was always quick to spot items of rare quality, and Marion brought home a little mother-of-pearl crucifix. It came from Goa where the apostle St Thomas had founded a Christian community in India many centuries before converts were made in Britain. For Marion and her parents the highlight of their visit to India took place in Calcutta where they joined the Inchcapes as guests at Viceregal Lodge. They arrived there for the Christmas season which Marion recalled:

> It was a great insight into the last days of the British Raj. Everything was gaiety and luxury, if you were

British, and there was no sign of any grudge on the part of those who were less fortunate.

Lord Reading was Viceroy and entertained us most hospitably. At dinner a magnificent Sikh stood behind every two chairs all the way round the table, in full dress. I remember chiefly their splendid turbans and the immaculate long white gauntlets which rested on the belt of the sword as they stood motionless as statues. We ate off gold plate and curtsied to the Viceroy as representing the power of the Raj, and his invitation to dance with him was a royal command. This was not really a dance but entailed sitting and talking to him during a dance. He was charming and 'easy' and no effort for a greenhorn like myself. How well spent the time of the initiated to the uninitiated; it is always remembered with gratitude.

While young Marion was being enthralled, the Viceroy probably enjoyed her conversation as much as she enjoyed his. During her life William Burrell's daughter was destined to meet a succession of outstanding people. Lord Reading had risen with meteoric success. Though he and his wife presided with all the grace of royalty they had been born Rufus Isaacs and Alice Cohen, both offspring of London merchants. After ten years in parliament, Isaacs had been raised to the House of Lords as Baron Reading of Erleigh, then Viscount Reading, and would yet attain the rank of Marquess. Having served as Solicitor General, Attorney General and Lord Chief Justice in addition to numerous diplomatic posts, he had been appointed Viceroy of India in 1921. Amid Viceregal glory the teenage Marion was enjoying the time of her young life:

We danced all night and every night during Christmas week and even followed this with breakfast parties at Tollygunge, the polo ground. At the races the Viceroy drove up the course in state – as the Queen does at Ascot. There were dinner parties at a variety of houses every night and then on with the dance.

Under the auspices of the Inchcapes, the Burrells were lavishly entertained. According to his biographer, Lord Inchcape was in a position of considerable influence and during his career came close to being appointed Viceroy. At Vice-regal Lodge Lord Reading held sway in a magnificent palace flanked by pavilions which were connected to the central block by curved passages. In sumptuous state rooms marble columns reached up to ceilings which were royally embell-ished with gold. This Palladian creation was a masterpiece of British supremacy and said to resemble Robert Adam's design for the Curzon seat at Kedleston Hall in Derbyshire.

Once the Christmas festivities were over the Burrells sailed from Calcutta to Rangoon on a British India ship and were welcomed at Government House by Sir Harcourt Butler, Governor of Burma (now Myanmar). Marion was growing accustomed to this kind of attention, taking it all in her stride. Rangoon was celebrating the Chinese New Year with ceremonial dragon dancers and fireworks. During the visit she went with her parents to see working elephants skilfully rolling and stacking logs, and then watched them luxuriating in the river while they were bathed and scrubbed by their faithful mahouts. Having enjoyed more entertainments the three Burrells were wreathed in garlands of flowers when they set out for a three day trip on the Irrawaddy.

We went on a stern-wheeler from Mandalay and alongside we towed another boat much as a motor bicycle with a side car. The boat alongside was for natives and these were very friendly and came over to see us when they felt like it. There was a dear old woman from the Shan States who wore their traditional costume. I don't think she had seen many white people before and she picked up my hand and stroked it comparing it with her dark one. She was a dear old thing.

There was a Burman who also came over to our boat and he smoked a pipe with a long stem and a jade bowl. My father's quick eye got onto this piece of jade and he bought it then and there – right out of the smoker's mouth!

We tied up every night; the first night was at a place called Katha, and wishing to stretch our legs went for a walk along the river bank and only learned when we got back that Katha is one of the worst places in Burmah [sic] for snakes.

When freed from formality Marion was carried away by her love of adventure.

Bamoh [sic] was only 30 miles from the Chinese border and the influence of China was very much in evidence. There was a temple with a round doorway in the wall and an upward curving roof. In the bazaar the conical hats of China were worn, the wearers looking like so many mushrooms as they squatted in circles on the ground. The tribe here appeared to be Kachins who looked more suspicious and unfriendly than our gentle Shans on the boat. The women dressed in red and black with an endless number of black wooden rings round the waist. This seemed to have something to do with age or status, as a mother would have many more of these rings than her daughters.

As we proceeded down-stream we passed rafts composed of logs being floated down to the mills. Sometimes there was a tiny cabin for the boatman. This seemed very necessary as there was one of the worst thunderstorms imaginable. It was rainless and most spectacular with huge flashes of light.

The Irrawaddy is almost impossible to chart, as the bottom is constantly changing, so it was not surprising we ran aground on a sandbank. One would have thought this was a perfect opportunity for dacoits [bandits] to board us as we were helpless. However, by getting into reverse we managed to get off only to run into a sand storm. This was much more unpleasant as the sand penetrated everywhere, beds and food and everything.

Back in Rangoon, my father refused to go to the Shwedagon Pagoda, as the Buddhists were insisting on everyone taking off their shoes, and he maintained this was purely political. I have always regretted this very much as the Burmese, especially the ladies, made an unforgettable spectacle in their vivid coloured silks and parasols, even the poorest wearing pure silk.

Being accustomed to giving orders Burrell resented receiving them, especially from foreigners whose motives he suspected. Sadly for Marion, her father's intransigence continued to influence her life. She often felt drawn towards the people she met and, for the rest of her life, preserved a collection of bags and sashes made in Burma from brightly coloured silks. It seems that she never found a use for them as they were the kind of things that a tourist will sometimes buy in a rush of generosity when hoping somehow to improve the lot of an impoverished hawker.

From Rangoon the Burrells sailed to Madras, and then on to Ceylon (now Sri Lanka). Returning from a full-day journey to see the elephant carvings at the Caves of the Nine Pagodas, they almost failed to ford a fast running river. When Marion and her parents had explored Ceylon with its mountains and paddy fields, tea plantations, shrines and temples their travels finally came to an end. Colombo was their last port of call, and before leaving for home they bought precious gems.

> There was a jeweller down on the quay-side whose name was Seidel. Ceylon was in those days a land of precious and semi-precious stones and Seidel's shop was a virtual Aladdin's cave. He took no precautions against theft. There were common kitchen mixing bowls filled with gems of every sort. You could pick them up in handfuls and allow them to trickle through your fingers. My father bought two sapphires, one of which I still have. The Ceylon rubies were rather poor in colour – the best being the 'pigeon blood' of Burmah, the mines now alas worked out.

The tour had been demanding and the accumulation of luggage was an ongoing worry. A cabin trunk was pilfered when a thief cut a hole through the back and a number of items went missing before anyone spotted the crime. In the holy city of Benares (Varanasi) where Hindu burials take place on the sacred River Ganges, all the Burrells went down with dysentery. No reports reveal how Constance coped with tropical hazards and ailments or with the heat and the creepy crawlies, but she must have been less fragile than she seemed, considering the arduous itineraries she tackled. Thanks to Lord Inchcape's kindly influence her family had been provided with every comfort and attention it was possible to bestow. The opulence of the Raj was said to exceed the court of King George V so, for Constance Burrell, the pleasure of being royally received by the Viceroy had been sublime. Her self-esteem had soared and future possibilities were already entertaining her mind.

For all of them the tour had been a thrilling adventure. Young Marion had regained her sparkle. She had been entranced by India and responded with vivacity to the grandeur of the British Raj. For her, the Christmas season at Calcutta had been tremendous fun; a 'fishing fleet' of young British ladies was there to hunt for husbands while bachelors serving the Raj were equally keen to find wives. Though Marion's parents did not seek an army officer or a member of the Indian Civil Service for a son-in-law, they had been taking note.

From Colombo the Burrells sailed for home in the SS *Morea*. The sad episode of Leslie Watson seemed to be safely buried and the time had come to look ahead. The next objective would be to rent a property near Hutton Castle until the alterations were completed. Now Marion could not wait. When they were at sea the mournful exercise book was brought out again. This time the young traveller poured her heart out in words of her own by writing 'A Cry to Dunbar'.

I want to be out on the links once more. I want to feel the soft springy turf under my feet and see the long expanse of the links stretched out before me and beyond – the blue, blue sea with its fringe of rocky wave swept shore. I want to see the tall white column of Barness Lighthouse shining in the sun; and behind me the little fishing town with its beweather-cocked Town Hall; the harbour against whose massive stone walls the waves of the North Sea lash themselves in vain. I want to feel a club in my hands; to play one really good shot and feel the little thrill of satisfaction trickle down my spine. I want to hear the pro say that it is a good shot – reluctantly – with that Scots inborn dislike of praise – I want to fill my lungs with clean pure air; to feel the blood coursing through my veins like wine. I want to feel the keen sharp wind like a whetted knife whipping the colour into my face.

It isn't a fashionable place. Nobody goes there. It's only a little fishing town.

But I miss it so.

I want it so.

I love it so.

I'm unutterably homesick without it.

CHAPTER 7

Great Expectations

In 1923 the Burrells returned from the tropics to a familiar landscape where the soft, damp air smelled of bluebells and newly mown grass. As spring burgeoned into a temperate Scottish summer, Marion prepared to forge a new beginning for herself. There could be no going back. Had she been contemplating a reunion with her lost lover, all hope was now gone, for during her absence another young lady had taken her place as Leslie Watson's bride. Now Marion longed to break away from the scene of her disastrous engagement. Recalling teenage days at Kilduff made her yearn for the east coast. For the time being her 'home' was at Rozelle, but the lease was coming to an end and while Hutton Castle continued to languish in its half-finished state another house had to be rented. Before the Burrells could move, all her father's precious works of art would have to be carefully assembled and crated. Wherever they lived, these items would multiply and the hassle of transporting them had become part of family life. The careful preservation of Burrell's famous collection was destined to be an ongoing source of worry.

Back in Ayrshire Marion began visiting her cousins and catching up on the local news. My parents had recently become engaged, and that summer Eva MacAndrew was to marry Captain Jim Thomson whose family had lived at Glentower before moving to Ayrshire. As soon as the girls were together, Eva asked Marion to be maid of honour at her wedding in June. Marion accepted enthusiastically, suppressing any hint of her own disappointment. The role of bridesmaid was one she was destined to perform many times. Jim's married sister, Adelaide Walker, lived near Ayr at Newark Castle where she and Archie had kindly provided him with a bachelor flat in their basement and even made house room for the monstrous heads of buffalo he had shot in British East Africa.

While celebrating their engagement, Jim and Eva called on the Burrells at Rozelle. When drinks were offered, Jim asked for whisky and soda. An interesting ritual then took place. Willie Burrell rang for the butler who carried in a tantalus with a row of decanters locked inside. While leaving the contents visible, these tantalizing contraptions were designed to prevent the evils of alcohol from corrupting servants. And so everybody sat and watched Willie extract a bunch of keys from his pocket and ceremoniously release the appropriate decanter. At length the whisky was poured and my father was finally served with a glass of Scotch. In large households a degree of pilfering and breakage was almost inevitable. Apart from whisky, Burrell was loaded with possessions both valuable and vulnerable. As he and his wife often spent weeks and months away from home, the obvious solution was to lock everything up. The collector became obsessed by his need for security. When Burrell's immense wealth became publicly known he soon realized that sharks would be out to hoodwink him, and after that he was always on his guard.

Jim and Eva were married in Ayr on 25 June 1923. Marion looked fetching in a modish headdress she had created for herself from a satin brow band flanked by two bunches of rosebuds. Like the chief bridesmaid, each member of the wedding group had come from a background of wealth derived from coal, iron, industry or trade. Though some might hesitate to admit it, the majority of Scotland's gentry owed their prosperity to the Industrial Revolution, and much of it came from Glasgow. But that was not what the Burrells were seeking for their daughter.

In the wedding photographs Marion smiled as brightly as anyone there. When Eva was changing to leave for her honeymoon, her bridesmaid was rapturous. But the bride was less starry eyed; she too had been subject to parental pressure. Jim was a mature bachelor and family friend who had swept Eva off her feet before she realized that her mother had been surreptitiously promoting their romance. As so many young men had been lost in the war Bessie MacAndrew had been desperate to see her youngest daughter married. But Eva could not forget a young naval officer who had died at Zeebrugge. They had met on his leave, fallen in love and regardless of parental approval, secretly planned to announce their engagement on her sixteenth birthday, even though her mother would have thrown a fit! Since this tragedy, the charming and cultured Captain Thomson had fallen for Eva and deftly claimed her. He was a talented and scholarly man, but would always be dogged by the mental scars he had received when serving at Gallipoli as ADC to General Hunter-Weston. At 43 he was more than twice the age of his bride. Eva was only 20 and made the most of her lot, though she could not help feeling miffed when Jim boasted that the suit he was wearing was older than his bride.

Wedding presents on display were said to be 'numerous and valuable', and when Marion asked her what she would like, Eva said she craved a jade necklace. Ragtime was all the rage, and girls liked to 'Charleston' and shimmy while twirling long strings of beads. But Marion's gift was not what Eva had expected – it was a short necklace with stones which were knobbly and irregular. Eva was disappointed and exchanged it later for one of the long ones which she preferred. Marion, who had brought the gift from India, recognized it later in a Bond Street window. When she went in and asked the price, the assistant replied 'This necklace isn't jade, madam. These stones are uncut emeralds!' When Eva was told she refused to believe it, and perhaps it is just as well that the value of the emeralds has never been divulged! In India during the time of the Great Moghuls, gem stones were polished rather than cut, and they often retained irregular shapes. To the untrained eye, these uncut stones are remarkably similar to the jade tourists buy today. William Burrell would have known what he had bought, but having collected a hoard of purchases, Constance and Marion may have found by the end of their tour that some acquisitions had lost their appeal. Eva suspected the necklace was handed on because Marion didn't like it either.

It was not long before William Burrell had made arrangements to rent a house in East Lothian, and after spending Christmas at Rozelle the family moved there early in 1924. Marion clearly welcomed the change:

Broxmouth Park belonged to the Duke of Roxburghe and was the dower house for Floors Castle. It was a charming Georgian house facing south onto Doon Hill, half a mile distant. Behind the house to the north there was a wood of mixed trees, protecting the house very successfully from the cold N.E. winds. Beyond that was the domesne [sic] wall and beyond that the golf course. The ground for this had been sold by the Duke of Roxburghe with the proviso that any players from Broxmouth could start playing at the 6th hole where a door in the wall gave on to the course. When you had completed the course, you played the first holes last which brought you back to the door in the wall. This privilege was useful, but not desirable if the course was crowded.

The Broxburn ran through the grounds and out to the golf course where it formed a hazard to the 6th green. During the summer months there was always a man with a long pole with a wire netting bowl at the end of it, who would fish out any golf balls from the stream for a penny! He also had a key to the door in the wall and a clever black retriever. This dog knew his job so well that his owner told me he retrieved 35 golf balls in one morning. Inside the wall the little stream was the haunt of kingfishers and on the lake in the middle of the wood were a pair of swans. These birds had a rather endearing habit of flying off to Dunbar, where at the Temperance Hotel a bowl of porridge was put out for them daily.

Dunbar abounded with tales from the past and Broxmouth also had a colourful history. In 1650 Oliver Cromwell had marched his troops north to quell the Covenanters and made his headquarters at Broxmouth during the disastrous Battle of Dunbar in which 3,000 Scots died. On a happier occasion in 1878, Queen Victoria had stayed there as a guest of the

Duke and Duchess of Roxburghe, while her faithful ghillie, John Brown, occupied the adjoining suite. To commemorate her visit the Queen had planted a cedar tree in front of the house.

Broxmouth provided a welcome retreat, because progress at Hutton Castle was not going well and the problems seemed endless. To get the work finished Burrell had engaged another architect. This time the plans for his future home were put in the hands of Reginald Fairlie, who had been a pupil of the ill-fated Robert Lorimer. The change of architect did not go well because Burrell became infuriated once again, and it was not long before Mr Fairlie fell from favour and was made to follow his predecessor. In the end, Lorimer's rejected schemes were proved to be sound and by seeking alternatives Burrell was left with a compromise which lacked the character and harmony which his former architect, and one time friend, had sought to achieve. In the course of time, Burrell may have recognized his errors, but it was not in his nature to alter a course he had chosen. Once Fairlie had attended to his client's basic requirements, other experts were employed to create baronial interiors and get the project completed. As the whole thing dragged on it became plain to Marion, and everyone else, that the remodelling of William Burrell's medieval dream house was going to take a very long time.

While they were living at Broxmouth Park the Burrells held a garden fête. There were marquees, stalls and sideshows and crowds of local people came to join in the fun. A gypsy caravan proved a popular attraction, with Marion and her friends disguising themselves as fortune tellers. The 'gypsies' looked alluring with knotted head scarves and jingling ear rings, and Marion was in her element enticing customers to come and be bamboozled by mysterious predictions as the gypsy girls consulted playing cards and peered into a crystal ball. The diversion was progressing well until one of the fortune tellers started itching unbearably and they suddenly realized the caravan was hopping with fleas. The unfortunate victim was so overcome she had to phone for her family chauffeur to come and drive her home. Luckily, the infestation did not wreck the fête.

The Burrells were glad to be involved in county life. While local pursuits revolved around the hunting scene, their family did not incline in that direction, so Marion's father turned his attention to shooting.

It was while we were tenants at Broxmouth Park that shooting became a great interest to my father. The 5 miles from Dunbar to Thornton Loch has always been looked upon as the best potato country in Europe. The cultivation did not run too close up to the hedges thus giving room for the game to nest. It was therefore very good partridge shooting and the climate the second driest in Scotland [and] conditions for the birds were almost as good as East Anglia.

Although there was excellent pheasant and partridge shooting at Broxmouth, the real excitement began when Burrell rented a grouse moor. Marion supported the enterprise with enthusiasm:

Sixty miles of Lammermuirs lay between East Lothian and Berwickshire and again conditions were good for game. My father was asked to shoot at Mayshiel on one of the smaller of these moors and for some reason I was asked to come along. The day was unpropitious,

dull and cold, a poor show of birds and correspond-
ingly poor bag. From memory it was somewhere in
the region of 60 odd head. The owner decided to rent
the moor and my father took it from 1926 to 1937
and during this time it rose to its peak from getting
60 odd in 1925 to 929 birds on Aug. 12th 1933.

In this male-dominated activity Marion was happy to be out
with the guns. She became interested in grouse management
and enjoyed handling dogs. At ease in a butt (a grouse shooting hide) or trudging through heather, Burrell's daughter
looked elegant in well-cut tweeds and stout brogues. Though
most of her father's guests were older married men, she met
bachelors too and as usual she turned heads. Officers of the
Royal Artillery were stationed at Dunbar and Marion could
watch their horses at exercise, drawing gun carriages on the
shore near Broxmouth Park. Soon she was meeting young
officers at local parties and being invited to partner them at
tennis. But those who warmed to Miss Burrell's irresistible
charm were liable to be stopped in their tracks by a powerful
rebuff from her parents. Once again William and Constance
were growing worried, but this time they were not unprepared.

A new development had been taking shape since that
memorable Christmas season in Calcutta when they had all
basked in the glory of the Raj. Thanks to introductions made
through Lord Inchcape, William and Constance began to
adjust their ideas. A prestigious marriage was their aim for
Marion, but the problem was to find a worthy suitor. If their
daughter was to meet acceptable candidates, they decided
she would have to be taken south and encounter the social
grandeur of a full London Season.

Marion's parents were determined that she should achieve a station in life where her talents would be used to full advantage, and they were convinced that the route to this goal would be found among the ranks of the aristocracy. In this field Burrell's perception was acute. Nobility was not for him; although he discoursed with influential people and liked to move within their spheres he did not try to curry favour or conceal his Glasgow roots. Nevertheless, it paid to aim high because rank can open innumcrable doors. He observed that the power and privilege embodied in the House of Lords had been created through generations of selective breeding, and that blue blood was continually revitalized through fresh infusions of beauty, brains and wealth. Burrell knew his daughter to be amply equipped with attributes desired by that exclusive club. William and Constance firmly believed that the course they had chosen was the greatest gift they could bestow upon their daughter.

Marion was now 21, while the majority of debutantes were aged about 18, but there were no set rules. Most girls were 'brought out' by their mothers, but the Burrells were not au fait with London society, and as Constance had not undergone the ritual of a court presentation she lacked the entitlement to present her daughter. Like other parents in their position the Burrells enlisted the service of a qualified chaperone. Once again the Inchcapes were able to give advice, having launched their own daughters, including Marion's friend Elsie.

In due course an arrangement was made with Florence, Lady Garvagh, a mature chaperone in her seventies. She was a Danish aristocrat, the daughter of Baron Joseph de Bretton of Copenhagen and the widow of an Irish peer, Baron Garvagh of Garvagh, County Londonderry. Having served as lady-in-waiting to Queen Alexandra her manner was nothing less than courtly. As a hostess in diplomatic circles she was known to the Inchcapes and came to be highly regarded by the Burrells. If debutantes found her old fashioned and perhaps a little eccentric, her richly upholstered bosom contained a heart of pure gold. After meetings and consultations the Burrells agreed that a suitable London residence would be required for Marion's introduction to society, and so 40 Grosvenor Square was rented for the Season. This former London residence of the Earls of Strathmore was an elegant mansion in the heart of Mayfair, and came complete with a ballroom hung with crystal chandeliers. Marion delighted to tell her friends that the outrageous Margot Asquith, who became the wife of one of Britain's prime ministers, once rode her horse into the marble hall.

Following normal procedure, Burrell would foot the bill while Lady Garvagh managed his daughter's 'debut'. Marion's chaperone was an old hand at presenting and 'bringing out' young ladies of quality. She was kind and not over exacting with the girls who were delivered into her charge, so Marion warmed to her readily, thankful to be under the auspices of a lady other than the mother she found so hard to endure. From the start, she was invited to address Lady Garvagh as 'Aunt Florence', and to look upon her as a godmother. Press reports described Marion as Lady Garvagh's goddaughter and even her niece. Her bond with 'Aunt Florence' was a happy one, and Marion later became godmother to Lady Garvagh's grandson, the Hon. Victor Canning, younger son of the 4th Lord Garvagh.

A sense of excitement pervaded the Burrell household as preparations were made for events ahead. Constance could now take pleasure in her status as the mother of a society debutante, while her husband made sure that she was attired in all the finery befitting a lady in her position. She felt elated when choosing fabrics, issuing instructions and fussing over details. Precious gemstones were made up for her in a range of co-ordinating tiaras, necklaces and earrings to complement every evening dress that she would wear. Although these costly adornments might have become heirlooms, the jewels provided for her daughter were more restrained.

For Marion, a London Season offered a welcome escape from parental oppression, and whatever lay ahead, she intended to enjoy it. Once again, William Burrell took charge of all expenses while the leading fashion houses provided his daughter with a wardrobe of fabulous outfits and a galaxy of glamorous hats. As only the best would suffice, several ball gowns were created by Victor Stiebel. Joyce Grenfell, the actress niece of Nancy Astor, also patronized the royal couturier, and considered him 'the most distinguished of the top London designers'. Beauticians and hairdressers were also required to ply their arts. Being groomed as a debutante was a thrilling experience for Marion and she revelled in it all.

The Burrells took possession of the London house they had rented in good time for the Season which began in May 1925. Having settled their daughter and her noble chaperone in this lordly residence, William and Constance quietly withdrew along the road to Claridges Hotel. Grand townhouses which were designed for entertaining could be short of comfortable accommodation, and the Burrells felt more at home in a first-class hotel. For one thing, William found the plumbing infinitely preferable. The manager at Claridges had recently installed the latest bathroom fittings in order to satisfy American guests.

When a dance for Marion was arranged at Grosvenor Square, Lady Garvagh was given full rein to invite guests on behalf of the Burrells, protecting Constance from unnecessary stress. Being unfamiliar with the London Season they were content to maintain a low profile while Lady Garvagh took the strain. It was becoming clear that hobnobbing with the Viceroy of India did not guarantee acceptance among the higher echelons of British nobility; aristocrats operated on a different footing. Constance felt ill equipped to compete with the network of matchmaking mothers and lacked the personality to penetrate their circle. An expert with inside influence was indispensable.

Invitations arrived at Grosvenor Square, whirling Marion into a maelstrom of luncheons, dinner parties, cocktail parties, country house parties, 'thé dansants' and balls. The year 1925 would long be remembered as a brilliant one because more that 700 girls were presented at Court, the largest assembly of debutantes known in a London Season. The parents of these post-war debs were even more determined to promote their daughters, as about 25 per cent of eligible bachelors had lost their lives in the Great War and many who returned were maimed. As this damaged generation emerged, the shadow of disaster still lingered so that the festivities which followed had an undercurrent of tension. Many survivors of the war set out to break away from the past and compensate with high living. The 1920s were described as madly 'gay' in the old meaning of the word, because the young were fired by a zest for life which sometimes verged on hysteria.

For Marion's mother the frantic social pace was disconcerting and arduous, and new acquaintances sometimes found her cold and withdrawn. Being held by Mrs Burrell's steely eye was said to be unnerving. Once again maladies seemed to arise, and William would offer his habitual explanation, 'My wife is unwell'. Throughout the Season gossip columnists were at work recording their daughter's progress and the daily papers had begun by proclaiming:

> Miss Marion Burrell is being taken out by her godmother, Florence Lady Garvagh, by whom she will be presented. Miss Burrell, a very pretty girl, is the only child of Mr and Mrs Burrell who are giving a dance for her. Mr Burrell, a wealthy ship owner, has lent his collection of French and Dutch paintings to the Tate Gallery. Some time ago he bought Hutton Castle, Berwick-on-Tweed, and he and Mrs Burrell will go there when the alterations are completed.

William Burrell's willingness to lend works of art might explain an unusual purchase he made at this time, *The Charity of a Beggar at Ornans*, painted by Gustave Courbet before 1868. This harshly rendered depiction of a vagabond giving a coin to a starving child may have struck a personal chord with Burrell because, since the sufferings of his impoverished forebears, he had acquired treasures which he was now able and happy to share. It was pleasing for Burrell to receive recognition for his collection and for Hutton Castle, of which he was so proud, but frequent references to his wealth annoyed him as, little by little, he found himself wondering whether the right message was being conveyed. Because he preferred to avoid publicity, he resented Marion being advertised as if she were up for grabs, rightly suspecting adventurers were at large and would gladly marry her just to get their hands on his fortune. But the launching of Marion

Burrell was underway and she was already gliding down the slipway. William Burrell could not restrain her impetus any more than he could hold back a new Strath Line ship from entering the ocean.

Marion encountered new names and faces every day. At dances, bejewelled chaperones rustled around arranging introductions and then retired to gossip on gilded chairs while young couples waltzed dreamily to the strains of 'Some day I'll find you' or stepped out jauntily to 'Ain't we got fun?' The Royal Caledonian Ball was a spectacular affair with Highland dress and regimental uniforms offset by a flock of pretty debutantes arrayed in white dresses. Marion was invited to join a formal set reel led by Captain Neil Ritchie of the Black Watch. She was partnered by Mr Philip Dundas, and the other young ladies in the set were Miss Stewart of Ardvorlich, Miss Jean Graham Stirling and the Hon. Margaret Forbes-Sempill. The dancers made a procession into the ballroom and formed eight eightsomes round a sixteensome reel in which the Duchess of Norfolk was partnered by the Earl of Dunmore. Then, pipers skirled as kilted dancers twirled their partners till their tartan sashes were flying like the banners of warring clans.

There were dances almost every night, as well as house parties out of town. Marion's celebration was on 11 June. There were six 'coming-out' dances that evening but hers was a triumph. At No. 40 Grosvenor Square flower-decked salons came alive to the sound of music as William and Constance Burrell emerged to receive over 300 guests. Resplendent in her gorgeous jewels, Constance was surrounded by magnificence; Marion's ball was almost like a coronation. Flanked by liveried footmen, the Burrells lined up with Lady Garvagh while the major-domo announced a succession of guests which included five princes and princesses, seven dukes and duchesses plus numerous nobles and most of the diplomatic corps. The preceding dinner party had been graced by the Duchesses of Norfolk and Hamilton, the Marquess and Marchioness Carisbrooke, the Earl and Countess of Dunmore and the Earl of Munster. The delectable Marion had meanwhile been happily surrounded by a score of young lords, ladies and Honourables, including her friend Elsie Mackay.

The dancing was in full swing when the whole building was suddenly plunged into darkness. There were shrill cries and gasps from the guests who began to wonder if gangsters were staging a hold-up to steal their priceless jewels. Eventually somebody found the fuse box. The debs were rather disappointed that the diversion had ended before anyone called the police. Next day newspapers gleefully reported the 'Scare in Mayfair' while applauding the splendour of Marion's dance and including the blue-blooded guest list.

And so the festivities progressed. For debutantes the presentation ceremony at Buckingham Palace was the major event of the Season; ladies who had been presented at Court were invited to royal garden parties, admitted to the Royal Enclosure at Ascot and received in British embassies throughout the world. To be presented at Court, a lady had to be sponsored by another who had already undergone this formality and was thereby entitled to submit an application to the Lord Chamberlain. Once Lady Garvagh had set the wheels in motion her guidance on Court procedure was invaluable. Marion required a full-length gown with a train and a headdress of three white Prince of Wales ostrich feathers from which a veil hung down her back, reaching as far as her fingertips. Long white kid gloves and an ostrich feather

PLATES 36. Photographers snapped Marion wherever she went. At the races it was reported that 'Miss Burrell wears her tweeds well'.

Miss Marion Burrell is Sir William and Lady Burrell's only child; her home is Hutton Castle, in Berwickshire. She had one of the best tweed suits at Musselburgh

Marion Burrell has dress sense, the sylph silhouette and hosts of friends

PLATE 37. Craigievar Castle where Marion stayed with Lord and Lady Sempill for the Highland Gatherings.

PLATE 38. Captain Allan MacGregor-Whitton.

PLATE 39. At the Games. Left to right: Lord and Lady Sempill, Miss Burrell, the Earl of Dumfries, the Hon. Miss Margaret Forbes-Sempill, Lady Jean Crichton-Stuart and Captain MacGregor-Whitton.

Three broken engagements

PLATE 40. *Above left*: Captain Leslie Dundas Watson.

PLATE 41. *Above right*: The Hon. John Benson, heir to Lord Charnwood. Portrait drawn by Simon Elwes.

PLATE 42. *Left*: The Hon. Patrick Balfour, heir to Lord Kinross, as an undergraduate at Oxford.

Always a bridesmaid

PLATE 43. The marriage of Captain Geordie Gordon-Duff to Miss Rosemary Craven. Marion is on the right.

PLATE 44. The marriage of Major Douglas Beresford-Ash to Lady Helena Rous. Marion is on the left.

PLATE 45. The marriage of Mr Eyre Chatterton to Miss Elisabeth Anne Hunter Blair, Marion on the left.

PLATE 46. *Above*: Hutton Castle after Sir William Burrell's alterations.

PLATE 47. *Left*: The drawing room at Hutton Castle.

PLATE 48. *Bottom*: Bedroom No. 1 at Hutton Castle. Note: no reading lamp!

The lovers

PLATE 49. *Above left*: Major Sholto Douglas.

PLATE 50. *Above right*: José Luis Plaza.

PLATE 51. *Left*: This snapshot taken at Hutton was found amongst Marion's possessions. Could this be 'Matthew'?

PLATE 52. Marion sunbathing at Beech Hill.

PLATE 53. Mrs Ruth De Pree, who died in 1944 when Beech Hill was destroyed in a wartime disaster.

PLATE 55. Digby's daughter, the Hon. Pamela. After successive high flying affairs and marriages, Pamela Harriman became the American ambassador in Paris.

PLATE 54. Sir William Burrell mounted, accompanied by Lord Digby while grouse shooting at Mayshiel.

PLATE 56. *Top*: Marion acting as hostess at the Mayshiel shoot.

PLATE 57. *Above*: Counting the bag.

PLATE 58. *Right*: Sholto Douglas preparing for action.

The godchildren

PLATE 59. The Hon. Victor
Canning, lived 1924–44.

PLATE 60. David Pitcairn,
lived 1939–44.

PLATE 61. Gavin McGill, Marion's
post-war godson.

PLATE 62. Marion with the author at
Hillhouse in Ayrshire, 1935.

PLATE 63. *Right:* Mary Mitchell, Marion's aunt, at Perceton.

PLATE 64. *Below:* Mona Mitchell (left), Mary's daughter, who married the author's Uncle Charlie MacAndrew (right).

PLATE 65. Sir William signing the Deed of Gift in 1944, with his wife, Lady Burrell, and Lord Provost James Welsh.

Wartime

PLATE 66. Peel Hospital near Selkirk, where Marion served as a VAD.

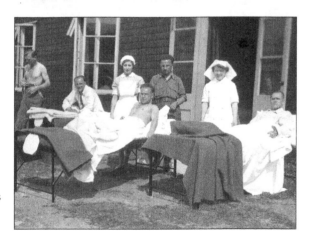

PLATE 67. The operating theatre at Peel Hospital.

PLATE 68. Wounded patients and their nurses enjoying the sun.

PLATE 69. Matron Burrell at Newlands Preparatory School for Boys, 1950–51.

PLATE 70. *Right*: Miss Burrell, having changed her name to Silvia, addressing the guests after cutting the sod at Pollok Park for building to begin on the new Burrell Collection museum, 1978.

PLATE 71. *Below*: Meeting the Queen at the opening of the Burrell Collection, 1983.

PLATE 72. Silvia enjoying a visit to the Burrell Collection.

PLATE 73. At Pollok House, with Burrell Trustees in the front row.
Left to right: Alan Mitchell, Lord Muirshiel, Miss Burrell, Trevor Walden and Merrick Mitchell. In the back row is Councillor Robert Logan.

PLATE 74. The naming of the RNLB *Silvia Burrell* at Girvan, 16 October 1993.
Left to right: Mr AM Mackenzie, 2nd Coxswain Stuart Moffat, Sue Stephen, the
Duke of Atholl, Mr Sandy Grant Gordon and Coxswain Roddy Leitch. The
author performed the ceremony, proudly wearing the turtle brooch which her
godmother had received after launching the *Strathlorne* 80 years before.

fan completed her outfit. While wearing this regalia she had to learn how to walk and perform a full curtsey. In the presence of royalty this was a complicated process which required her to end by stepping gracefully backwards without tripping over her train.

The big day arrived in June, and the whole of the Mall became congested by a long procession of limousines slowly proceeding to Buckingham Palace. It was thrilling to drive through the iron gates and finally gain admission. Beyond the royal portals there was gilt and red carpet everywhere. Having been ushered up the grand staircase Marion and her chaperone were admitted to the state rooms where Gentlemen-at-Arms stood to attention at every doorway. The ceremony took place in the great ballroom which was already thronged by the diplomatic corps, resplendent in gold braid and decorations. In a long continuous line of bobbing feathers, the debutantes and their sponsors were gradually ushered forward until they finally came into the royal presence where King George V and Queen Mary were beheld in rigid majesty upon their gilded thrones. Crowned by a massive tiara, the queen's head seemed to be held erect by a towering choker of pearls as they both stared stonily before them. Marion's chaperone handed her card to a gentleman in waiting who announced their names 'Florence, Lady Garvagh, presenting Miss Marion Burrell'. Lady Garvagh swept forward and curtsied first to the King and then to the Queen while Marion breathlessly followed at the requisite number of paces behind her. After her presentation had been safely executed she sighed with relief as their trains were scooped up and draped over their left arms so that they could proceed to an allocated drawing room and be served with 'light refreshments'. Miss Barbara Cartland, later to become a novelist, was also being presented, and was amused to discover that the uniformed waiters had been recruited for the day from the Joe Lyons chain of popular tearooms.

As the days passed in a giddy round of dances and visits to races at Ascot and rowing at Henley Marion was making new friends. Being older and more experienced she could converse with ease and feel more confident than some of the younger debs, but the age difference meant she was sometimes out of step. Some looked down on those who employed professional chaperones, rudely referred to these ladies as 'bear-leaders', a term formerly used for tutors who escorted young gentlemen of rank on Continental tours. Marion's extraordinary upbringing had made it difficult for her to fit in, because she had never shared the rough and tumble of a normal family life. The new freedom she discovered under Lady Garvagh's supervision affected her rather oddly. Although she appeared sophisticated and was popular with other girls, there were times when they found her strangely naive and unworldly. As she loved fun and mischief she developed an irresistible tendency to become disorderly and sometimes even abandoned. A fellow deb at a house party was extremely shocked to see Marion, like a fleeing nymph, streak half naked down a corridor with her open dressing gown flying out behind her.

The Burrell parents, like many of their generation, frowned on make-up and cigarettes, so Marion of course indulged in both. Needless to say she hoped to conceal these habits from her parents, but Willie Burrell was no fool, and whatever she tried, he always managed to find out what she had been up to. Whenever he discovered make-up he immediately destroyed it; her father's persistent interference may explain why Marion in later life was inclined to apply her lipstick like a gesture of defiance, and sometimes with less precision than panache! Repression made her want to break out and at one time she posed for a series of photographs while languidly smoking a cigarette. While Constance looked up to William and complied with his wishes, it worried him to have a daughter who refused to conform and the situation made him increasingly wary.

When it came to men, Burrell was even more alert. During the Season eligible bachelors were always in demand, and seldom short of invitations. Free dinners were particularly popular with ex-servicemen who were hard up after the war and this caused more anxiety for William Burrell. Lady Garvagh on the other hand was not fussy about Marion's comings and goings, and as marriage was the object of the exercise she liked to encourage romance. Marion, being a bit of a devil, often preferred the rakish types of whom her parents would not approve. As usual, her father tried to limit her escapades, and when she was invited to house parties in the country he would pay her rail fare, but refuse to give her any money to spend when she got there. This embarrassed her acutely and she became more impetuous than ever. William Burrell's ambitious scheme had created a rebel in a gilded cage.

While all these things were happening to Marion, Jim and Eva Thomson were also living in London. They had rented a house in Chelsea while Jim was taking a course at the London School of Economics. After graduating from Cambridge he had qualified as a barrister, and now hoped to pursue a political career. London was new to Eva and her life there was not like Marion's. In the evenings she and Jim would make up a four at bridge or dine out and go to the theatre. In town they rode in Rotten Row, attended polo events at Hurlingham and played tennis at Queen's where young Dan Maskell, the future professional champion, was their ball boy. From time to time there were visits to the stately homes of friends in the country. Like Marion, Eva had been presented at Court and admitted to the Royal Enclosure at Ascot, but she was finding married life dreadfully dull because her husband's friends were old enough to be her parents.

On one occasion, when Marion was taking a rare evening off from her dizzy social round, Jim and Eva were invited to dine with the Burrells at 40 Grosvenor Square. Though dinner was 'en famille' it was served in style with butler and footmen in attendance. Eva was intrigued to see the splendid house, and glad to catch up on the glamorous life of her friend while Jim was discoursing with their hosts. Willie Burrell had supplied his own staff as well as the linen and silver which was, of course, superb. When Jim expressed delight in Willie's Georgian pepper pots, his host immediately invited him to borrow a set and have them copied. Eva, meanwhile, was agog to hear about the wonderful time Marion was having and could not help feeling envious. She would have been thrilled to receive an invitation to one of those glamorous London parties, but if she felt excluded, she was not alone, because not one of Marion's young cousins was invited to join in any part of her London Season. Relations could have no place in the Burrells' ambitious designs for their daughter – Marion should only mix with the cream of society.

And so the round of balls and dances continued as introductions led to even more invitations. When Lady Garvagh roped her in to sell poppies in the Ritz, 'Miss Burrell's splendid effort' was reported in the press. At a charity sale at the

Royal School of Needlework Miss Burrell was pictured buying an embroidered cushion from the young Duchess of York. Thanks to an unusual act of paternal indulgence that day, she had enough cash to purchase it from the future Queen. And once the London Season was over, the grouse and salmon seasons began as the smart set gravitated north for even more social activities. In Scotland, Marion enjoyed race meetings, Highland gatherings and balls where eager young bachelors clamoured to attend her. For some of the Season's debutantes weddings were already being planned, but that year brought no engagement for the vivacious Marion Burrell.

CHAPTER 8

Noble Prospects

In 1926 the Burrells were back at Broxmouth Park when they received the news that Lady Garvagh had taken ill and died, less than a year after that glamorous London Season at Grosvenor Square. Besides being sadly missed in London society, Florence, Lady Garvagh, was widely mourned. In her widowhood she had worked tirelessly for the Red Cross and during the Great War she had handed over her London house to be used as a hospital for wounded soldiers. For her outstanding service the gallant lady had been awarded the OBE.

That May London was disrupted by the General Strike. A massive protest staged by the miners had brought all the trade unions out in sympathy, and for weeks the capital was in turmoil. As public services ground to a halt there were ugly scenes. Troops were called out and special constables enlisted to keep the peace so that volunteers could direct traffic and man transport systems. As the crisis continued, society ladies ran canteens while undergraduates learned to drive buses and underground trains and would-be debutantes were diverted to serving soup. It was not a promising year for the London Season.

Though the strike had caused widespread alarm, life at Broxmouth Park continued much as usual. Both Hutton Castle and Mayshiel Moor could easily be reached by car. William Burrell became the owner of two Rolls Royces and, according to Marion, both of them were gifts. His black Phantom II was said to have been a present from his wife, and the white one from an 'admirer' whose identity was not divulged – and neither was the motive for this surprising act of generosity. Two chauffeurs were employed to drive William and Constance about; a cheeky Irish chauffeur who thought nothing of the Burrells once drove a car up to the door without having cleaned the far side, but he was soon relieved of his employment. In addition to their chauffeur-driven visits to neighbours at Paxton House, Ladykirk, Duns Castle, Bughtrig and Chirnside, Burrell was able to supervise the work at Hutton Castle and also devote time to managing the grouse moor at Mayshiel.

Fox hunting was another popular county pursuit, and about this time horses cropped up again in Marion's life. This latent interest may have been aroused by Hugh, 4th Viscount Gough, one of the desirable young men introduced by Lady Garvagh. The Burrells had accompanied Lady Garvagh to see him in training at Rodzianko's Riding School near Windsor, where they watched him take his horse over formidable jumps. Lord Gough had been awarded the Military Cross for war service in which he was badly wounded and lost an arm. Before returning to the hunting field he had been taking a riding course, and his intrepid performance may have encouraged Marion to ride because she too received tuition. Needless to say she was immaculately kitted out, but while she learned how to look well on top of a horse and appear an accomplished horsewoman, she never actually became one. Like other ambitious parents, the Burrells may have committed the classic error of providing a mount which had been bred and schooled beyond the ability of the rider. As the venture met with failure, no romance developed with the equestrian Viscount and the Borderland hunting scene gave Marion no pleasure.

While the Burrells began to settle into county society their ambitions for Marion's future were stronger than ever. They were like countless overzealous parents who devote their energies to promoting a talented child and end up by getting it wrong. But William Burrell had set his course and nothing was going to stop him. He and Constance were still convinced that the road to a successful marriage lay south of the border, and so they decided that their daughter should be given a second London Season in 1927. Marion was now a sophisticated lady of 24 with a circle of London friends so the prospect was much to her liking. Another dowager was called in and this time the outlook, in Marion's view, promised to be even better.

Lady Clodagh Anson was a daughter of the Marquess of Waterford, and possessed all the credentials the Burrells could have desired. She was a granddaughter of the Duke and Duchess of Beaufort and began life with the impression that 'Your Grace' was just another term for 'Granny'. As an aristocratic chaperone Lady Clodagh turned out to be splendidly unconventional, but she did know the ropes. In particular, she understood the significance of elder sons. Before her mother married the Marquess of Waterford, Granny Beaufort had told her teenage daughter she might flirt with his siblings but 'You must marry their elder brother'. The Waterford family seat was at Curraghmore House in County Waterford and Lady Clodagh, having survived the Irish Troubles, fraternized with the Prince of Wales and begun her married life on a Texan ranch with rattlesnakes under the floor, seemed to be fazed by nothing. Being a lively lady and still in her forties she believed that being cheerful kept one young. She was strongly in favour of a bit of devilry and claimed that boredom was exhausting. The memoir she eventually published was entitled simply *Book,* and when everyone found it hilarious she followed it up with *Another Book.*

Marion's broadminded chaperone liked the young to go off and enjoy their own amusements. But when Lady Clodagh was not engaged in formal gatherings she was running a soup kitchen for down-and-outs near the Thames Embankment where her smart friends would sometimes fetch up after a night on the tiles. She was greatly concerned with the homeless, and Marion, being a dedicated champion of the underdog, readily sympathized with vagrants. This midnight refuge may have inspired her enduring desire to befriend fellow beings from every walk of life.

That summer there was another visit to Buckingham Palace when her father received a knighthood from King George V in recognition of his 'Public and political work and for services to Art in Scotland'. William Burrell had by then become a Trustee of the National Galleries of both England and Scotland. In their new capacity as Sir William and Lady Burrell, Marion's parents spared no expense in promoting their daughter in another attempt to find a noble match for her. As Lady Burrell, Constance would now have more in common with the aristocratic ladies she would be meeting in London.

This time Norfolk House was rented for the Season. Like the Strathmore mansion in Grosvenor Square, this colossal Palladian style residence no longer exists. It was built for the

Duke of Norfolk in 1756 and once occupied an entire side of St James's Square. The splendour of the French Rococo interiors was said to have been breathtaking. In the eighteenth century, when the ducal palace was first opened to guests, Horace Walpole, the celebrated writer, reported that they had all gazed upwards and trod on each other's toes as if 'transfixed by the sight of a comet'. In 1927, the cream of London society arrived in hordes when Lady Burrell and Lady Clodagh arranged a ball, although the latter admitted with hindsight that a guest list of 1,200 was perhaps a little excessive. The party was shared with her own pretty daughter who was the same age as Marion. The girls were good friends and 'Little' Clodagh, being six feet tall, was a perfect match to Marion. The pair looked sensational receiving guests amidst the setting of gilded magnificence.

As the great plan proceeded Marion was, as usual, deliberately severed from her relations and family friends in Scotland, but Lady Clodagh seemed to know everyone in London from the nobility to the underworld. There were plenty of introductions and Marion developed an insatiable appetite for making new acquaintances. She became a dedicated collector of people, and as her chaperone imposed few restraints there was no shortage of fun. It was the era of outrageous escapades, motorized treasure hunts and varsity hoaxes. Marion loved to go wild. She sparkled and dazzled and waltzed around London enjoying the social whirl. Soon the glossy magazines were displaying photographs – 'A striking figure was Miss Burrell of Hutton Castle, her gown of Linden green was sashed with coral to match her coral finger-nails'. On this occasion no parental recriminations were reported. While following the latest trends, Marion was also learning ways to avoid detection.

Meanwhile the press reported that 'Miss Burrell is being chaperoned by Lady Clodagh Anson as Lady Burrell is not strong'. While the Season progressed under the benevolent eye of Lady Clodagh, Sir William and Lady Burrell had been content to take a back seat and await developments. As Constance continued to languish more society engagements were announced and more marriages followed. Marion served her time as a bridesmaid but again it was not her destiny to be a bride. When the London Season was over, returning north to Berwickshire held no pleasure for her. In later years she recalled her feelings on moving into Hutton Castle.

> Alas! The day came in the summer of 1927 when we had to leave Broxmouth and move to Hutton. The workmen who were adding a new wing were still there and the discomfort was acute. The doors had as yet no handles and wouldn't shut, or if they did wouldn't open! The only rather ineffective way to control them was by a piece of string, strung through the keyhole and tied in a loop. The stairs, which were of course uncarpeted had rough planks of wood at the edge to prevent you from taking a toss, or was it to cause one?

There was even more trouble when the newly laid oak floor boards warped and buckled so that all the flooring had to be replaced. Problems continued when the water in the Hutton well was found to be suspect. Marion was intrigued when a diviner was called in, but he failed to produce the desired result and engineers were summoned to bore for another source. Having penetrated 100 feet a specimen was sent to the lab and declared unfit for human consumption. The water supply caused continual problems; in drought conditions the chauffeurs were made to take the cars down to the river and wash them in the Bluestone Ford. At Hutton Castle the bath water was rationed, and the household had to make do with baths which were only two inches deep. This was rather a comedown after Burrell had installed ultra-modern sanitary ware which even included bidets.

When it came to finishing the interior he finally stopped quibbling and no expense was spared when Wilfred Drake and Frank Surgey were enlisted to oversee the interior decoration and bring the scheme to completion. Drake was well known as an expert in stained glass and Surgey had served with the firm White Allom on interiors at Buckingham Palace. At Hutton Castle, massive stone chimney pieces were installed, stained glass windows were fitted and several rooms were enveloped in linen-fold panelling. But installing the collection brought even more worries. When Sir William required two tradesmen to transfer a work by Crawhall (*The Black Cock*), the men were indignant at the fuss he made over shifting a picture of 'twa bloody hens!' Then he insisted that the ground floor windows should be secured against burglary by installing iron bars. Two-way bars were being fitted when Frank Whyte, the Hutton village 'bobby', pointed out that the horizontal ones made a perfect ladder, smartly shinned up to demonstrate. Poor Willie Burrell was so upset that he abandoned the project and his medieval security system was never completed. Meanwhile Constance was recovering from a second London Season and suffering from phlebitis. The situation at Hutton was doing nothing to improve her health.

Poor Marion was thankful when autumn approached and

she was able to escape to the company of friends. It was the time of year when sportsmen took to the moors and hills and the southern gentry moved north for the annual round of Highland Gatherings, race meetings and balls. Marion's parents seemed happy for her to join the house parties of families they favoured, but this was when her troubles really began.

A young Scots nobleman captured Marion's admiration and soon found the way to her heart. He was George Harley Hay, 14th Earl of Kinnoull, and his additional titles of Viscount Dupplin, Lord Hay of Kilfauns and Baron Hay of Pedwardine seemed more than enough to satisfy her parents' aspirations. When still in his teens Kinnoull had succeeded his grandfather and became rather wild with a passion for performing daredevil stunts in a light aeroplane. The sober residents of Perth were shaken when he suddenly zoomed over the River Tay and nonchalantly touched down upon the South Inch, a misdemeanour which landed him in court. Marion found the roguish earl utterly delightful, but other ladies had featured in his life, and he had come to regret an early marriage which had been recently dissolved. As divorce was a social stigma at that time Marion's parents became concerned about her new attachment. They had also heard rumours that the high-living nobleman was said to be running short of funds. Sir William began to fear for his fortune and another romance was scotched. Like former suitors, Kinnoull was warned off and once again Marion's hopes were dashed.

The following year the Earl chose to marry a girl who was not an heiress. His new Countess was the daughter of an Irish lady who did not share Burrell's inhibitions, the celebrated Mrs Meyrick who had achieved fame from minimal resources. Coming from a family of impoverished Irish gentry, she had married a successful Dublin psychiatrist, but after he took to philandering the couple had parted. She raised their six children and had them all educated at Harrow and Roedean but by the end of the 1914–18 war Mrs Meyrick was really hard up, and so she used a loan to start a thé dansant in London. When she realized larger profits could be made from selling alcohol, she launched a succession of West End night clubs and learned to make even more money by bending the licensing laws. Though this habit made her spend a lot of time in gaol, Mrs Meyrick remained undeterred by police raids and frequently hid her young customers under the tables, having first supplied them with champagne.

During the 1920s, the '43', 'The Silver Slipper', 'The New Follies' and 'The Little Club' became the hotspots of London night life while this sparky little lady in her famous green velvet wrap presided over a glittering clientele of royalty, millionaires and celebrities which included Steve Donoghue, Augustus John, Rudolph Valentino and Tallulah Bankhead. 'Bright Young Things' were rarely exploited. When a newly demobbed officer couldn't afford to bring his girlfriend for an evening out, the thoughtful proprietress slipped him some money so that he might take the young lady to a less expensive establishment. 'Ma Meyrick's' kindness was not forgotten – when a staffing crisis arose, her clients willingly buckled to and helped by filling in for the waiters. Miss Barbara Cartland recalled the triumphal song:

> Come all ye birds
> And sing a roundelay
> Now Mrs Meyrick's
> Out of Holloway.

The young Meyricks were sometimes involved in their mother's establishments and, after leaving their smart boarding school, the girls helped to look after the upper crust customers and got to know them. Though their enterprising mother never made a fortune and ended her business career as poor as she began, all four of Mrs Meyrick's daughters married into the aristocracy. But Marion Burrell's parents would hardly have approved.

By this time the luckless Marion was growing accustomed to having her suitors seen off by her father. She tried to make the best of it by attending Highland Gatherings at Braemar and Aboyne, Aberdeenshire. When she stayed at Craigievar Castle as a guest of Lord and Lady Sempill, photographers at the Games snapped members of the party defying a steady drizzle to witness the traditional tossing of the caber. While the handsome Earl of Dumfries was present, eyes were drawn to another dashing bachelor who radiated authority in his splendid Highland dress. All the girls were fascinated; it was impossible not to notice the glamorous Allan MacGregor-Whitton who looked and carried himself like a prince. Although he could not claim nobility, Captain MacGregor-Whitton was popularly known as 'The uncrowned King of Scotland'.

At the Aboyne Ball Miss Marion Burrell was greatly admired 'in white, with flowers embroidered in lettuce green ribbon, finished with a belt and streamers from the back of the neck', and she had not been slow to take note of this handsome man who laughed and joked with everyone while he casually smoked a pipe. Allan's flamboyant style was much to her liking. He flaunted Highland dress, jauntily combining different tartans, and Marion was highly amused when he instigated a long distance spitting competition from the battlements of Craigievar. The MacGregor-Whitton family home was Ardchoille on Loch Earn, and Allan's father was another merry prankster. The old colonel had a long white beard and dressed like an ancient Highland chief. When cars came along the road in front of his property there was a blind corner where he would lurk behind the wall and suddenly sound a motor horn to startle approaching motorists.

Despite the wild streak which ran through Allan's family, his military bearing was genuine as he had given gallant service in the war. Though he took pleasure in baiting fellow officers by ordering a piper to rouse them from their tents, his conduct under fire was exemplary. He had been wounded in action and repeatedly decorated. As an officer in the Royal Scots Fusiliers he had served overseas as ADC to the Lord Lieutenant of Ireland and also as Assistant Military Attaché to the Embassy at Rome, for which he was awarded the Italian Order of St Maurice and St Lazarus, 5th Class. This was probably the elaborate 'gong' which he liked to hang from his neck at dances. Young ladies were impressed and Marion was no exception. The attraction was mutual and in no time another affair of the heart began to flourish.

That autumn Marion was invited to stay with the Craven family at Aldourie, by Loch Ness. Rosemary Craven had been a fellow debutante and had recently married Captain Geordie Gordon-Duff. Her parents had arranged a house party and when Marion joined she was delighted that Captain MacGregor-Whitton was among the guests. He was in high spirits and publicly courted Miss Burrell, though everyone was well aware that trouble lay ahead. While friends watched the romance progress word went round that an elopement was being planned. It seemed a great lark because clandestine marriages frequently featured in society news.

Marion enjoyed romantic scandal so the idea appealed to her immensely. She was longing to break away from her stifling home life and could not wait to be free of her domineering parents. Companions who were in the know were thrilled by the prospect of a drama unfolding in their midst and awaited the outcome with bated breath. For Marion to escape at last from bondage and be carried off by the dashing hero who set every girl's heart aflutter seemed almost too good to be true. It was.

As usual her suspicious father had kept his ear to the ground. Nothing seemed to deceive him for long, and having got wind of the plot he lost no time in making it known that, if his daughter should marry without his consent, he would have no hesitation in cutting her off without a penny. Without a share of the Burrell fortune Captain MacGregor-Whitton could not hope to maintain Marion in the manner to which she was accustomed, let alone benefit from her wealth, so he took the hint and hastily withdrew. The whispered schemes and secret preparations were all in vain when no one turned up to carry Marion away. For Allan, it may have been little more than another light-hearted prank, but when her elopement came to naught, Marion's hopes lay once again in tatters.

The Cravens were distraught when the Burrells blamed them for causing the trouble. After that, no member of their family was received in the Burrell household. It was a sad rift because Rosemary and her parents had been guests at Hutton when she was presented at Holyrood on her marriage to Geordie Gordon-Duff. In later years their first child, Patrick, became a great favourite with Marion, but he could only be an 'honorary' godchild.

Marion returned in disgrace to Hutton Castle where the

atmosphere was far from happy. In September 1927 her uncle George Burrell suddenly died on a fishing holiday. His health had been failing, but the news of his death was particularly sad because during the latter days of Burrell and Son the brothers had not been in accordance concerning the final sale of the Burrell fleet. William Burrell was once again becoming distanced from members of his family. Soon there was another shock when Marion answered the phone to hear the news that the River Thames had overflowed at Mill-bank and was threatening to flood several of Sir William's paintings which had been stored in the basement of the Tate Gallery. He travelled south on the night train, but his luck prevailed and the damage was less serious than feared. Somehow the packing cases had floated free and the paintings managed to stay above water.

Then there came horrifying news of Marion's friend Elsie Mackay. Without telling her parents, Elsie had drawn £5000 (nearly £250,000 today) to purchase a light two-seater plane and set out on a secret attempt to fly the Atlantic piloted by a young Captain Hinchcliffe. In the 1920s lady enthusiasts had been financing daredevil ocean flights, and three had lost their lives in the previous year. Knowing that her parents would be bound to try and stop her, Elsie had deliberately kept them in the dark. The plane departed from Cranwell in Lincolnshire, but failed to reach its destination in the USA. There was no radio and it was never traced.

The newly created Earl and Countess of Inchcape were in Egypt when Elsie's father received the ghastly news that both their daughter and the plane were missing. Trying hard to spare his wife he concealed the news from her for several days, desperately hoping that Elsie might be rescued. When the full story came out they were utterly heartbroken by the loss of their vivacious madcap daughter. To create a living memorial, Lord Inchcape planted rhododendrons to form the letters of Elsie's name so that they might watch them flower each year on the hillside near Glenapp. Marion was deeply saddened by the death of her friend but she could not help admiring Elsie's spunk. The escapade was one that she might have been tempted to emulate if her own father had permitted her to possess a bank account.

1929 was the year of the slump, but Sir William was hardly deterred by the collapse of the Wall Street Stock Exchange because his money was in gilt-edged stock and not in equities. While he was busy adding to his collection Hutton Castle buzzed with phone calls and telegrams; from his business room he kept in touch with dealers and galleries every day. It was said that his brain was like a calculating machine and he counted money like a banker. 'Take care of the pennies' he said, 'the pounds will take care of themselves'.

His negotiations with dealers were remarkably successful because he made each of them believe himself to be the collector's prime adviser. Frank Partridge brought him more purchases than any other dealer. John Hunt was an expert on medieval items. Frank Surgey and Wilfred Drake were paid commissions and became his friends, while Muirhead Moffat operated for him in Glasgow. Some dealers were so keen for Burrell's patronage they frequently approached him with items of interest. On one occasion he was waiting at Berwick station for the night train to London when fellow travellers were astonished to see two Lebanese dealers turn up and spread carpets out on the platform. The place began to look like an oriental bazaar while Burrell made a thorough inspection and eventually took his pick before departing. He was always on the lookout for a bargain.

As already mentioned, Sir William was publicly acclaimed for his loans to British galleries, but when he tried to distribute his increasing collection through his home at Hutton Castle, he had trouble finding enough space. Works of art spread throughout the house and the drawing room was like a show room with fabulous carpets laid out five deep. Fine paintings overflowed into the servants' quarters, where a wing had been added for staff. Even staff bedrooms were provided with the hot and cold running water which was piped throughout the house. About ten domestic servants were employed, including a butler and a liveried footman. Gardeners, gamekeepers and chauffeurs were housed on the estate. Sir William could never understand why his cook gave notice when her bedroom enjoyed the unsurpassed benefit of a stained glass window created by Sir Edward Burne-Jones. Like some of Burrell's other possessions, this window is not in the Burrell Collection.

Burrell was considered to be a fair employer, but he was also cautious and exacting. When important items were to be cleaned he demanded meticulous maintenance, and due to his constant desire for security while cleaning took place, servants were sometimes said to have been locked into rooms and searched before being released. As waste was deplored Burrell controlled his electricity supply by imposing a curfew. A master switch was fitted in his bedroom and the household was plunged into darkness at precisely 10 pm. Those who were caught out had to make do with candles or torches. For further economy, the lights in each room were controlled from a separate box for which he retained the master-key.

Burrell became notorious for his meanness and as the years passed the stories increased. In the city, he preferred to walk rather than pay for transport. One day he was seen taking change from a cloakroom attendant's bowl of coins when he was reclaiming his hat. Having been caught without an appropriate coin, he would not have been the first to drop in a larger one and help himself to change, but because he was so rich his action seemed shocking. When one of Marion's girlfriends teased him, saying, 'Is it true Sir William that you drove all the way to Berwick to buy a new spade because it was cheaper?' he just laughed and replied 'There could be some truth in it, but I'm not mean: I'm just careful'. He enjoyed having his leg pulled and would readily laugh at himself.

But the home he created at Hutton Castle could not be described as a cosy place. The massive outer walls with their bleak barred windows conveyed all the friendliness of a medieval prison, while the gloomy interiors were hardly more inviting. Marion never felt at home there, though guests were welcomed and lavishly entertained. Sir William was a charming host, but Lady Burrell sometimes seemed rather artificial because she was inclined either to gush profusely or to fall silent and fix her guests with that glassy stare. Within the castle there was strict prohibition regarding animals. When Marion's cousin Ruth Mitchell came to stay she arrived with a small West Highland puppy. Her Uncle Willie was horrified and ordered it to be sent at once to the kennels. Ruth had other ideas, and quietly sneaked the pup into her bedroom. Unknown to her host, her four-legged friend spent a comfortable night reclining on a precious piece of seventeenth-century crewelwork.

The castle was like a museum filled with wonderful exhibits. If a visitor showed interest in a jade figurine, a drinking horn or perhaps an alabaster Madonna, Sir William would take enormous pleasure in showing it off and beguile each willing listener with intriguing information and entertaining anecdotes. His pawky sense of fun was often reflected by his acquisitions, and one of his favourite toys was a medieval imprisoning chair. He kept it in the dining room and raised a laugh each time he invited an unsuspecting guest to sit on it as they would become entrapped when he surreptitiously worked the levers. But one day a quick thinking lady outwitted him and Burrell was caught instead. 'Aha! Sir William!' she cried in triumph 'Now I have you at my mercy!'

Lady Burrell was glad to be the doyenne of a castle filled with fine furnishings and objets d'art. The décor supervised by her husband was both sumptuous and restrained but the domestic china and linen left to her own choice were rather more elaborate. Visitors were courteously attended by servants and welcomed with displays of flowers, the finest tableware and exquisitely embroidered bed linen. But Constance did have reservations. While visiting ladies and married couples might slumber in richly embroidered sheets, single male shooting guests were given plain linen ones marked 'shoot' with indelible ink to avoid them being mixed with the best ones!

In addition to the Hutton estate, the woods and farmland at Blackburn and Whiterig provided pheasant shooting over the winter months. Guests occasionally slept in the old pele tower where mysterious occurrences sometimes took place. Marion recorded that:

There was a shoot that year (1927) on Dec.10th at which the guns were Sir Wm Burrell, Sir Michael Malcolm, Admiral May, Maj Sholto Douglas, Ken Murray and B Maxwell.

It was on this occasion that for the first time

anything supernatural at Hutton came up. Sholto had been given the top room of the pele tower and on being asked the following morning if he had slept well, he admitted to a very disturbed night and asked if we'd been making whoopee about 1 am. No one had of course and the servants, who worked very hard at the time of a shoot, had gone to bed early. I asked him what sort of noise and he said a confused sort of stamping and shouting. It was well known that when cattle thieves were known to be approaching the cattle (as many as could) were driven into the ground floor room.

This noise of confused shouting was also heard by Teddy and Ella Stevenson on another occasion. My father was never told of this as he refused to believe anything supernatural and made fun of those who did, saying they needed to have their heads examined. This was odd as his mother was rather psychic.

As to the shoot I see we got 3 partridge, 143 pheasant, 19 woodcock etc, with 6 guns.

William Burrell had a lively imagination and normally made the most of any interesting aspect which concerned the castle's colourful past. He even installed a stained glass panel of Beatrix van Valkenburg in the tower because spurious evidence had led him to believe that her stepson, Richard Plantagenet, once slept there when his cousin Edward I had famously spent the night at Hutton Castle in 1296. Although Burrell was not told of the manifestation, his dismissive attitude towards 'strange happenings' may have been due to his constant desire to avoid upsetting his wife. Marion, who had no inhibitions, investigated the mystery on the anniversary of the Hutton pheasant shoot and later added this footnote.

> I was much intrigued by this and decided to see if I could hear anything, so on 9th and 10th of December, which were the dates on which the noises were heard, I had a large fire lit in the unused room and duly went to bed. The furniture was all of oak, and as the fire died down the oak contracted with pops and bangs. Each time I sat up hopefully, but no supernatural excitements happened!

By this time Marion was becoming a serious worry to her parents because their plans for her future kept going awry. In spite of all the money and effort they had invested in their daughter's future she kept attracting unsuitable men. Now her behaviour was becoming embarrassing, and they were at their wits' end to restrain her. But, just when the situation was beginning to seem hopeless, the ideal man appeared on the scene and all the Burrells heaved a sigh of relief when at last an engagement was announced on 14 May 1929.

Everybody spoke well of the Hon. John Roby Benson, and he must have seemed the answer to the Burrells' parental prayers. He was heir to a peerage, being the elder, and only surviving, son of Baron Charnwood of Castle Donington, a successful politician with a baronial seat at Stowe House, Lichfield, and a London house in Eaton Square. The engagement made headlines in the popular press, describing the charming bride-to-be as 'exceptionally tall and good looking with pretty fair hair' as well as being a considerable heiress and daughter of a wealthy ship owner who was also an art connoisseur. The wedding was expected to take place in London two months later, in July.

Marion probably met her fiancé through the late Lady Garvagh – John had been among the guests who dined at Grosvenor Square on the evening of Marion's coming out dance. He was a burly six-footer, and different; amusing and companionable without causing mayhem, but while sober and orderly he was also inclined to be unpredictable. Having sprung from a political background, he became fascinated by science during his schooldays and found infinite pleasure concocting alarming experiments in the Eton labs. At Oxford he read medicine and tinkered with motorbikes. Then he qualified as a mechanical engineer and began a career in the motor industry. In later life he studied optics and developed a passion for sailing yachts. All this was unfamiliar to Marion, who had been reared on the arts and though her lively mind would seize enthusiastically upon almost any subject it is hard to tell what drew these two together. Could Marion Burrell have been swayed by parental pressure? Or was she driven to escape the restraints which she suffered at home?

John probably appealed to Marion's maternal instinct because he was rather a lovable character who seemed to need a good woman to look after him. A friend once described him as 'a big shambling teddy bear'; he had been a polio victim and walked with a slight limp. Though game for a spot of tennis John preferred to avoid the dance floor, and this could hardly augur well for the effervescent Marion who loved to blaze and shimmer through ballrooms in her gorgeous evening gowns. He found her exuberance hard to take, soon realizing that her passionate nature was much too hot for him to handle. There was no fire in their romance, and the chemistry was wrong. This time it was Marion who broke the engagement, confessing later, 'I suppose I didn't love him enough'. John Benson was said to have been immensely relieved. It was a bitter blow for Marion's parents to have to cancel their plans for her wedding. After the worries they had endured over their daughter's unsuitable boyfriends the future Lord Charnwood had displayed all the attributes of a genuinely 'nice young man'. The Burrells took themselves off to Vienna in the hope that a summer vacation would help them to recover from their disappointment.

Back in the gloomy confines of Hutton Castle Marion tried to put her shattered life together. With sadness she learned that the ship she had launched in her childhood had finally been sold. *Strathlorne* had been the last remaining Burrell ship. Was it the memory of that day which made her father preserve that ship? Marion had followed *Strathlorne's* progress throughout two decades. In 1930 she was sold to Greek owners who changed her name and her luck changed too. The end came in 1940, but not through enemy action. When the engines and steering gear failed, the ship drifted for five days off the west coast of Ireland and was finally lost on the rocks.

After World War I Burrell's ventures in shipping had virtually ceased, and during the 1920s he had closed most of the company down. Having operated on a much reduced scale as agents and brokers Burrell and Son was finally wound up in 1939. After the death of his brother George, William's decisions had been made without consultation, leaving no prospect of employment for George's sons. When Burrell's autocratic actions reduced their incomes, some family members resented it. As her father's career in the world of shipping finally came to an end Marion was left with a feeling of loss. A brilliant era was over, and in spite of the painful conflicts between them, she never ceased to take pride in her father's phenomenal success.

In 1930 women were rediscovering the curves they had lost during the 'flapper' years. Cocktails, cigarettes and make-up were in vogue, so Marion returned to her social set and took every opportunity to indulge. Her father, freed at last from commercial commitments, devoted himself to adding even more fabulous items to his collection. His reputation had travelled far. Sir William casually confided to a friend that he also collected for 'The Old Lady' – he was referring to Her Majesty the Queen.

For once Sir William seems to have given in to the temptation to show off and that September, Hutton Castle was honoured when Queen Mary graciously accepted his invitation to visit his collection and come for tea. But despite the excited preparations, the presence of royalty was kept strictly under wraps until the visit was safely over, when a report appeared in the local press. The event caused Sir William more than a little anxiety. Queen Mary's keen interest in objets d'art was well known, and so was her habit of admiring a precious artefact with such enthusiasm that the unfort-unate owner was obliged to present it as a gift. By the time the royal entourage arrived, Burrell had taken the precaution of putting his most valued treasures out of sight. The Queen was ceremoniously received and given a tour of the famous collection but having admired the magnificent contents of the drawing room she chose not to take tea in that echoing cavern and made for the warmth of the dining room fire. It was a wise choice, because the drawing room chairs were said to be so uncomfortable that their occupants frequently suffered from cramp. When tea was being served she turned to her host. 'Sir William, I believe you have some very fine Ming', she enquired hopefully. 'Indeed Ma'am', he smoothly replied, 'It is true that I used to have some'. Sir William was delighted by the royal visit, and commemorated the occasion by flying the saltire from his flagstaff every year on Queen Mary's birthday.

While Burrell's collection was receiving the royal seal of approval Marion was in circulation again. From nearer home a new man had appeared, and this time she was enthralled – his personality seemed to suit her own in every way. Though they probably met in London, the Honourable Patrick Balfour was a Scot, the eldest son and heir of Lord Kinross, 2nd Baron of Glasclune, a law lord of the Scottish Bar, Sheriff of Dumfries and Galloway and a director of the Bank of Scotland. At last Burrell's daughter was doing the right thing, or so everyone thought. There was general rejoicing on 10 February 1931 when the engagement was announced.

The wedding of Patrick and Marion was to be held in London at St George's, Hanover Square on Tuesday 17 March at 2.15 pm Lady Clodagh Anson had kindly offered her London house for the reception. No time would be wasted, and everyone looked forward to a prompt and happy ending to this arduous marriage trail. Five weeks might seem a short time to arrange a wedding but Marion's previous engagement, to John Benson, had been announced only two months before the date of the marriage. Engagements of that length were not unusual then.

Patrick's family home was not far off, at Heriot Row in Edinburgh, so the Balfours and Burrells were soon on good terms. Patrick Balfour was a lanky man, six foot four inches tall, and dark with sensitive, finely chiselled features and a quizzical smile. He was talented and entertaining with a quicksilver wit. Lady Burrell was charmed by his easy manner while Sir William warmed to his knowledge and discerning eye, realizing that here was a man who understood art. But the Burrell treasures may have been at risk because when Patrick became over enthused he was inclined to wave his arms about and knock things over. He was notoriously clumsy, and said to be the only man who could lean backwards while going forwards, and then proceed sideways.

Being a journalist his social circle was extensive, and this was ideal for Marion, who loved meeting interesting people and revelled in lively company. At Oxford, Patrick had mingled with the Bloomsbury set and joined the guests of Lady Ottoline Morrell to stroll among peacocks on the Garsington lawns in the company of Bertrand Russell, Lytton Strachey, Aldous Huxley and Virginia Woolf. His fellow undergraduates had formed a gathering of enlightenment which included Evelyn Waugh, Kenneth Clark, Osbert Lancaster, Harold Acton, Cyril Connolly and John Betjeman. Theirs was the talented gang which became notorious for wild escapades and elaborate hoaxes during the 1920s, and Patrick had been in the thick of it.

When young Balfour came down from Oxford in 1924 his parents had sent him off to Paris to polish up his French at the Sorbonne, but life at the Ritz proved more to his liking. Back in Scotland he became an apprentice journalist at the *Glasgow Herald* but was soon drawn south to London where he took a studio flat in Yeoman's Row and became a gossip columnist. Although his learned father showed displeasure, Patrick had no regrets. From the *Weekly Dispatch* he progressed to the *Daily Sketch*, *Sunday Dispatch*, *Evening Standard*, *Harper's Bazaar* and *Punch*. Malcolm Muggeridge, later the editor of *Punch*, commented 'Gossip-writing is a most instructive occupation, probably the best liberal education now available', and having collaborated with Balfour he recalled, 'We were a composite personality who was supposed to have been everywhere and to know everyone', adding that 'the public assumed that our readers were all old Etonians, changed for dinner, went grouse-shooting and hunted in due season'. Patrick had discovered his element, while Evelyn Waugh, in return for personal publicity, fed him scandalous tales of his plan to elope with Evelyn Gardner, knowing that readers would be intrigued by the news that she was the daughter of Lady Burghclere and niece of Lord Carnarvon of Tutankhamun fame. When their subsequent marriage was not a success there was even more material for gossip columnists.

Cyril Connolly had become a literary journalist and for a time came to reside with Patrick at Yeoman's Row, but when Connolly tired of Patrick's frenetic social life the arrangement ended. In 1929 John Betjeman moved in, as he and Patrick had become the closest of friends. Betjeman was broke and unemployed at the time, and his mother wrote an effusive letter to Patrick thanking him for his kindness. During the summer of 1930, Betjeman had joined Patrick's family during a holiday on the Isle of Skye and afterwards he wrote a letter of thanks to Lady Kinross while he spent two hours waiting for his car to be repaired in Kyle of Lochalsh. Depressed to be leaving, with the misty Cuillins still in sight he concluded 'Oh I did like Skye' but 'What a vulgar place Gleneagles is! I could hardly believe such horror existed'. In letters to Patrick, Betjeman confided roguish attachments to girls whose fathers would not have considered him an acceptable suitor. By 1931 Patrick was also treading on dangerous ground, and it was not long before Marion Burrell's father began to hear alarm bells.

With the prospect of a London wedding in March the Burrell family was swept into a whirl of activity while Patrick and Marion snatched precious hours to plan their future together. Then, with only 12 days to go, Marion's world fell apart when she discovered the devastating newspaper announcement declaring that her marriage to Patrick had been cancelled.

There had been no change of heart between the young couple; once again William Burrell had stepped in and settled the matter himself. This time he had taken drastic action to protect the interests of his daughter. Within a month of giving his blessing Sir William had begun to have doubts about the marriage. Having been disarmed by the heir to a peerage Burrell was taken aback by his future son-in-law's unconventional lifestyle. Not only was Patrick a gossip columnist, it was also rumoured that he had been gambling and got himself deeply in debt. Burrell had not forgotten the shameful fate of his gambling ancestor. Fearing that an irresponsible son-in-law might reduce his own fortune to a similar fate, he enlisted the services of a private detective. Burrell's fears were soon confirmed. When Patrick continued to run up debts, Lord Kinross, being a shrewd man with limited means, had flatly refused to pay them. As Burrell insisted that his detective should leave no stone unturned, further undesirable aspects of Patrick's life came to light.

During the 'Roaring Twenties' Oxford undergraduates were said to fall into two categories, being either 'aesthetes' or 'hearties' – brain or brawn. In that male domain where few women were admitted, it was not unusual for friendships among aesthetes to be homosexual. Although Patrick could charm the ladies, his inclination towards other men was well known among his friends. To the straight-laced William

Burrell, the revelation came as an ugly shock, and aroused grave concern for his daughter's happiness. In his eyes her marriage was doomed, and the only solution would be to rescue her from this unfortunate alliance.

There could have been few fathers in William Burrell's situation who would not have shared this concern, and it would have seemed rational to suggest to Marion that she should break off the engagement. But the subject of homosexuality was considered to be unmentionable in the presence of ladies. An elderly father of Burrell's generation would have had a hard time discussing the problem with his daughter, let alone with a strong-willed rebel who could not wait to be freed from parental influence. Marion would never budge. There was a genuine attraction which drew Patrick and Marion together and fired their determination to be joined in a lovingly eccentric companionship. Their untamed spirits shared a bond which made them sparkle together, and both were dedicated to a union which would bring freedom to Marion and solvency to Patrick. But would it have worked? Was Burrell wrong to sever this alliance? Neither Marion nor Patrick forgave him.

Patrick vented his wrath by publishing scorching articles decrying 'The Stupid Lives of the Rich' – 'The desire to obtain money and the fear of losing it are the all-absorbing emotions of the life of the average man today. A man's success today is judged by the amount of wealth he possesses. Luxury is not life', he declared, adding pointed references to the sins of suspicion, snobbery and meanness. Unknown to her parents, his banished bride preserved the cuttings and pasted them into her scrapbook. Though Patrick showed no mercy to Sir William and Lady Burrell, he never ceased to speak kindly of Marion. In after years he continued to admire her spirit, averring that, in spite of her father's enormous wealth, she had never become spoilt.

In 1938 Patrick married the beautiful Angela Culme-Seymour but the union was short lived. John Betjeman's daughter, Candida Lycett Green, named her as the prototype of the notorious 'Bolter' in Nancy Mitford's novels *The Pursuit of Love* and *Love in a Cold Climate*, though Angela was not the only lady to be accorded that celebrated title. Patrick had succeeded to the peerage by World War II when he served as Squadron Leader in the RAF and was mentioned in despatches. A celebrated writer, his works include humorous novels and weighty volumes on political history. As Lord Kinross, he published *The Ottoman Centuries* in 1977 and dedicated this erudite tome to the writer and traveller Freya Stark. Marion was advanced in years by the time she read this work, and more than four decades had passed since she had been torn from the man she had hoped to marry. A contemporary photograph of Patrick had been pasted into the copy which was proudly displayed among her books.

CHAPTER 9

Open Conflict

When Marion's engagement to Patrick was forcibly ended her fury knew no bounds. In a single sweep, her father had destroyed her dreams and exposed her to public humiliation. However well intentioned his motives may have been, Marion could interpret his actions in no other way. War broke out in the Burrell household as she raged at her parents and accused them both of wrecking her life. 'I will never marry', she proclaimed. Gossip spread through the drawing rooms of Berwickshire while tongues wagged in the clubs and cocktail bars of London. Marion avoided her friends and while she took refuge at Hutton Castle, William Burrell tried to explain her sudden absence from society by announcing in *The Scotsman* that his daughter was required in the family home to entertain his guests. It was a futile gesture and nobody fell for the story.

Devastated by their daughter's reaction and dreading further trouble, Marion's parents were as wretched as she was and equally embarrassed by the situation. They racked their brains to think of ways to restrain her from ruining their family reputation. It was an agonizing time for them all, and a permanent rift set in between Marion and her parents. Constance seemed incapable of motherly love, and now that Marion was deprived of the kind chaperones who had once befriended her there was no sympathetic bosom on which to shed her tears.

Patrick had been a staunch ally, but now the rock on which Marion had intended to build her life had gone. The atmosphere at Hutton was becoming unbearable, with her father beside himself and her mother on the verge of collapse. In desperation the Burrells left home and spent eight months travelling on the Continent. Marion was miserable, and no matter where she was she felt desperately alone. The love for which she longed had again eluded her, and nobody could give her solace, least of all her parents.

In desolation Marion turned to the albums in which she had used to record each stage of her life; year by year, her story was told in pictures of remembered faces and events. All her friends were there, the engagements, the shooting parties, her fabulous clothes. She tried to recapture moments of happiness by poring over the weddings and house parties fondly displayed along with the cartoons, quotations and poems she had captured for posterity. Like her father, she had, in her own way, become a compulsive collector by preserving thoughts, passions, triumphs and disasters in books. One album was entitled 'Grave and Gay' because hers would always be a bitter-sweet collection.

What did the future hold for Marion Burrell? Fate took an unexpected turn, since not many miles away deliverance was waiting. On this occasion, it was to a father figure that she turned, an old family friend and contemporary of her father who often stayed at Hutton as a shooting guest. She had known Major Sholto Douglas from her girlhood, and the connection between them was something of an enigma.

'Major Douglas' had been named on her Christmas shopping list in 1927, almost like a godparent. She kept studio photographs of Sholto as a handsome young captain in dress uniform, but the signatures he added had been coyly scratched out. More recent photos showed him grey haired and still a fine-looking man, clad in comfortable country tweeds and accompanied by his dogs.

Sholto Douglas had served with distinction in the Royal Artillery. During the South African War he was awarded the DSO at Ladysmith and twice mentioned in despatches. In civilian life he became Chief Constable of the Metropolitan Police, and in 1914 was appointed Chief Constable of the Lothian and Peebles Constabulary. Furthermore, he received the King's Police and Fire Services Medal as well as the CBE. To the hero-worshipping Marion, Sholto stood for all that she admired. His gentle eyes and welcoming smile assured her that he was the one true friend to whom she could unburden her anguish. He befriended the desolate Marion and listened to her sorrowful tale with compassion.

Behind the Major's strong military bearing lay a soft and susceptible heart, and the fondness which Marion felt for him was not without reciprocation. With avuncular benevolence he had watched her grow up and never ceased to find her enchanting. Without hesitation he charged to her rescue, and before either of them realized what was happening he had taken her to his heart, not as an uncle, nor indeed a godfather, but as her lover. This sudden rush of passion might seem strange in a couple whose ages were more than 30 years apart, but in his sixties Sholto was still a vigorous man and immensely appealing. In the aftermath of Marion's broken engagement, this unimaginable rebound could hardly have been more catastrophic. Not only was Sholto a respected and longstanding friend of her parents, he was also a married man.

Many years later Sholto confided his story to a member of his family. He had met Grace Wolfe Murray in India when serving as a young army officer, and they had married, like Marion's parents, in 1901. Grace had been unhappy due to trouble with her mother and, longing to escape from a miserable home life, she had proposed marriage to Sholto. He gladly accepted, but the marriage did not turn out well. Romance was quickly stifled when Grace found she had no inclination for the physical realities of marital life. Without children to bring the pair together a void pervaded their relationship.

While Sholto was Chief of the Metropolitan Police the couple had lived in London but when he transferred to Scotland they settled in Edinburgh, making their home in George Square. Though Sholto and Grace were an ill-matched pair they had remained together while following separate lives. Grace was gifted and artistic, and city life suited her. She could use her talents as an interior decorator while running a fashionable gallery, 'Bondy', in Queen Street, where she displayed and sold beautiful furnishings and exotic artefacts imported from foreign parts. Her friends were intellectuals, aesthetes and homosexuals. Sholto did not feel at ease with them. He was an outdoor man who enjoyed country life and, being a good shot, welcomed invitations which took him and his dogs out of town.

The lovers maintained their liaison, enjoying hill walks to forts and cairns and quiet fireside hours while Sholto's ill-founded marriage began to fall apart. When a separation followed he fervently hoped that his secret assignations with Marion would one day end in marriage so that they might raise the family for which he had always longed.

When Marion arrived on the scene Grace Douglas had withdrawn to her circle of friends. Living among artists, writers and poets, she fallen under the influence of an erstwhile companion of Oscar Wilde, John Gray, a carpenter's son. Gray had become a writer, and during the 1880s his flowing locks and fancy clothes had caught the roving eye of Oscar Wilde. Soon he became one of 'Wilde's boys' while Wilde supported his literary career. When *The Picture of Dorian Gray* was published, young Gray claimed to have been the subject of this darkly sinister novel, and invited other members of their circle to call him 'Dorian'. The author promptly denied his claim. Gray was offended and became even angrier when he discovered that his place in Wilde's affections had been usurped by Lord Alfred Douglas, known as Bosie. This precocious undergraduate was the son of the Marquess of Queensberry, who eventually had Oscar Wilde tried for sodomy and thrown into Reading Gaol.

The jilted John Gray transferred his devotion to a rich Russian aesthete called André Raffalovich, and having found a new sponsor he and Raffalovich became lifelong friends. Gray then became a Catholic priest and settled in Edinburgh where his Russian benefactor built for him St Peter's Church in Morningside. Unfortunately this chain of events spelt disaster for Sholto and Marion, as Grace Douglas decided to follow John Gray by embracing the Catholic faith. Because divorce was forbidden by the Roman Catholic Church, so long as Grace continued to live, Sholto Douglas could never be released to marry Marion Burrell.

This obstacle could not be overcome because, at that time, to 'live in sin' was socially unacceptable. If they had resorted to cohabiting, a public scandal would have followed.

Marion would have been denounced by her family and friends, and Sholto could not allow her to suffer that disgrace. The situation was bad enough already. Though their meetings remained hidden from the public eye, sooner or later William Burrell would get to know what was going on.

While their meetings continued the lovers indulged their pleasure in books and Sholto gave Marion several, including *The Ballad of Reading Gaol* by C.3.3. (Oscar Wilde) and *The Works of William Shakespeare*. Her feelings of rebellion were at their height when he gave her a new novel by AJ Cronin. *Hatter's Castle* is a Victorian tragedy set in a Scottish town where an absurdly ambitious man makes his house look like a castle and mistreats his daughter by banishing her suitor and making her a prisoner in her own home. Marion made pencilled notes indicating parallels with her own life. The girl's mother was described as 'Unstable as water, and as shallow, she reflected merely the omnipresent shadow of another stronger than herself'. Like Constance, the fictitious mother tried to manipulate her daughter by instilling feelings of guilt. Constance had grown fiercely jealous, and Marion was almost in despair.

At Hutton her situation had gone from bad to worse. It was inevitable that her parents should get wind of her association with Sholto Douglas and she was treated with total mistrust. William and Constance were distraught because their plans for Marion's future had been destroyed again, and they feared their reputation was being threatened by their wayward daughter. Their only child had proved to be a devastating disappointment and her ingratitude seemed unendurable.

At 29 Marion was beyond control. To turn her out would have caused a scandal and, while it might have been a relief to wash their hands of her, it seemed safer to keep her at

home. Her elderly parents tried to restrain her by withdrawing privileges and withholding funds – Marion had to ask
her father for permission to use a car and come to him for
pocket money, just like a little child. When servants were
present and witnessed her requests she felt deeply humiliated.
To live at Hutton Castle without cash or transport made her
feel like a prisoner, but within and without the Burrell household, appearances still had to be preserved. Friendly invitations
could not be ignored and guests continued to arrive from
time to time. Marion grasped every opportunity to be with
her friends, and those who knew about her problems did
their best to help her. Often she had to borrow money or
try to sell her possessions. To clothe herself she had been
allowed accounts in department stores while her father paid
the bills, so she learned to invite a friend to use her account
in Jenners in exchange for cash. Marion became skilled in
the art of subterfuge, and for a time the secret encounters
managed to continue. The frail Lady Burrell was hardly cut
out to be an effective gaoler and Sir William had other work
to do.

By 1932 the furbishing of Hutton Castle had at last been
completed. Now that Burrell's dream of medieval grandeur
had been realized, it would have seemed logical to consign
it all to posterity by willing his estate, with the castle and
contents, to his only child. Had Marion fulfilled his hopes
by marrying a worthy aristocrat, Hutton Castle might have
become a noble family seat, but after all the attention he had
lavished on her, his daughter had failed him and fallen from
grace so his plans for the future were changed. Marion was
cast aside and now that her prospects of marriage had ended
in disaster Burrell came up with a different idea. Having
achieved recognition as a leading collector in Europe he

made a momentous decision which would bring him world fame. Early in the 1930s William Burrell resolved to endow his entire collection to the British nation.

With this stupendous goal in view, the importance of his collection increased. Refusing to be deterred by his daughter's failure to live up to his expectations, the prospect of crowning his achievements by providing a national legacy made him more active than ever. Buying widely, and on a rising scale, his outlay peaked in 1936 when his annual expenditure on the collection reached £80,000 (nearly £5 million today). Across the globe new sources were attracting him while Hutton Castle overflowed with objéts d'art from French ivories and silver chalices to rare Chinese jade and carved shabti figurines from Egyptian tombs.

And success awaited Burrell in other directions. The grouse moor at Mayshiel was approaching its zenith. It spread across about 3,300 acres of the Lammermuir Hills and Burrell was determined to achieve maximum results. Expert management had been enlisted and the shoot became a triumph during the decade between 1926 and 1937. Each year in August, the grouse shoot on Mayshiel was an almost continuous three-day event, when more than a thousand birds could be shot. A keeper reported that afterwards the moor would remain un-shot until the following season. On the Glorious Twelfth of August 1933 conditions were so good that a record Mayshiel bag of 465 brace was shot on that single day. Nine guns with loaders made up the party and Burrell invited first-rate shots. He was extremely competitive about the seasonal records at Mayshiel. Though equipped with the best of guns from Purdey, Burrell had been a late beginner in the sport and the standard of his shooting never matched that of his guests. Humbly, he admitted 'I just move the birds around'.

Having reached his seventies he rode a Highland pony to get to his butt. Eventually he accidentally peppered a beater and decided to hang up his gun.

For Marion, the shoot was a welcome diversion, but in the end she grew tired of the slaughter and preferred the freedom of the moor after the shooting was over. She longed to walk alone to commune with the elements and observe wildlife at peace. Being an ardent nature lover she yearned to run free. When an opportunity arose she would throw off her clothes to swim in a river or sunbathe naked on a roof. During a scorching August day on the shoot there was an awkward incident when she surreptitiously removed her stockings. Willie Burrell was so shocked that, in the presence of his guests, he ordered his daughter off the moor. Unceasingly he strove to hold her in check and keep undesirable influences at bay. A grouse moor should offer few temptations as his shooting guests were mostly married men and considered to be thoroughly respectable, but there were no guarantees with Marion.

In 1934 Eva Thomson gave birth to a daughter called Susan, and I come into the story now because Marion kindly agreed to be my godmother. Having a female godchild was a new experience for her, and the relationship was a long and happy one. She was not only the best of godmothers but also the truest of friends. More and more of her circle were getting married and as usual Marion was out of step. The De Prees of Beech Hill were regular guests at Hutton, and when their offspring began to join the marriage stakes the Burrells wished that their daughter would do the same. Soon there were christenings, but William and Constance could only be outsiders at these happy events.

Willie Burrell might have become a devoted grandpa,

delighting small people with the mischievous bunnies on his medieval tapestries and the naughty tricks of Reynard the Fox. Instead, he became interested in falconry accoutrements and bought a magnificent seventeenth-century set to add to the Burrell collection. Some of these items are said to have been a gift from King James VI and I to Sir William Pope of Wroxton Abbey. What grandson would not be intrigued by the exquisite hoods, gauntlet and lure, and what granddaughter could resist the embroidered flowers with which they were decorated? Burrell knew how to get on with children. One day while walking by the river he came upon a small boy and asked him 'Would you be thinking of poaching here laddie?' and heard him reply 'Och no Sir! The man at the big hoose wouldna like it'. After that the boy received a letter from Sir William permitting him to fish that stretch of the river for the rest of his life.

Constance Burrell had enjoyed reading stories to small nephews and nieces and the prospect of knitting baby clothes for a grandchild could have been the therapy she needed. Instead she used basic paper patterns and sewed simple garments for herself. Although she valued quality and took pleasure in beautiful things, Constance did not share her daughter's creative imagination. Depression made her withdraw from company so that William often had to explain 'Her ladyship is unwell'. But while he continued to cosset her, Constance became ever more dejected, devious and demanding, her mind tormented by the delusion that she was being neglected and victimized by her daughter. Now she regretted that Marion had been indulged with opportunities she herself had never known. Marion could do nothing right, and Constance continually sought to punish and exclude her.

The household at Hutton Castle was rarely a happy one, and Constance had problems retaining domestic staff. In desperation she even attempted to hijack her neighbour's cook! But the Hutton gardens were an ongoing success because William Burrell employed the best of gardeners. For many years, when the gardens were in their prime, Peter Freeny served as head gardener with at least six men employed under him. Burrell had the highest opinion of Freeny, and as he lacked close friends with whom he could share his troubles, when life was getting him down, his head gardener was the person in whom he confided.

Sir William did not easily fit the role of a country gentleman. As the laird of Hutton Castle, he cut a curious figure. Wearing grey flannel plus-fours and an ancient fur lined coat which had belonged to his father, he strode about his domain with a barley sugar walking stick. Burrell appreciated good service and several devoted employees stayed with him for years. John Pringle served on the estate while Jimmy Wallace was the Hutton gamekeeper. Jim Guthrie maintained the castle generator and helped Sir William to arrange heavy items in the collection. During the 1930s a young farm girl called Ethel Shiel became his trusted secretary and personal assistant. Ethel biked seven miles to work each day and hand-wrote letters because Sir William hated the sound of a typewriter. After she left to do war work Freeny's daughter Janet filled her place. Lexie Lesenger was another local girl who entered domestic service at Hutton Castle but also helped with the office work.

Constance loved to be among the flowers; the Ladies' Walk led through overhanging trees to magnificent wrought iron gates which formed the entrance to the walled garden, but gardeners were banned from the walk and made to go round by the road. There were long herbaceous borders, massed rose beds, flowering trees and a range of hothouses yielding exotic fruit and prize-winning blooms. In summertime the garden was a haven of tranquillity, but the long winters at Hutton Castle were becoming arduous.

In 1934 Doctor MacLagan recommended that for the sake of her health Lady Burrell would benefit from a warmer climate. Sir William gladly took her off to spend the winter in Jamaica and so they spent December, January and February abroad. For those who could afford to go, Jamaica had become a popular wintering place. Early in the century Elder Dempster & Company had been subsidized by the British and Jamaican governments to run a steamer service delivering tourists and returning with cargoes of fruit. The company also held an interest in the Constant Spring Hotel which occupied a large estate with banana plantations and well-tended gardens at the foot of the Blue Mountains. Having been the first Jamaican hotel to install electricity and running water the management now offered every luxury the Burrells could desire, including haute cuisine, swimming, golf and even a concert hall with a resident orchestra. Voyaging on a 'banana boat' was a pleasant means of transport and the Burrells found the Caribbean sunshine so beneficial that the sojourn was repeated every winter until World War II.

As Marion was not included in this health cure she remained to face the Hutton winters alone. Ever resourceful, she vacated her chilly bedroom and had her things brought down to her father's business room on the ground floor of the tower where she could live cosily and enjoy the warmth of a fire. Her parents had made sure that her activities would be restricted as far as possible by making her live on the same subsistence wages as their staff. Her only transport was a

bicycle. Luckily there were sympathizers in the neighbourhood and from time to time she devised ways to get away.
Marion was leading a miserable life, and while her mother
continued to fuss and complain her own health had begun
to suffer. Having previously enjoyed a strong constitution
she began to suffer from digestive problems and irritating
skin conditions, and she sought help from the Thomson
Nature Cure Clinic in Edinburgh. When Dale Carnegie's
book on *How to Win Friends and Influence People* was
published in 1936, she noted that 'Hatred is never ended by
hatred but by love'.

Marion was suffering a tortured existence. Though her
secret affair with Sholto Douglas had been concealed from
outsiders, her parents would have been electrified to learn
that an old and trusted friend of their own generation had
been dallying with their daughter, and the fact that Sholto
was a married man as well as a respected member of society
was even more shocking. Though Marion's bond with
Sholto would always endure, the lovers knew there was no
future that they could ever share. Marriage was out of the
question, and while her faithful protector was approaching
old age, Marion was in her thirties and still in her prime.
From her enforced confinement at Hutton the outlook
seemed hopeless, and without the warmth of Sholto's
galvanising embrace to comfort her she felt utterly forlorn.

Having tramped alone through woods and fields Marion
sought consolation among the hothouses of her father's
garden where the warm air hung heavy with the fragrance
of lilies and jasmine. Her spirits rose when she picked armfuls
of sweet-scented carnations to brighten her temporary quarters in the castle. But when her parents arrived home from
their winter vacation Constance was outraged because her

daughter had purloined the beautiful blooms which should have been reserved for herself. In response to his wife's fury Sir William gave orders that the carnation house must remain permanently locked against their daughter. Constance had learned to exert her influence and her ever-loving husband was like putty in her hands.

During one of their winters in the sun she had suffered a nasty insect bite which hurt when she walked, so William enlisted two obliging natives to carry her about in a sedan chair. This form of transport appealed to Constance so much that she decided to continue it at Hutton Castle, thereafter insisting on being carried upstairs every day for her afternoon rest. The butler and footman were made to heave her up the awkward spiral stair on a chair supported by two long poles. This activity was not popular with the porters, especially when Lady Burrell reappeared downstairs just after they had carried her up. Robert Lorimer's warnings had been well justified, but it was only after Sir William fell down his own stairs that he finally installed a lift. Needless to say, he also fitted it with a lock. But Constance still chose to be carried aloft in her chair although she preferred to come down in the lift.

The tortured existence of Marion Burrell continued in a strange parody of normality alternating between Dickensian austerity and social meetings with friends. Today it seems almost unbelievable that a lively and intelligent young woman could become isolated and subjugated in the ways in which Marion undoubtedly was. Around this time she is said to have driven a 1935 Hillman Minx but, as usual, her father supplied the petrol and she was only permitted to use the car about once a week.

The De Pree family at Beech Hill were among the

friends who gave her sanctuary from time to time. After Goda De Pree married Captain Andrew Pitcairn, Marion acquired another small godson, David Pitcairn, and proudly attended his christening. On her visits to Beech Hill, Miss Burrell always received a special welcome from the butler, who, being of a literary bent, wrote flowery odes to the beauties of nature and presented them to her with the utmost reverence. Sometimes she joined the family for a day at Lanark Races. On these occasions she would dress elegantly and her striking appearance continued to command attention. Yet again press cameras clicked and it was reported that 'Miss Burrell wears her tweeds well'.

Marion also looked smart in uniform when she became involved with the Girl Guides and played her part as a Guide Commissioner. She was said to be an efficient organizer and her infectious enthusiasm made her popular with the girls whether signalling by semaphore, transporting a casualty or demonstrating how to light a campfire with only two matches. At one time her mother was called upon to preside over the Berwickshire Red Cross. Although the frail Lady Burrell had little capacity for administration, her dignity and fine looks befitted a figurehead and her elegant manners carried her through. Constance raised funds for the charity by selling 1,000 daffodils which had been picked at Hutton Castle.

The Burrells supported the local community when Sir William generously provided Hutton with a Village Hall and presented it in the name of his wife. They were regular attenders of the parish church where Burrell had one of the pews altered to accommodate his long legs. His commitment as an elder was greatly appreciated though he drew the line at visiting parishioners. On Sundays Lady Burrell wore black and they both seemed a little stiff. When the collection was due, Sir William would delve in his pocket to extract some coins and then hand one to his wife and one to his daughter to put in the offering plate. Miss Burrell was invited to open a sale of work in the new hall and made a masterly speech in which she raised the subject of 'economy'. Having begun by extolling its merits, she made the audience laugh by telling them to put economy out of their minds and give unstintingly to the Church funds that day. Did her father note the jibe? The festivities ended in a village dance. Marion had good friends among the Hutton people and she badly needed some light-hearted moments.

During this period providence took another unexpected turn and romance began to bloom when a new and younger man swung into her orbit. He would become the great passion of her life through stolen meetings snatched during her parents' absences from home. Marion carefully covered her tracks and never recorded more than her lover's initials, JLP. He appears in numerous snapshots with unnamed adults and children, but only dates and place names were recorded. He was smartly dressed; a sturdy, muscular man with a handsome Latin look; pensive with heavy features and darkly brooding eyes. But who was the mysterious 'JLP'?

Some lengthy detective work was required but my search began to progress when, almost by accident, a succession of clues came to light among Marion's books. A receipt which fell out from one revealed that 'J L Plaza Esq.' had lived at 61 Knightsbridge and bought two dozen handkerchiefs from Robinson and Cleaver in 1935. Then I discovered a card from a florist in Chelsea in a packet of British Museum postcards depicting the Elgin Marbles. This cultural visit must have gone well, because at Lady Clodagh Anson's London address

Marion received a bouquet of pink carnations, like the favourite Hutton flowers from which she had been banned. The florist's shop was in 'Whitelands House', a block of Art Deco flats in the King's Road, Chelsea, which was identified inn snapshots of Marion's lover.

In her albums JL Plaza's image kept cropping up among Valentine cards, mementoes and cuttings from theatre programmes which spanned the decade between 1935 and 1945. Eventually I showed the pictures to my aunt, Mona MacAndrew. She seemed to recognize him, but only recalled that he had a funny name which sounded like 'Horsey'.

Some photos showed Marion and her boyfriend with three school-age children, and I dreaded unearthing another broken marriage. They appeared to have been cycling at a place called 'Newnham' and again at 'Westbury' where the village church had a separate bell tower with a strangely crooked spire. As luck would have it, there are about six Newnhams in England and at least two can be paired with a nearby Westbury. After some abortive investigations my husband happened to spot another Newnham near a West-bury in our road atlas while we were motoring near the Severn. This observation prompted an unscheduled detour which led us at last to the thirteenth-century church with the crooked spire at Westbury-on-Severn. Along at the Newnham post office we made enquiries about the village school and achieved a major breakthrough when contact was established with John Billings, son of the late headmaster. A friendly correspondence followed. By sheer coincidence, the family in Marion's photographs had spent most of World War II living next door to the village schoolmaster. The two families had become close friends, although the children in Marion's photos never attended the Newnham village school. Instead they had gone to a Roman Catholic convent because they were Spaniards.

At last I was able to identify the people in the photographs, and as John Billings' family had kept in touch the trail eventually led to Spain, so an interpreter was called in. One of the girl cyclists was married and living in Vigo. When we were able to trace and phone her, the interpreter became redundant because Lolita Luengo de Pestana spoke perfect English, having completed her education at North Foreland Lodge in Hampshire. José Luis Plaza had died in 1993. He was the children's uncle and still a bachelor when he and Marion met. A Spanish diplomat who came from Cartagena in southern Spain, he served as First Secretary to the Spanish embassy in London. As Lady Clodagh Anson lived near the embassy she might have known and introduced him.

In 1935 José Plaza's elderly mother came to England with her daughter and family to escape from the troubles of the Spanish Civil War. Señora Plaza spoke no English and José's sister and brother-in-law were also disadvantaged, but the three children soon learned to converse fluently. Señor Luengo, José's brother-in-law, was a pharmacist, but his command of the English language was not good enough to allow him to follow his profession in Britain. The elderly Señora Plaza had lived with her daughter's family in Chelsea at one of the flats at Whitelands House until the start of World War II when they all moved to Newnham. José kept closely in touch with his family, and on some of his visits Marion had accompanied him.

Marion lived for the times they could spend together. She was continually strapped for cash but when she contrived to join him José was able to subsidize her. He was a man of means, and also immensely cultured – he enjoyed music, the theatre and the arts and works by Picasso and Modigliani were among his possessions. While Marion's parents were wintering abroad he came to Hutton Castle, and she was proud to show him some of the items in her father's collection which had not been locked away. In the late 1930s before World War II broke out, her bicycle was joyfully abandoned while they toured in his car visiting Scottish castles and stately homes. In London there were outings to museums, galleries and the theatre when Marion's school friend Jean Forbes-Robertson played the lead in Ibsen's *Hedda Gabler*. Together the lovers visited exhibitions and travelled to the Rijksmuseum in Amsterdam.

Marion found José a charming and immensely interesting man. At last she had discovered a true soul mate who enjoyed the interests she had loved to share with her father. José had travelled widely and spoke several languages. He began to educate Marion on Spanish politics and encouraged her to read in French the works of Victor Hugo, Balzac and Flaubert. Perceiving her interest in ships he introduced her to the sea-faring stories of Eugene O'Neill. José was a serious thinker and sometimes inclined to be depressed, so he understood Marion's troubles and made her smile with the story of *Ferdinand the Bull*. For a decade the lovers met whenever they could. Stolen sojourns between this vibrant young woman and the brooding, hot-blooded Spaniard created a passion made all the more poignant by the soul-destroying circumstances which Marion was forced to endure at home. While their ardour reached great heights no prospect of marriage seems to have been entertained. Marion was not the only woman in José's life, and as he was neither noble, British nor Protestant, her parents would have opposed him to the end.

Meanwhile Europe was entering a period of unrest as Adolf Hitler gathered his forces in the run up to World War II. There were more weddings when Marion's cousin Ruth Mitchell married Alec Mackenzie and my bond with Marion was strengthened when Ruth's sister Mona Mitchell married my uncle Charlie MacAndrew, a politician who later became Deputy Speaker in the House of Commons.

In 1939 when war was declared Marion achieved certificates from the Red Cross and St John's Ambulance Brigade and enlisted in the Voluntary Aid Detachment (VAD) to nurse at Peel Hospital, near Selkirk. As a VAD, she was able to live away from home. It was testing to be under orders and on her feet all day, but she threw herself into it whole heartedly and felt instantly drawn to the wounded men in her care. Her life was changed by the cheerful companionship of experienced nurses as well as her fellow VADs. Because she was tall she suffered through constantly bending over hospital beds and lifting patients made her back ache. When her shift ended, she would retire exhausted to her cubicle where a large photograph of José in polo gear was pinned above her bed.

In September 1939 signs of a German air attack were already threatening Scotland, and Mrs De Pree witnessed a dogfight in East Lothian with fighter planes above Beech Hill. After an air raid warning, gunfire could be heard coming from the Firth of Forth. Suddenly a Heinkel came into view, closely followed by three Spitfires. The noise was deafening when a fourth Spitfire joined them, all rattling bullets into the doomed Heinkel which finally crashed onto Longnewton Hill. Afterwards, the smell of gunpowder lingered in the Beech Hill garden. Four German airmen survived to be taken prisoner by the local constable, but the mechanic and wireless operator had been killed. Next day, hundreds of cars arrived with queues of people wanting to see the wreck and it had to be cordoned off. Ruth De Pree was a niece of Earl Haig, and her military background prompted her to record a lucid account of the 'Battle of Beech Hill', of which Marion received a copy.

On the Firth of Clyde the prospect of air attacks threatened Clydebank. The Thomson family shipyard, which caused the town to be built, had since achieved fame as John Brown's of Clydebank. As the shipyard was a prime target for enemy bombs the neighbouring community would soon be at risk, and so children were being hastily removed to places of safety. My home was at Hillhouse in Ayrshire where my parents were struggling to cope with wartime conditions in a large and isolated country house. It had plenty of available space but almost all of the staff had gone off to serve in the war. My mother hardly knew how to cook when, with consummate irony, the Thomson household was allocated a busload of two dozen evacuees from the slums of Clydebank. The unfortunate children were not only tired and hungry but grubby and verminous as well, so with the experienced help of my nanny, my frantic mother rounded them up two at a time and systematically bathed the lot. It was a harrowing experience for everyone concerned. Food and beds were eventually prepared, and next day my mother bought a set of new clothes for every child. Although she learned to deal with many crises it was hard to tell who had been more traumatized that day, Eva or her 24 unexpected guests. The alien countryside made the children pine for home, so most of them were returned to Clydebank in time for the devastating Blitz which shattered the town in 1941. As country houses were being requisitioned for hospitals or other wartime purposes, my parents took the initiative and converted Hillhouse into flats for the families of serving officers while land girls occupied the stable buildings where the chauffeur and grooms had lived.

There were more surprises when we woke one day to find our house surrounded by road blocks with armed soldiers hiding under rhododendrons and creeping through the woods. Unknown to us, British troops were rehearsing the D-Day invasion of Normandy and, after crossing the Firth of Clyde in a fleet of landing craft from Arran, Hillhouse had been their first objective.

It would be interesting to consider how the Burrell Collection might have fared if Hutton Castle had been subjected to an invasion of evacuees or destructive manoeuvres by army tanks, let alone damage from enemy bombs. Luckily, despite the castle's history of conflict the Burrell household escaped serious disruption. Somehow José and Marion still managed to meet, even through the blackout, when London was thronged with ARP wardens and uniformed personnel. Precious times were shared at sandbagged galleries and those small theatres which defiantly stayed open to boost public morale with performances of *Blythe Spirit* and *Arsenic and Old Lace*. While hostilities continued, their love affair was conducted without the inhibitions of those furtive meetings Marion had held with Sholto Douglas. Caution was thrown to the wind when José booked them into hotels as a married couple. When Charlie and Mona MacAndrew spent a night of their honeymoon at the Grand Hotel in St Andrews they were more than a little surprised to discover Mona's cousin breakfasting with her Spanish boyfriend at the next table. Years later my aunt seemed mildly amused by the encounter and recalled a later occasion when Marion brought José to visit them at Newfield. The meeting was not a success as other cousins who were present had reservations about Marion's irregular attachment and José's foreign background made them ill at ease. Marion was hurt by their reaction. After that she was chary about introducing her friends to members of her family, but it made her cousins suspect that she was being secretive.

Meanwhile, the Hutton villagers were actively engaged in war work, supplying comforts and raising funds to entertain the troops while the surrounding countryside became transformed by camps for Polish soldiers and German prisoners-of-war. Girl Guides met each week to stitch blankets and knit army socks in a blacked-out hall lit by paraffin lamps. When she was free to do so Marion taught them first aid. At Peel Hospital wounded servicemen arrived every day and she worked long hours, also taking turns on night duty. Sometimes when the patients were asleep she found time to read, and José sent books to sustain her 'For the long nights'. Once, during the small hours, she was sitting alone when she became aware that a young patient was fully conscious and seemed to be watching her. The wounded soldier had not spoken a word since arriving at the hospital so Marion began to talk to him and gently persuaded him to reply. For the first time he began to speak and told her he had been an army boxer. Then he asked about her own life and proceeded to draw her out with an extraordinary powerful understanding. Gradually her story poured out as they talked quietly together through the night till eventually the young man grew drowsy and fell asleep once more. Having unburdened her soul, Marion was left with a feeling of peace and found herself armed with new confidence. The following morning the man seemed unaware that anything had passed between them.

At Hutton Castle Marion's aging parents coped with wartime restrictions as best they could. When their cook suddenly departed they had no idea how to prepare the meat she had left in the larder, and so the gardener, Peter Freeny came into the kitchen and cooked mince and gravy to feed his employers. Afterwards Sir William and Lady Burrell gratefully assured him that the meal had been delicious. The flower beds in the walled garden had been planted with vegetables which were sold to buy fuel for the boiler. In the meantime, Sir William took every opportunity to continue collecting, knowing that good bargains could be found in wartime. While his collection kept increasing his storage problems increased as well. His castle was already overflowing and after some frantic digging, a good many of Burrell's treasures were buried in trenches under the lawns of Hutton Castle. More perishable items were crated and stacked in outhouses and the crypts of local churches. Once it became safe to do so, he solved some of his problems by lending works to galleries in other parts of Britain. When her father sent French and Dutch paintings to the Art Gallery at Berwick Marion believed that some of them would eventually come to her, but she was to be disappointed.

Having decided to donate his collection to the nation, Burrell was faced by further problems. How and where was it to be done? This was to prove a lasting headache. As time went on, sites in London and the Home Counties were rejected. The City of Edinburgh suffered the same fate because Sir William had been infuriated by the Edinburgh authorities when they took away the gates and railings from Hutton Castle to use as scrap metal to support the war effort.

As compensation for the sacrifice of his valuable ironwork Burrell had been offered a paltry sum of £3. Edinburgh was never forgiven. Eventually, in 1943, Sir William Burrell paid a handsome compliment to his home town when the city of Glasgow was finally chosen to receive the Burrell Collection. His generosity was acclaimed with great rejoicing and a formal celebration took place in 1944. But almost at once Sir William became concerned about security and the endless difficulties of finding a suitable site for the museum. Soon he began laying down conditions and restrictions which were destined to cause trouble for everyone involved. The years were beginning to take their toll, and now that he was in his eighties the future of his fabulous collection never ceased to worry him.

Away from the public eye Marion continued to meet José, and when the south of England was beset with flying bombs he took her to Newnham where they enjoyed a summer break with his family and cycled with the children through the quiet lanes of Gloucestershire. Those dark days of the war brought sadness for Marion when two of her godchildren were killed in 1944. That May, Lady Garvagh's grandson Victor Canning, a Lieutenant in the Grenadier Guards, died in action while serving in Italy at the age of 20. Then, in October, a disaster occurred at Beech Hill. Marion's friend Goda was already a widow as Lieut. Colonel Andrew Pitcairn had also died in action. Goda was staying with her parents at Beech Hill along with five-year-old David and his nanny when, late at night, after most of the family had gone to bed, a low flying aircraft was heard overhead. Suddenly a terrific explosion shook the house as the plane crashed and set the whole building ablaze. Beech Hill was wrecked. This time it was not an enemy plane but an

RAF Mosquito which came to grief, and two British airmen were killed. Little David Pitcairn and his nanny died in the fire, as did his grandmother, Ruth De Pree, and her brother Colonel John Haig of Carnoch. Along with members of the household staff Colonel De Pree survived the tragedy; his daughter Goda was spared because she had gone downstairs to refill a vacuum flask.

During the last two years of the war Marion transferred from Peel to Edenhall Hospital in Musselburgh, a rehabilitation establishment for service men and women who had suffered amputations or other disabilities. They received specialist care and physiotherapy while learning to cope with their handicaps. Marion was a great encourager as well as a sympathetic nurse and, like thousands of others, she was awarded medals for her nursing service when World War II finally ended in 1945.

After the troubled years of gloom and anxiety, Britain erupted into glorious celebrations. At last the lights came on again and people began to rebuild their cities and their lives. But for Marion it was also a time of sadness because, when the war ended, her meetings with José ended too. They had come together from distant poles and their lives were to lead them in different ways. Without animosity they agreed to part, although it was painful to end a rapturous interlude which neither would ever forget.

As the war was ending José arranged for the Luengos to take his mother and their young son to live in South America while he took charge of the two girls' education at an English boarding school. Plaza resigned his position at the Embassy, and when his relations were reunited he also moved abroad and married a lady who shared his interest in the arts. Like the Burrells, the couple were blessed with an only daughter but, even after his experience of consoling Marion through her family strife, José turned out to be another unrelenting father. When his own daughter embarked on a scandalous affair he rejected her, and in due course they too became estranged.

When José departed from her life Marion mourned her loss. Her world had been shattered once again, but the mysterious thread which had drawn them together would never be destroyed.

CHAPTER 10

Escape

For Marion the return to Hutton Castle could hardly have been joyful, but it was tempered with some parental warmth because, in July 1945, when Japan capitulated and VJ Day finally marked the end of World War II, her father gave her a set of ten framed Crawhall prints of *The Fables of Reynard the Fox*. William Burrell had acquired the original illustrations in 1935, and these are now in the Burrell Collection. The prints were ones Marion had enjoyed in her nursery days at Great Western Terrace. The gift was timed to welcome her home from the war with a tribute to the service she had given as a VAD.

Her return to the family fold meant changes for them all. Each week the Hutton Castle order from the fishmonger was delivered by the local bus and Sir William announced that his household would now be requiring 'an extra piece of fish'. He failed to keep abreast of the cost of living in post-war Britain; and his supplies of ready cash were no longer replenished with sufficient regularity, so local tradesmen were sometimes underpaid. Understandably, they resented this. Delivery vans still called at the castle, and when Lady Burrell declared the butcher's chicken was too costly she may simply have lacked the requisite cash.

As Marion's parents grew older her life at home became grimmer than ever. Her father's sight was failing and his health had begun to deteriorate, but in spite of his frailty his enthusiasm for collecting was undiminished. In 1948 Burrell reached a second peak when he spent more than £60,000 (nearly £2 million today) on new acquisitions. Even as an elderly man he continued to order people about and pursue his goals, but he resisted change and doggedly adhered to concepts he had valued in the past. Despite his active brain William Burrell was not the man he had once been. For years Constance had been ailing and demanding attention, and now that her husband was becoming dependent on others her influence over him increased, allowing her more opportunities to orchestrate their dealings with Marion. Little by little the power that her parents exerted gradually dominated her life.

So why did Marion return? Today a woman in her situation would be expected to break away and lead a life of her own, but like many women who suffer abuse she remained invisibly chained to the source of her misery. After the war was over her parents were aged approximately 85 and 70, and as their lives were drawing to an end Marion believed it her duty to care for them. It would have been hard for her to do otherwise since she depended entirely on their financial support. As usual, they kept her pitifully short of money and refused to trust her, fearing the freedom that money could bring would lead her into even more trouble. They firmly believed they were protecting her as well as themselves.

Rationing continued for almost another decade and petrol was in short supply. The two Rolls Royces remained jacked up in the garage while the car which Marion sometimes used was officially reserved for her parents. Being deprived of both money and motorized transport Marion had to pedal her bike for four miles when she was invited to play bridge at Paxton House. Having no cash to cover her losses she borrowed money from her father's chauffeur. She went about in worn tweeds and walked out with a shepherd's crook to visit her friends on foot. Local people knew she suffered, staff gossip leaked out and it was no secret that Lady Burrell made the cannonballs which Sir William fired.

Marion spent her time devising ways to raise cash. Kind friends helped her to sell her clothes; her expensive riding gear had long been redundant and she was happy to part with it. Knowing her father would pay the bills she would ask her dressmaker to overcharge so that she could pocket the surplus. After this ruse met with success she tried to persuade a loyal ally to charge her son's school uniform to her Burrell account at Jenners. When her father settled the bill Marion hoped to receive the equivalent cash from her fellow conspirator, but her friend had the sense to back off. Then Marion tried another scheme, and began framing old prints taken from antiquarian books. With minimal outlay, she used sheets of glass and strips of passe-partout to make sets of framed pictures. Exotic birds and flowers were used as well as aquatints of historic views. Some were intended to be table mats, which was hardly a practical idea, but Marion made the most of her skills and even her line in recycled Christmas cards managed to be pleasing.

Lady Marioth Hay, who lived nearby at Chirnside, accepted an invitation to lunch at Hutton Castle and found herself in an extraordinary situation. As her father, the Marquess of Tweeddale, had collected fine art Lady Marioth got on rather well with Willie Burrell. She was also a friend of Marion's and had helped her sell clothes and furs to a London shop called Pandora. As soon as their guest arrived Marion took her aside to discuss how she might sell the prints she had framed. Then, during lunch, Lady Burrell announced that she intended to sell some jewellery. After inspecting the handwork of her cash-strapped friend, Lady Marioth was dumbfounded when a servant brought in a tray laden with jewels which looked worth a king's ransom. The matching tiaras, necklaces and earrings had been set with coordinating emeralds, rubies and sapphires for Lady Burrell to wear during those splendid London Seasons. Now that such finery was no longer required Constance reckoned she might as well sell it all and reap the windfall. While his wife picked over her glittering hoard Burrell looked on in silent indulgence.

Marion had learned to 'make do and mend'. She also stitched and knitted garments to clothe herself and with her well-trained eye she applied a good deal of flare and ingenuity. The local dressmaker proved a staunch ally, repairing and re-styling outdated clothes. Now she was slimmer than ever before – as her parents ate frugally the Hutton menus were excessively meagre so the bonus of any game shot for the pot was always welcomed. Though Marion was capable of basic cookery her parents insisted on employing servants. If staffing problems arose they just moved out and stayed in hotels. When Sir William found hotel food too rich, he ordered porridge. There were no more visits to the West Indies or to the Continent, but Britain still had comfortable hotels where the Burrells could live for weeks or months while Sir William would visit dealers and salerooms or prowl around old country churches. When they were away from home Constance demanded even more attention, so Marion

Marion's relations

PLATE 75. *Left*: Grandma Burrell, from the somewhat daunting portrait of William Burrell's mother (née Isabella Guthrie) painted by George Henry in 1903.

PLATE 76. *Below left*: Grandma Mitchell, Constance Burrell's mother, was born Marion Miller. This picture dates from the time of her marriage to James Mitchell when she was 18.

PLATE 77. *Below right*: Aunt Mary. William Burrell's favourite sister was painted by John Lavery in 1895.

PLATE 78. *Right*: Suzani embroideries were much admired by William Burrell, and at Hutton Castle some were used as gorgeous bedcovers.

PLATE 79. *Below*: *An Arab Raid*, c.1888, by Joseph Crawhall.

PLATE 80. 16th-century brass alms dish of the type described by Robert Lorimer.

PLATE 81. Mother-of-pearl box, the lid carved with fishes.

PLATE 82. Detail from *Camp of the Gypsies*, a tapestry probably from Tournai, c.1520. A gypsy is reading the gentleman's palm while her charming friend is stealing his purse.

PLATE 83. *Peasants Preparing to Hunt Rabbits with Ferrets*, a South Netherlandish (possibly Brussels) tapestry, c.1470–90. The game of bunny spotting has delighted generations of children.

PLATE 84. *Left*: Life-size luohan, Chinese polychrome figure, AD 1484.

PLATE 85. *Below*: 'The Temple Pyx', a 12th-century bronze gilt.

PLATE 86. *Bottom*: *The Stag Hunt*, Lucas Cranach the Elder, 1529.

PLATE 87. *Alfresco Banquet*, South Netherlandish or French tapestry, c.1510. Can you find the frog?

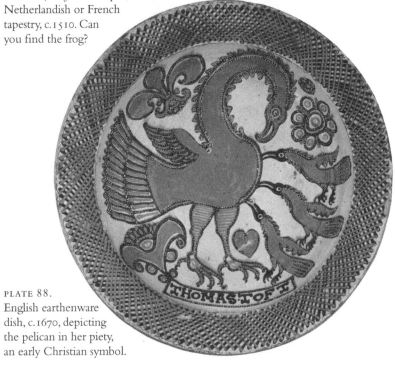

PLATE 88. English earthenware dish, c.1670, depicting the pelican in her piety, an early Christian symbol.

PLATE 89. An illustration by Joseph Crawhall of the *History of Reynard the Fox*. Marion loved these stories and remembered the prints in her nursery.

PLATE 90. *The Empress Eugenie on the Beach at Trouville* by Eugene Boudin. Marion helped her father to buy this painting.

PLATE 91. Goanese mother-of-pearl crucifix probably acquired by Marion when the Burrells toured India, Ceylon and Burma during the winter of 1922–23.

PLATE 92. Marion was educated at Heathfield near Ascot. This devout Anglican school made a deep impression which contrasted with her Presbyterian upbringing at home.

PLATE 93. Confirmation candidates. Marion is on the left.

PLATE 94. The school chapel at Heathfield.

PLATE 95. Magpie and jay painted by Marion in her biology exercise book. She was awarded 'A. Very Good'.

PLATE 96. Burrell's dream. Hutton Hall in 1889. Watercolour by an unknown artist. 'He's dying to get hold of an old castle', wrote Robert Lorimer.

PLATE 97. Beatrix van Valkenburg. A stained glass panel which Burrell believed to have connections with Hutton Castle.

PLATE 98. The imprisoning chair which Willie Burrell used to tease his guests. English 16th-century style.

Paintings from Marion's bedroom at Hutton Castle

PLATE 99. *Left: Woman with a Parasol* by Edgar Degas, c.1880. Marion's father owned 22 works by this artist.

PLATE 100. *Below: Washer-women on the Banks of the River Touques* by Eugene Boudin, c.1883–87.

More paintings from Marion's room

PLATE 101. *Portrait of a Lady* by Edouard Manet, c.1882–83. Marion was with her father when he bought this portrait, made by the artist shortly before his death in 1883.

PLATE 102. The Flight into Egypt, bought by Burrell as a Memling, but now known to be by The Master of the Prado *Adoration of the Magi*.

PLATE 103. *Fruit* by Gustave Courbet, c.1871–72.

PLATE 104. *Shipping* by Camille Corot, c.1830–40.

PLATE 105. *Above*: *The Black Cock* by Joseph Crawhall, c.1894. When decorators were working at Hutton Castle they could not understand the fuss Burrell made over shifting 'twa bloody hens'.

PLATE 106. *Right*: Rhyton jade drinking cup with clambering felines in high relief, Ming dynasty.

PLATE 107. The Wagner Carpet. This famous garden carpet once belonged to John Holms of Formakin. It was sold after Holms became bankrupt and later Burrell grabbed his opportunity to buy it.

PLATE 108. *Right*: Ewer, Ming dynasty. Queen Mary expressed her interest in Ming when she visited Hutton Castle.

PLATE 109. *Below*: Falconry accoutrements including embroidered hawking pouch and gauntlet, early 17th century.

PLATE 110.
Above left: Vale Royal heraldic stained glass medallion.

PLATE 111.
Above right: Virgin and Child, painted and gilded oak, Netherlands, c.1500.

PLATE 112.
Left: Polychrome fangxiang tomb guardian figures, Tang dynasty, 8th century AD.

PLATE 113. Marion's jewellery. The pendant earrings were 18th-century Portuguese chrysoberyl. The ruby ring weighed 13.77 carats. The butterfly brooch c.1890 came from Aspreys of Bond Street.

PLATE 114. Marion loved to wear the huge diamond and emerald ear studs. The emerald ring weighed 9.87 carats. The ruby and diamond bee brooch is c.1900. Along with her three-strand pearl necklace and another ring, these items were sold by Sotheby's after she died.

PLATE 115. The pearl and diamond turtle brooch which William Burrell chose for Marion after she launched the *Strathlorne* when she was seven years old.

PLATE 116. Replicas of the 18th-century silver tableware used by Sir William and Lady Burrell. At Sir William's invitation, these copies were made for the author's father.

PLATE 117. *Charity of a Beggar at Ornans* by Gustave Courbet, 1868.

preferred to remain at Hutton and seek the company of friends.

Sometimes she would live on short rations for a week in order to invite friends in for a meal, requesting them to bring a bottle of wine because Sir William locked up the cellar. When a visitor's dog caught a rabbit Marion gladly retrieved it for her supper. A neighbour who dropped in for tea was concerned to find Burrell's daughter had become so fearful of her father's wrath that a minor mishap like burnt toast or a chipped cup seemed to distress her. There must have been some devastating family rows. Constance's mental state was verging on paranoia, and now that William was growing frail his constant submission to her whims was affecting his judgement. Marion's friends were appalled by the life that she was leading, but in spite of her troubles she was loath to speak ill of her parents. Her true feelings were nevertheless revealed in a copy of *The Works of William Shakespeare* which she kept with her Bible at her bedside. Significant passages were marked in pencil along with personal comments:

'Hutton'   And hath detained me all my
                  flowering youth
              Within a loathsome dungeon there
                  to pine.
                          [*Henry VI,* Act II]

[no caption] O, Beware my lord, of jealousy;
              It is the green-eye'd monster that
                  doth mock
              The meat it feeds on.
                          [*Othello,* Act III]

'Portrait of Old	Alas poor princess
Green-eye'	What thou endurest
	Twix a father by thy step dame
	governed
	A mother hourly coining plots.

[*Cymbeline*, Act II]

Marion kept the nickname 'Old Green-eye' to herself, although she admitted in later life that her mother had been insanely jealous. Once she managed to slip away for a brief break in London, having been lent a flat in Dolphin Square by her Berwickshire neighbours, Jock and Susan Askew of Ladykirk. When she and Marion were together Susan was concerned to see her friend collapse in tears and become utterly inconsolable. Marion's troubles had suddenly over-whelmed her while she lamented the deaths of two godsons and the many wartime tragedies which had befallen her dearest friends. She appeared to be on the verge of a break-down. When she was staying alone in the Askews' flat their cleaner arrived on schedule at 10 am, but Marion refused to let her in and after a heated argument the poor woman found herself being sacked. The autocratic trait had been inherited by Burrell's daughter and she was clearly reaching the end of her tether.

During this unhappy stage in her life Marion sank almost to the depths of despair. At Hutton she was unbearably isolated and felt herself falling apart. But in her darkest hour, when life seemed utterly devoid of meaning, a glimmer of light briefly eased her misery when, unexpectedly, a fellow sufferer reached out to her and gently offered sympathy and love. This man has remained an almost total mystery – neither his surname nor his place of origin is known. Though it could only be a transient liaison, their unlikely affair was far more than a wild impulsive fling because the lovers showed tenderness and genuine devotion in the letters which continued to pass between them. The man was obviously foreign and he wrote in an untutored hand; he could have been one of her father's employees and might have worked in the kitchen. Polish soldiers had been stationed near Hutton but changes of staff were frequent and no one has identified this man.

In their letters this oddly matched pair had used nicknames: Marion was 'Darling Marchen' and he signed himself 'Mattichens', which may have derived from 'Matthew' because she recorded the date of 'Matthew's birthday' and preserved 'Matthew's key' among her keepsakes. After they parted he wrote to her from London, having gone to live in Maida Vale while working in a restaurant in the City. Marion's lover may have been one of the many unhappy exiles from war-ravaged countries who had lost their homes and families during the conflict and now hoped to make a new start in post-war Britain. From her experience of nursing foreign soldiers she would have understood these problems and sympathized deeply. The couple seem to have met as two sad and lonely people drawn together by their need of love and consolation. Afterwards they kept in touch, as Marion was always loyal to the people she loved.

After 'Matthew' departed there came a time when Marion could no longer bear her life at Hutton Castle. From the events which followed it is clear that she had reached breaking point and was hardly capable of rational thinking. The next part of her story is so bizarre it seems best to let her describe what happened in her own words. The following letter was found among Marion's possessions after she died. Its contents had been intended for the Right Honourable James Chuter-Ede, who was Home Secretary at the time. There seems to be no record of the letter having reached him, and every reason to suspect that Marion was persuaded not to send it.

THE HOME SECRETARY

At the request of the Berwickshire Police I wish to make the following statement about

ERICH HOFER

When I returned to my home Hutton Castle, Berwick on Tweed on Jan 3rd 1950 after a visit to London, I found that Erich Hofer and his wife Maria had entered my father's employment as butler and cook respectively. Gradually the man Hofer began for no apparent reason to persecute me, and make my life in my home unbearable; by flouting my smallest request, and by rank insolence. The following are some examples of his behaviour towards me.

The first occasion of any definite act of hostility was on April 10th when I asked him to clean my antique steel fender in my bedroom, as this was part of his duties. He looked sulky and said he could not do it that day and I replied that there was no hurry as I realised it took some time to do thoroughly. As he had not previously cleaned it I pointed out that emery paper was needed for the steel and for the brass metal polish. He seemed displeased and scarcely answered. Three days later the fender was returned, very badly done, the whole scratched including the brass which had wrongly been cleaned with emery.

For many years I have been in the habit of making my own tea so as not to allow my own engagements to interfere in any way with my aged parents' routine. The Hofers are not expected to be on duty the whole afternoon and on April 15th I entered the kitchen as usual to make my own tea. I found the cupboard in which the bread was kept had been locked and the key removed. I called upstairs to Maria Hofer and she answered me, but it was Hofer who came down and when I asked him why the bread cupboard was locked he replied that I was to use the stale piece of bread in the larder which he fetched. I refused this and asked for the cupboard key but he refused to give it to me. I said I should have no alternative but to complain to my father about his attitude. He then shrugged his shoulders and said that I could go to my father. I was very angry and told him to leave the kitchen while I was preparing my tea, and he replied that I could 'get out' myself. That evening when I returned home after being out, he at once emerged from the pantry and began singing 'Deutchland, Deutchland [sic] über alles' in a loud tone.

At this time my father who is 88 was confined to his bed ill and my mother aged 74 was away from home also ill. Hofer took full advantage of this situation and assumed not only the management of the house but everyone connected with it and went so far as to order our chauffeur, Phillips, who is aged about 60 and had been with us for 4 years out of the house while he was carrying out his duties. Things went from bad to worse as he got more and more self important. I avoided him as much as possible but he went out of his way to intrude his presence in order to be insolent and irritating.

When I left him a note it was ignored and pinned upon my bedroom door and on another occasion it was screwed into the top of my hot water bottle [vacuum flask?].

When I met him in the passages of the house or on the drive or the road to the village he noisily cleared his throat and coughed. His bedroom was over the side door to which I have the latch key and whenever I went out he coughed loudly and suddenly in order to startle me. During all this time I attempted to complain to my father but felt I ought not to say too much because he was ill and so he was inclined to dismiss the matter as rather trivial and I did not press it. By June 4th my father and mother were both sufficiently recovered to go away for a period of convalescence and as it was a sudden decision and I already had other engagements to fulfil, I was unable to accompany them.

On June 6th when I returned to the house for luncheon I found the side door bolted. There are three doors. The front door which is always kept bolted, the side door which is used by the family [and] the back door which is used by the staff. Before leaving home my father had given orders regarding the doors and had told Hofer the side door was not to be bolted, but that I was responsible for doing this when I entered the house with my latch key for the last time each day. When I rang Hofer came and unbolted and unlatched the door and walked away without opening it.

On June 7th I was again bolted out and I therefore fetched Phillips the chauffeur to come with me as a witness. I rang and the door was undone as on the previous day. I told Hofer that if he bolted me out a third time I should have to send for the Police. Hofer replied rudely that I was 'crazy' and that I must not call him Hofer as he was MR Hofer to me.

At luncheon that day the cutlery was not set out on the table but placed in a heap. I spoke to him about it and he answered that I could put it right myself and left the room.

After dinner I found that the telephone had been disconnected from its usual place and it was impossible to make a call without going to the switchboard outside the kitchen door. I placed a note on the uncleared dining room table asking that the telephone should not be disconnected from upstairs. After giving him time to clear the table I returned to the telephone to find that my instructions had been ignored. I therefore went down to the switchboard myself. Hofer was on the lookout for me and had taken up a very menacing attitude, the intimidating insolence of which I find very difficult to describe. He was standing over the switchboard guarding it against me. His right shoulder slouched against the wall, feet nonchalantly crossed, left hand on hip and in his right hand a cigarette which he smoked on seeing me. I felt afraid by his intimidating attitude and did not try to get near the switchboard and since I was cut off from any help by not having the use of the telephone, I began to feel genuinely frightened and immediately left the house and went to the Police.

On June 8th when Hofer heard me coming up the stairs he came out of the dining room and threw my letters and newspapers towards me managing to convey the impression that he would like to have thrown them at me – some of them fell on the radiator and some on the floor. I left them untouched for the Police to see as I expected them that morning.

The telephone was still disconnected, and although Hofer said he was in charge of my father's incoming calls, I have ascertained that friends who telephoned to me could get no answer.

On June 8th Hofer also said he refused to allow his wife to cook for me. I then decided I could no longer tolerate my position in the house as apart from everything else it was affecting my health and I could not sleep.

Several of my friends were very concerned about me and begged me to go and stay with them. Miss Stewart of Broadmeadows, Lady Wilson of Meadowhouse Mains and Sir Michael and Lady Malcolm of North Berwick; all of whom except Lady Wilson have known me most of my life.

On June 9th I went to Lady Wilson and she, Phillips and I went to the castle at 2.35 pm to do my packing. We again found the door bolted and Hofer repeated his usual performance. I packed and left at 4.30 pm.

In conclusion I should like to point out that because of my father's great age and the ill health of both my parents I have never been able to push my complaints to them too far. Particularly as at all costs they wished to keep an adequate staff in the house and were for this reason not disposed to listen to my complaints against Hofer. None of this was lost on Hofer who summed up the situation very accurately. I need hardly add that at my parents' age it is difficult to make them realise that it is possible for a man like Hofer to have the power to bully and intimidate their daughter to a point where she felt she had for safety to leave her home. It is for this reason that I am appealing to you to take what action you think fit, as this alien is not the type who should be allowed in my opinion to remain in this country.

Marion Burrell (Miss)

Broadmeadows House,
Berwick on Tweed.

Marion's story ranges from domestic trivia to the creepy horror of a Hitchcock film. The imperious attitude learned from her father shows through, although she was wrestling with her growing fear from being persecuted in her own home by malicious servants. Marion described the Hofers as 'aliens' because they were Germans who had entered Burrell employment less than five years after World War II. Images of prison camps and the Blitz were still vivid and, to many people in Britain, recent enemies remained unwelcome. The staffing problem at Hutton must have been dire for her parents to chose to take them on. In spite of her complaints about Erich Hofer, Marion said that Maria Hofer was Prussian and the worst of the pair. Having bullied their employer's daughter, the couple continued to taunt her by sunbathing in front of the house when they should have been working. When confronted by police officers Hofer was reduced to tears, but by the end of the interview the insufferable butler was smoking a cigarette.

Marion's parents had ignored her appeals and finally rejected her. Her involvement with a working class man, who may have been one of their servants, would have made them consider her beyond redemption. Once Sir William and Lady Burrell felt well enough to travel, they went away and left their daughter to her fate while Hofer managed the household to suit himself, taking pleasure in tormenting her. For Marion, escape seemed her only solution, and while she considered the prospect 'Matthew' had written from London:

(a quick one that you not wait too long)

Friday 8th [June]

Darling Marchen

Thanks very much for your letter and I was glad to hear about you even if it was so sad. I am in the same repression [sic] because life is so hard.

Well Marchen you must well consider but if you go you will have peace and freedom. With the policeman it is good because you are sure that they would try to make you trouble. Where you like to go depends on you only, but you would do good to stay with Miss S. and she would employ you as a driver or house care-keeper that is so near it would gie [sic] your parents the biggest blow in the face because all would get to know about and they would be very shame that you go somewhere else they would say you went for pleasure, so I think well. I am sorry for

Phillips and liked him at first but he had been too
selfish and proud of himself but I am real sorry for
him. I will write you next week – and will send you
the butter.

God bless you and send you more luck

your ever loving
Mattichens xxxxxxx

Denied food from her parents' kitchen, Marion was now
relying on food parcels from London. Sir William and Lady
Burrell left home on 4 June and five days later, shortly before
her forty-seventh birthday, their daughter departed from
Hutton Castle never to return. Marion claimed to have fled
from her parental home on her bicycle, the only means of
transport she possessed. Accounts of her escape seem to vary
due to confusion among her rescuers because she immediately went into hiding from her parents. Although this reaction might seem absurd in an adult woman, few could
imagine the trauma she had endured. Knowing her parents
would go to almost any length to subjugate her Marion was
resolved that all contact would be ended.

After Lady Wilson and Phillips the chauffeur had assisted
her removal, Marion took refuge in the home of a neighbour, collapsing into the welcoming arms of Miss Emily
Stewart of Broadmeadows House. This kind-hearted maiden
lady lived only a couple of miles beyond Hutton village and
near to the home of Sir Gordon and Lady Wilson at Meadowhouse Mains. Marion arrived with no money and very
few clothes or possessions. Being emotionally and physically
drained she had become ill and would neither eat nor take

aspirin, and so Dr MacLagan was summoned. Suddenly she was surrounded by kind people who wanted to do everything in their power to help, and after the anguish of the past months her contrasting feelings of shock and relief almost overwhelmed her. During the days which followed, Miss Stewart and her staff tenderly cared for her while the Broadmeadows chauffeur helped to transport the rest of her possessions. As her books and belongings were removed from her former home, the Wilsons provided storage space and continued to help her. With sadness she said farewell to the paintings she had grown to love on the walls of her room in the castle.

While Marion was holed up at Broadmeadows and beginning to recover, news of her flight began to reach her friends. One of the first to hear from her was Jock Askew who wrote from London on 17 June saying he was glad that she had got away safely. He would be returning shortly and was ready to give help, but meanwhile advised her 'Don't whatever you do, weaken in any way, don't have remorse, and know that the whole countryside backs you'. A letter arrived from another friend, Hy Wilson of Belchester. She wrote on 4 July offering a warm welcome and saying 'Rumours are flying around that you have cast adrift from the parental roof at last but I fear it may only be wishful thinking'.

Marion's hideout remained a heavily guarded secret known only to a few trusted friends. Any mail addressed to her at Hutton was intercepted and covertly passed on to her. Phillips, the chauffeur, was of course 'in the know', but nobody told the Hofers where she had gone. They were kept in the dark, no doubt wondering where Miss Burrell was and whether she would reappear. Meanwhile Phillips continued to guard her secret: a brave deed which was destined to cost him his job. By the beginning of July Marion had been lying low for a month and so it was essential that Sir William and Lady Burrell were told that their daughter had absconded.

It was a shock for them to learn that Marion was at large, having taken her possessions and gone to ground. When Sir William became aware of the trouble he sent a telegram from Weybridge on 9 July.

to MISS MARION BURRELL HUTTON CASTLE
BERWICK ON TWEED

PLEASE ARRANGE STAY IN EDINBURGH HOTEL
TILL WE RETURN

I SHALL PAY BILL DADDY

Constance immediately took command and adopted a different approach. Almost at once a letter was sent, but there was no mention of Marion's predicament.

Oatlands Hotel   10th July
Weybridge
Surrey

My dear Marion,

You will be sorry to hear that Daddy has been ill with pluerisy [sic] and pneumonia. I have had a nurse and still have her for night duty but she goes home at 7.30 each morning and I take on day duty then until she returns in the evening at 9 o'clock. She is a good nurse and I have got a very good doctor. Daddy is getting pennicilan[sic] and another medicine and is now improving but I have been so worried. The temperature is going down now as he has been in his bed now for ten days. We were all packed up to travel home when this happened. He is now getting on and today the doctor is very satisfied with his progress. I hope you are well. Everyone here is so kind and all wish to help me in any way they can. I don't know where you are but am sending this to Hutton to be forwarded.

Your affect
Mother

This unexpected news of her father's illness was worrying but Marion did not respond to her mother's tale of woe and ignored the cry of alarm. On 10 July she had gone to seek help and advice from her cousin Merrick Mitchell, as having lost her only source of funds she was totally dependent on the generosity of her family and friends. By this time she had written the story of her escape in the letter which she intended to send to the Home Secretary but Merrick expressed reservations about her sending it. Their meeting had taken place in his Glasgow office at Edmiston and Mitchell, and after Marion returned to her hideout further contact between them was delayed. When Merrick told his family of Marion's plight lengthy discussions followed because the situation threatened to become even more complicated. Without approaching the Home Secretary, Marion could still have prosecuted Hofer but doing so would have created a public scandal. Eventually Merrick sent Marion a letter:

Perceton   17.7.50

Dear Marion,

I promised to write you after I had spoken to Mother
regarding our conversation in the office ten days ago
and apologise for the delay in writing but I have been
kept terribly busy recently and have been working
late at the office practically every night last week, so
you must excuse me.

I had a long talk with Mother after I saw you and
she fully agrees with the advice I gave you and does
not see that anything would be gained by your pros-
ecuting the matter.

She was most upset to hear what had happened
and sends you her love and sympathy. She asked me
to let you know you are to treat Perceton as 'open
house' and come here whenever you like.

I sincerely hope that Uncle Willie dealt summarily
with Hofer on his return to Hutton.

The parents are both fairly fit and we all send you
our love and best wishes.

Yours ever
Merrick.

Aunt Mary was as good as her word, though her brother
Willie continued to employ the Hofers and sacked Phillips
instead. While Marion remained in hiding her cousin Tom
Burrell sent her a cheque to help cover her needs. Her cousin
Mona begged her to come and stay and also offered her the
use of the MacAndrew flat in London. Meanwhile Con-

stance waited in vain for a reply to her letter, and after two weeks sent another:

Oatlands Park Hotel   28th July
Weybridge, Surrey.

My dear Marion,

As I did not hear from you I wonder if you got my last letter telling you of Daddy's serious illness. Since writing you he has had two relapses and now he had to have an X Ray which gave a bad result that the pneumonia was still very bad at the base of the left lung. I have still his good nurse and doctor. He sleeps fairly well and eats moderately well but of course is in bed. Everyone here is so kind. The pleurisy is almost away but I do so wish the pneumonia would clear up but I am afraid it will be some time. I hope you are well.

Much love in haste
Your loving Mother.

As the saga progressed Marion's plight continued to be ignored and Constance was expert at sowing seeds of guilt. Tales of Sir William's illness might have drawn an anxious daughter to his bedside but Marion was devoid of funds and nobody offered to pay her railway fare to Surrey. Again she did not budge, but this time she replied and her letter bore the address of Sir Michael and Lady Malcolm. After another week Constance addressed a post office letter-card to Hutton with instructions: 'Please Forward'. It was posted on Marion's forty-seventh birthday.

Oatlands Park Hotel   4th August.

My dear Marion,

Thank you for your letter. Daddy has had another rise in temperature which worried us and now the doctor has put him off pennicilin [sic] and on to a new American medicine. So far it has improved the condition a little but if it fails I don't know what the doctors can then try. It is so disappointing in the lung which was ¾ infected with the pleurisy and pneumonia is still a good ¼ infected and unable to let the air into it at the thickened part. I managed to walk to Weybridge today in my short time off duty to buy a box of chocolates for your birthday and hope it will arrive safely. Many happy returns. Daddy is sleeping at the moment and I am afraid this is rather a scribble and shall send this home as I do not know if you are still at Milton Lodge.

In haste and our love
Your affect.
Mother.

The frantic medical reports were becoming monotonous but they could not be discounted. Throughout her life Marion had been subjected to her mother's wiles and the promise of a box of chocolates did not fool her. But Marion's mother had more tricks up her sleeve. After nearly a month had passed she sent yet another impassioned letter. It was her fourth attempt and a post office search for the missing chocolates would have made Marion even more sceptical.

Oatlands Park Hotel   30th August
Weybridge, Surrey

My Dear Marion,

parcel posted on 4th August

I sent for your birthday a little parcel and a letter-card
but I hear that the parcel did not arrive at Hutton.
The postmaster here is investigating about it and hopes
it may turn up as so many parcels now are lost in the
post. I have had a very anxious and worrying time
and still nearly a half of Daddy's right lung has pneumonia and it seems such a long tedious business. He
has been X Rayed 3 times already and in a few days
he has to go to London to a specialist who takes a
very wonderful X Ray photo of a certain type taking
sections of the lungs to see if since the last photo a
week ago any improvement has taken place. This X
Ray can only be done in London and no other where
so we hope and trust it will be satisfactory. We hope
you are well and send you our love.

Your loving Mother.

William Burrell's illness appeared to be serious and his wife
could hardly have done more to lure their daughter out of
hiding. But whatever his state of health, Sir William and Lady
Burrell had no wish to be seen rushing home because their
middle-aged daughter had finally flown the nest. While her
parents continued to sit tight Marion did the same. Then, in
September, two months after her escape, William and
Constance arrived home to find no trace of their daughter.

Hofer and his wife were still in charge at Hutton but despite their iniquitous guile they had no idea where Marion was hiding.

The Burrells hated to ask for assistance – they normally issued commands – so they were acutely embarrassed when Marion's friends clammed up. Rather than appeal to their neighbours they decided to call the police, unaware that Sergeant Whyte and his colleagues had become Marion's staunchest allies and were already aware of her situation. It was hardly a police matter to search for a missing forty-seven-year-old who was known to be living safely among her friends. Having failed to activate the Berwickshire Constabulary, the indefatigable Constance then announced the dreadful discovery that some of her precious jewels were missing. The suspicion of theft pointed at once to the absconding Marion who was well known to be in need of funds. As this was indeed a matter for police intervention the Burrells hoped their missing daughter would now be traced, apprehended and restored to the fold.

Having been asked to handle the case with all possible discretion Sergeant Whyte arrived at Hutton Castle with a Detective Inspector to investigate the theft. After interviewing Sir William and Lady Burrell and their staff, a thorough examination of the premises was required, so the officers needed access to the scene of the crime. As they were approaching Lady Burrell's room, Sergeant Whyte observed that she was becoming agitated, and when he watched her scuttle ahead of them and disappear from sight, he knew that something fishy was going on. Despite Sir William's attention to security it seems that the missing jewels had not been locked in a safe and Constance may have found it more convenient to keep them in a drawer. Sure enough, when the policemen checked, the jewels had gone and the subsequent search failed to find them.

Normal procedures appear to have been followed, but due to lack of evidence the trail grew cold and the crime remained unsolved. Years later, after both William and Constance had died and the rooms were being dismantled, a member of staff came upon the cache of jewels on an attic shelf behind a row of books. The treasure was assigned to John Logan, the family lawyer, and in 1962 the 'stolen' goods were auctioned by Christie's as 'The property of A Lady of Title, deceased'. In the catalogue, which Marion kept, the following items appeared: two pearl necklaces, three watches and a diamond and pearl brooch, also a cross made with emeralds, diamonds and pearls which fetched £105, and a pair of pearl and diamond ear pendants which went for £650. The jewellery which the lawyer recovered raised a total of £893 (nearly £25,000 today). It would seem out of character for William Burrell to be involved in this ruse, although there can be little doubt about the part that was played by his wife.

Meanwhile Marion continued to lie low while flitting between the homes of loyal friends. She desperately needed to support herself and, early in September, Marion Wilson offered her prospects of a livelihood. The post of sewing matron had become available at the prep school in Sussex which the Wilsons' two sons had attended. Marion had entered negotiations with the co-headmaster, when an urgent telegram arrived:

CAN YOU POSSIBLY COME NOW FOR A MONTH
AND HELP OUT? ALL TRAVELLING EXPENSES PAID.
UNDER MATRON ACUTE APPENDIX LAST NIGHT.

BOYS RETURN TOMORROW.

CHITTENDEN: NEWLANDS SCHOOL SEAFORD.

So Marion donned a white overall and found herself gainfully employed. When 'Matthew' heard from her, he feared she would find the work too hard and suggested she might fare better as a lingerie assistant in a smart London shop. But Marion rose gladly to the challenge, and was taken on for the rest of the school year. Her friends were delighted, and no doubt the boys were too because she was good with children. Being a Burrell, she knew how to wield the rod but she was also imaginative and entertaining, and never talked down to young people. They liked her because throughout her long life she never lost her infectious sense of humour.

During her first term a telegram managed to find its way to Marion's new hideout in Sussex.

ORDERED EASTBOURNE TO CONVALESCE. ARRIVED
YESTERDAY EVENING. EXPECT STAY ONE MONTH
AT CAVENDISH. PLEASE TELEGRAPH IF YOU WOULD
LIKE TO COME DADDY

The Burrells had no idea that their daughter was employed at a school just a few miles away from the hotel where they were staying. Marion's allies had established a secret chain of communication which would have been worthy of resistance fighters. While she continued to elude them William and Constance were at a loss, hardly knowing what to do or where to go. Now it was their turn to escape, and Eastbourne seemed a welcome retreat because their life at home was becoming increasingly unpleasant. Consternation reigned in the Hutton neighbourhood, and local feeling was hardening against them because their thoroughly decent chauffeur had been harshly dismissed while malevolent foreigners continued to be employed at Hutton Castle. Marion was deeply concerned about Phillips, and asked her friends to help her find him new employment.

At Christmas the under matron was allowed a ten-day break from Newlands School so she accepted an invitation to spend the festive season with the Mitchell family at Perceton. Over the holiday she wrote to numerous friends and relations explaining her situation and was immediately deluged with congratulations, sympathy and support. Lady Clodagh Anson signed herself 'Patty' in a chatty letter saying: 'We are thrilled with joy over your father trying to find out. I know him so well. He wouldn't admit to the world he didn't know where you were and yet he itches to find out! What a joke – it must have been hide and seek when they were at Eastbourne'.

Letters came from far and wide condemning her parents and promising to protect her secrecy. Some gave her financial assistance. Not one of her supporters could begin to comprehend why Marion had been, for years, so harshly treated. An outraged cousin was heard to say 'There's only one thing worse than Uncle Willie and that's Aunt Connie!' They all wondered why Marion had waited so long to free herself from misery.

There were many reasons, and one of them was pride. Her situation was humiliating because she had no money and, unlike women today, Marion had been groomed to be a lady at a time when ladies were not qualified to go out and earn their livings. Then there was taboo: some women took lovers and others eloped, but respectable ladies did not run away from home. And there were practicalities. Without money where could she go? Marion had been reluctant to throw herself on her Aunt Mary and her cousins and was loath to increase the antipathy which already existed between the senior Mitchells and Burrells. Above all she had been captive to the irresistible power of her father. When Burrell was in his prime, people who shared his enthusiasms had found him utterly compelling. He won admirers from every walk of life, and drew dealers like a magnet. From childhood Marion had been so enthralled by William Burrell and his conspicuous achievements that she had almost become 'possessed' by him. For the rest of her life, no matter how he treated her, her father's influence continued to dominate her.

After Christmas Marion received another letter from her mother:

Hutton Castle   29th December
Berwick on Tweed

My dear Marion,

I heard from one of the servants that you are at 'Broad-meadows' and hope you had a happy Xmas.
    Will you come on Sunday or any other day for either lunch or tea – Lunch is now 1 o'clock, just let me know you are coming.

Your loving
Mother.

Again, Marion made no response to her parents' attempts to reach her, and since they vented their rage against Miss

Stewart for harbouring their daughter, none of their neighbours wanted to speak to them. When Constance had tried to telephone Broadmeadows and Meadowhouse Mains she met with failure. The ranks had closed but Constance Burrell would not accept defeat and in the new year she tried yet again. A collaborator was eventually found within Marion's circle of allies. This lady was new to the area, having recently married one of the Burrells' close friends, and so she was anxious to become favourably established. Having supported Marion's escape she was also equally ready to sympathize with the grieving Burrell parents. Constance saw her opportunity and it was not long before the newcomer was invited to lunch at Hutton Castle. In February Marion received a chatty letter from her two-faced ally:

Dearest Marion,   7.II.51

What news? I have heaps to tell you! ... [on the second page the real news came]

  We went to lunch about three Sundays ago at Hutton! I put it off at first but your mother then said 'any Sunday' ... Well of course after lunch she asked me if I heard anything from you so said I hadn't. She then said she knows your address – that 'a man' who came to the house, gave it to her!! But she would not give it to me as she doesn't want you to know that she has it in case you change your job again as a result! ... She burst into tears at least 5 times while she spoke of you. I asked her to what she attributed your action and she said she had no idea except that she thought you were angry about your father supporting the German! What infuriates me is that a MAN has given the address. It would be! After your women friends have lied themselves silly not to tell! ... I pretended to know nothing. They have no idea your things are near by! ...

Knowing her mother's skill in artful wheedling Marion feared that she had been betrayed. She wrote at once to Marion Wilson because she was worried that her parents would cause trouble at Newlands School. A reply arrived promptly:

My dear Marion,   Feb 12th

... We have just been discussing your letter, and we think it would be best if you talked to Mr Manning. I did tell him, when I was suggesting you as a matron, that you had had a very unhappy home life – so it would not all come as a surprise to him. I wonder when your friend was over at Hutton Castle – because Dr MacLagan was here last week (Monday, I think) having just come from visiting your parents, and he remarked that your address was the best kept secret in Berwickshire – which did not sound as if your mother knew then. So let's hope she still does not know it. ...

Love from us both

Yours
Marion Wilson.

Then Marion received a very long typewritten letter from her 'supportive' friend:

Dearest Marion,   16th February 1951

… I don't quite know what to think of your mother and her 'address'. Certainly I considered the possibility that she was trying to trip me up, as soon as she said it: But, she did give rather a circumstantial account because I felt I had a right to ask her HOW she got the address after she had asked me so many times. It was not a man who 'came to the door' and I must have misled you there – it was, I gathered 'a caller' and he asked in the usual way 'How is Marion? How does she like her job etc.', THEN – said your mother – she decided to tell me that she did not know where you were – 'the man' having obviously been under the impression that there was no secret about it. … She would not tell me who he was. … Your mother told me she had tried to find out from the Doctor what your address was because she thought he could get it out of Miss Stewart as he is her Doctor too. As a matter of fact, IF it is any man at all who has produced the address there is one who seems to me the most likely. I shall try to do further checking. … Don't worry, Marion, he is not a valued friend of yours who has let you down but he is in a position where he could have got the address because no one would have suspected that he was going to give it to 'the enemy' any more than anyone else would. …

Being no fool Marion would not have been slow to realize who her 'valued' friends really were. In spite of the betrayal she seems not to have been troubled at Newlands School, as her parents were under the impression that she had found employment somewhere in a nursing home. The Hofers were employed at Hutton Castle for over a year before they finally departed to Leicester in 1951. Though Marion and her parents were never reconciled, her 'friend' maintained that the story had ended differently. Forty years later she still clung to a fantasy in which she had arranged a joyful reunion between Marion and her parents so that the Burrell family had remained together and lived happily ever after.

But no reunion took place. The Burrells continued to be estranged and when the secrecy ended Marion's parents kept their distance and withheld financial support. When the summer term ended in July Marion relinquished her post at Newlands School and took time off to visit her friends. Later that year she gratefully accepted another offer and went to live with her Mitchell relations at Perceton, and where Aunt Mary created employment for Marion so that she could support herself while assisting with the Mitchell household.

Mary was a loving aunt and Marion adored her, gladly caring for her needs with all the loyal attention that she had withheld from her ever demanding mother. It was a joy to share with her discerning aunt the pleasures in art which she could no longer share with her father. Marion was adept at cleaning and mending so she helped in every way she could, enjoying her aunt's company by driving her and attending to mail, as well as skivvying in the home. Perceton abounded with beautiful things and she fondly polished silver, mended china and touched up damaged picture frames. Simply to handle them was a delight.

At last she could enjoy a normal home life, and when Mitchell grandchildren came for visits she gladly joined their noisy games. Ralston and Mary were good to their niece and from time to time her female cousins helped to supplement her tired wardrobe with their own discarded clothes. Although Marion was immensely grateful she sometimes found it hard to accept the role of a poor relation. The family attended St Ninian's Episcopalian Church in Troon and Marion liked to join them. As a dedicated Christian she found comfort in the faith which had helped her endure so many hard times. The Rev. Jim McGill and his wife Rosemary became her friends, and when their fifth child arrived Marion was overjoyed to become a godmother to Gavin.

For about a year Marion's life at Perceton continued quietly with occasional breaks to visit friends, but there was anxiety in 1952 when her Uncle Ralston became unwell and then died in July. Willie Burrell never failed to attend a family funeral, so Mary knew he would come, despite his long-held resentment towards her husband, now compounded by the support that the Mitchell family had given to Marion. Mary feared that an awkward situation might arise if her niece attended Ralston's funeral so, very gently, she explained the problem to her and asked her kindly to withdraw. But Marion declared at once that she had loved her Uncle Ralston dearly and flatly refused to be dissuaded. She was adamant and nothing could be done.

Willie Burrell arrived just as Mary had predicted. When the service was over the mourners gathered at the graveside to witness the interment and hear the vicar pronounce his final words of blessing. Marion was among them as her father approached, half blind, and using a long white stick. When he became aware of her presence he moved behind her and reached out his stick, lightly tapping the back of her leg. It was the nearest they ever came to a reconciliation when at last Marion heard his voice shakily pronounce her name in the way he always did. 'Is that you Mary-on?' She froze.

Much as Mary Mitchell loved her strong-willed niece, her family realized that she was becoming wearied by Marion's devoted attentions. While they all remained good friends and supporters of their cousin, the problem was embarrassing, and nobody knew how it could be solved till Mona's husband, Charlie MacAndrew, came to the rescue. Everybody needed a change and no one more than Marion. As she loved adventure and foreign travel and also needed to support herself, he hit on a brilliant idea and gallantly offered to pay her fare on a voyage to South Africa. There she could join Isabel Hoult, the eldest of her five Mitchell cousins, who owned and managed a vineyard near Capetown. Marion jumped at the opportunity to break new ground and everyone heaved a sigh of relief.

Travels on a Shoestring

Another adventure began to unfold on 8 October 1952 when Marion sailed to Cape Town with the Blue Star Shipping Line on the *Fremantle Star*. It was not long before she began to meet her fellow passengers. Though her wardrobe of clothes was much restricted and she probably had to borrow some, she carried herself with the air of an aristocrat, and her lively conversation engaged everyone from the ship's captain down to his lowest deck hand. Mr and Mrs Frank Varian occupied a neighbouring cabin and it was almost inevitable that they should become friends. Frank Varian was a man of considerable standing who began life as the son of an elephant hunter in Ceylon (Sri Lanka), later establishing a successful career as a railway engineer in Africa where he devoted 30 action-packed years to pioneering the African railways. Marion was eager to hear about the great continent which lay ahead, and his stories were riveting. While enduring the hazards of laying railway tracks he had lived rough in the bush and shot game to feed his men. During his management lines had been established through the African continent so that Rhodesia (Zimbabwe), Mozambique, Angola and the Congo were now connected, while there was still hope of one day creating a line to link the Cape with Cairo. His memoirs, *Some African Milestones*, were published that year. Varian signed a copy for Marian and she kept it with her on what was to become a global working tour.

Travel excited her enormously and it may have been due to Varian's influence that during the voyage she acquired an itinerary for the overland journey from Cape Town to Luxor. Passengers on board the *Fremantle Star* could book this arduous trip which involved eight separate train journeys, another eight by boat and two by road. In Marion's situation the information could only be of academic interest. Her circumstances had changed dramatically since that fabulous passage to India 30 years before, but those days of her youth must have been remembered as she walked the breezy decks and then relaxed in warmer climes before retreating under awnings in the humid tropical heat.

When the *Fremantle Star* docked at Cape Town, the climate had become more temperate and Marion was entranced by her new surroundings as she took in the vista of Table Mountain on her way to visit Isabel Hoult in the Constantia Valley. Having left Scotland on the threshold of winter, she relished the change of climate and marvelled to see so many new and different plants, animals and birds. The cousins had not met for some time and Marion was warmly welcomed. When family news had been exchanged, along with the woeful tales from Hutton, Isabel set out to make Marion at ease by diverting her with all the good things South Africa had to offer. The Hoult vineyard was at Voorspoed, and while she watched the grapes ripening Marion became intensely interested in their cultivation as well as in the process of turning them into wine. Like her father, she wanted to learn about each new subject she encountered, and viticulture intrigued her. It provided the change she needed and she welcomed every opportunity to be involved.

The two cousins got on well – both were lively and slightly eccentric. On the Cape Peninsula they visited Hout Bay and Fish Hoek, and at the Orange River Gorge surveyed the plunging chasm. In the Kalahari Desert bushmen who cooked and ate meals outside their straw huts entertained them with a tribal dance. Marion was intrigued to learn that the males of the tribe are born and go through life with penises which are semi-erect. She also recorded a salamander, a ten-inch centipede and Isabel's dachshunds, but no picture of a unique strain her cousin claimed to have bred and named the Inka Pudinka.

Marion had armed herself with the addresses of possible contacts before she left home. Medical colleagues from her days at Peel Hospital were said to be in Cape Town then, but she recorded no mention of a meeting or of finding employment there. After eight months in the African sun she decided to move on to Australia. No special permission was required for 'citizens or nationals of a British Commonwealth country and of European descent' and she was assured 'Provided you are in sound health, of good character and can satisfy the Immigration Authorities that you are not likely to become a charge on public funds, a valid passport is sufficient authority for you to enter Australia and remain as long as you wish'.

So Marion enlisted as a stewardess and worked her passage on the TS *Arawa* which carried 274 passengers. She was determined to justify the generosity she had received by fending for herself and, at various stages during her travels, she was said to have paid her way as a lady's companion and as a governess. The ship sailed from Cape Town on 23 July

1953 and was scheduled to call at Fremantle before reaching Melbourne. After arriving at New South Wales, she travelled to Bathurst and found herself employment as a nurse at the District Hospital in a rural area about 100 miles west of Sydney. She lived in staff quarters and found the work hard. Bending over the patients' beds gave her back trouble again, so by October she was glad to take a week off to enjoy the Cherry Blossom Festival in Orange, a tourist resort in rolling farmland with a lake surrounded by orchards.

While Marion was keen to fit in with her fellow nurses, her cultured speech and elegant bearing made her stand out from the crowd. Combined with her dynamic personality and her ability to drive a car, these factors were probably considered when, later that month, she was offered a post as assistant housekeeper at the new Gilbulla Conference Centre near Sydney. A recommendation from the Commonwealth Employment Bureau had prompted the approach from Mrs Mowll, wife of the Archbishop of Sydney. Marion was pleased and flattered but the Centre was a charitable organization and could only offer a modest wage of Aus £7 (about £195 today) a week plus keep. Mrs Mowll may not have been aware that Marion possessed no private means when she regretfully declined the post. Hospital nursing was more remunerative and every penny she earned had to be saved because she was relying on her own resources. In later years Marion would say 'I'm not afraid of poverty because I know what it's like'. The struggle to support herself when she was far from home might have been a lonely one, but she did not lose her zest, and she made friends everywhere she went.

Meanwhile, back at Hutton her father was having a difficult time. In his nineties Burrell had become gaunt and skeletal, but kept in touch with dealers and galleries daily, though several of his trusted allies had died or moved else-where. For years there were disputes over possible sites for the collection and the worry of it all was getting him down. Industrial pollution can damage tapestries and fabrics, and he had insisted on a rural location somewhere near Killearn, Stirlingshire, and at least 16 miles north of Glasgow. Country estates were considered near Drymen, Balfron and Strath-blane, including Finnich Malise and Balfunning as well as Ballindalloch (my own home for 30 years). The castles of Mugdock and Buchanan also became contenders to provide the baronial setting Burrell keenly desired. After repeated disappointments, hopes were raised by Mrs Connell of Dougalston who generously offered the estate near Miln-gavie in the memory of her late husband, Charles Connell, the Glasgow shipbuilder. It seemed that Burrell's problems had been solved, but when a coal mining project was mooted nearby he instantly withdrew. Duntreath Castle was offered with a 25-year lease but it was not accepted either. One by one sites were rejected and though plans were drawn up for museum buildings none of them bore fruit. The years of tantalizing searches had been to no avail.

Having assigned the collection to the City of Glasgow, Burrell was distrustful of outsiders taking over his project. Soon he began to quarrel and fall out with his former ally, Dr Tom Honeyman, Director of Glasgow Art Gallery and Museum. There was a major row when, against Burrell's specific orders, Honeyman allowed paintings from the collect-ion to leave the British Isles and be loaned to a gallery in Switzerland. While disputes over the collection dragged painfully on, Burrell fell out with Andrew Hannah, the Depute Director, and eventually clashed with the Glasgow Corporation.

While Marion's father was addressing these problems he was also struggling with the heartbreaking burden created by his increasingly neurotic wife – shielding Constance was making him suffer more and more. Her troubled mind was plagued by delusions, and after their daughter left home her resentment of Marion continued to fester. Life at Hutton Castle became even drearier as rooms were dismantled and items in the Collection were packed up and taken away to Glasgow. Since his tribulations over Marion's escape Burrell's temper frequently got the better of him. He was becoming obsessed with security on every front. When he heard intruders trying to break into the castle he was so furious that, despite his failing eyesight, he grabbed his shot gun and fired both barrels out of his bedroom window. The burglars escaped without injury. Marion, thousands of miles away, knew nothing of her father's geriatric explosions. The collector lived to a very great age, and many of the anecdotes about him relate to his declining years and were told by people who knew him only slightly. By ordinary standards he often seemed mean and cantankerous, but William Burrell was no ordinary man.

Advancing blindness was a hindrance, and his problem with reading frustrated him. His store of knowledge had enthralled Marion, and in her youth he had been inspired to make charts for her, recording historical events. At Hutton many of the books he read were kept upstairs while his business room was lined with files and purchase books, along with the catalogues he used for reference. He distrusted academics, and preferred the advice of dealers, some of whom became his friends. Because he had grown used to success, thwarted negotiations now upset him, sometimes reducing him to tears. Failure was something Burrell could no longer handle. As his sharp acumen declined he did not adapt his strategem to hedge against inflation and only low yielding gilt-edged securities remained in his investment portfolio.

As his health began to fail he spent the mornings in bed. When he and his wife both became ill they were taken off to Berwick in an ambulance. After they had spent ten days in hospital a taxi was ordered to take them home again, but Burrell was enraged to discover that he was expected to pay. Yet while his spirit endured his humour did too. A dealer he encountered late in life recognized him as a Scot and enquired 'Do you know Sir William Burrell?' To which the collector wryly replied, 'Aye. I'm what's left of him!'

Peter Freeny, his faithful head gardener, eventually retired, and he and his wife went to live in Peebles. Devastated by the departure of his trusted confidant, Sir William pleaded with the couple to return. He even offered to build a house for them at Hutton, but nothing came of his frantic gesture. Burrell was 92 by then, and Mrs Freeny had no faith in an old man's promises. The Freenys' daughter Janet lived locally and continued to assist Sir William with his work on the collection. The Burrell Collection was everything he lived for and Janet supported him loyally, sadly aware that the task could well have been accomplished by her employer's daughter.

But Marion was far away. By November 1953 she had earned enough to tour Tasmania, although she had to budget with meticulous economy. She made careful plans when exploring new places, noting her impressions and experiences in the guidebooks which she continued to keep. From Melbourne she made the crossing in the *Taroona*, a ferry built for the Tasmanian Steamer Company by Alexander Stephen and Sons. In the Bass Strait the ship ran into a westerly gale and was severely battered for 22 hours. On reaching Launceston six hours behind schedule the captain declared it the worst crossing he had known in ten years. The local press reported broken deck seats and smashed crockery as well as seasick passengers. As Marion made no further comment it is hoped that she had inherited Grandma Burrell's sea legs and her indestructible constitution.

Although it was springtime in the Antipodes Tasmania turned out to be chilly. Undaunted, she wrapped up warmly and toured about while lodging in guest houses where dinner, bed and breakfast cost Aus£1 (£28 today) a night. Lord Rowallan, her former Ayrshire neighbour, was Governor of Tasmania and had she chosen to make herself known, she might have lived in better style, but explaining her reduced circumstances would have been embarrassing. Plenty of day trips were available. From Hobart she toured the Derwent Valley seeing mountains and forested gorges with giant tufted grass trees. There had once been a penal settlement on Sarah Island and pine logs which convicts had cut a hundred years before sometimes floated down the Gordon River. Kangaroos were seen among the trees near Georges Bay and, on the coast there were weird rock formations with blow holes. Aborigines had hunted freely in Tasmania before they were driven out by European settlers. The few who survived had been sent to a reserve on Flinders Island in the 1830s. Burrell's daughter took a dim view; throughout her life she was a passionate supporter of the underdog.

Back in Melbourne, where preparations for the 1956 Olympic Games had already begun, she visited a friend called Minnie who had come from Morningside in Edinburgh. To Marion she was also known as 'York', which would have been her maiden name and suggests that she had been a domestic servant when the Burrells were living in East Lothian. Being an enterprising girl who progressed to an office job, Minnie had married an Australian soldier after World War I. The reunion was a happy one, and they continued to keep in touch.

As Grandma Burrell's Australian adventure had remained strictly under wraps since that shocking solo voyage she had made in her youth, Marion may never have known she had Guthrie relations who emigrated to new South Wales in the 1880s. She admitted no knowledge of Burrells. In the 1980s, when a new aquaintance claimed to know 'the Australian Burrells', she promptly replied, 'I don't think I've heard of them!' The Guthries 'down under' had met with success – George Guthrie founded the Bendigo Pottery and his sister Mary's husband became a Member of the Australian Parliament. Though Isabella and her son Willie might have been in touch with them, Marion made no mention of these Australian relations and could hardly have met them without explaining the dreadful rift with her parents and her embarrassing shortage of funds.

By continuing to work hard Marion managed to save enough to go on a month-long tour in June 1954. From Sydney she travelled north to Queensland via Brisbane by Pioneer Coach and then by train to Mackay for a cruise round the Great Barrier Reef. From Cairns she recorded a seven-day coach tour with boat trips. Port Douglas was the most northerly point she reached and the tropical heat seemed to suit her. On Green Island she was enchanted by the sea garden of corals and anemones with shoals of darting fish which she was able to watch from a glass-bottomed boat. Crocodiles were seen on the Russell River and at Yungaburra

she counted 15 duck-billed platypus. There were huge irides-
cent butterflies, and around Innisfail the green fronds of sugar
cane seemed to her 'like the pennons of a marching army'.
Being a passionate 'people' person she was drawn to the
Aborigines, intrigued by their art.

After visiting Sydney, Marion felt ready for another
departure and sailed away to New Zealand where she
enlisted her services at Ravensthorpe Hospital in Auckland.
Nurse Burrell had acquired a good deal of experience, and
the wages she earned allowed her to make further explo-
rations before the eventual journey home.

Marion knew she had relations in New Zealand because
her Uncle Adam's family had settled there, but sadly no
meeting took place. Her uncle had left Scotland before she
was born, so she had never met him. Adam Burrell was said
to have been a clever man with a volatile temper. His relations
at Burrell and Son were displeased when he broke away and
left the family company to study medicine at Glasgow University. Once qualified, Adam sailed with Clarissa Jane and their
three young children to New York, where they were admitted
to the Ellis Island Immigration Station which loomed over
the harbour like a fortress with tall domed towers. Soon they
went to live in Laramie, and later in Saratoga, Wyoming, where
Adam's wife bought a pretty brick house for her family for
$1,000, which was said to have been a bargain. Another child
was born there, but having provided a medical practice Dr
Burrell appears to have fallen out with members of the local
community and decided to move on. This time the family
sailed to South Africa, where two more sons were born but
both died in infancy. Adam took to hunting big game, but
more trouble followed, and a spurious report alleged that he
had been attacked and eaten by cannibals. Having survived,

he set out once more when the family finally emigrated to New Zealand. They arrived at Methven in 1902, where the wandering doctor continued to practise medicine before moving yet again in 1905 to Akaroa and then to Oxford, where his youngest son was born.

In 1907, when Adam Burrell was 48, he met with an untimely death from blood poisoning contracted from one of his patients. Four years later the widowed Clarissa Jane married William McCulloch and after the years of frenetic roaming began to lead a settled life as the wife of a farmer. There would have been little incentive for her family to remain in touch with Burrell in-laws in Scotland, a home she had known for only seven years. Small wonder that Adam's niece did not know where her cousins were living, much as they would have welcomed her.

But Marion had longed to visit New Zealand, so in November 1954 she embarked on another month-long tour through a country which was spectacular and variable. Her notes describe a boat trip through caves lit by tiny glow worms at Waitomo. In the thermal region there were volcanoes, geysers and boiling mud pools where her father and grandmother had witnessed the devastation at Mount Tarawera 60 years before. Now Rotorua had a golf course with alarming hazards in the form of spouting steam jets. At Whakarewarewa Marion visited a Maori village where she watched the graceful poi dance and grunting warriors performing the haka and, in the springs of Paradise Valley, rainbow trout came to nibble bread from her hand.

In Tarawera she travelled the old coach road where the widowed Isabella and her son Willie had passed in the 1880s and continued her tour of New Zealand unaware of Grandma Burrell's girlhood escapade. At Wellington Marion saw the old capital with jumbled streets on a steep hillside above Cook Strait. Then she sailed to South Island and passed Ship Cove where Captain Cook had anchored the *Endeavour* and proudly hoisted the Union Flag in 1770. On her visit to the Arahura River she came upon the greenstone that Maoris had used to make tools. Then she climbed to 2,000 feet of Franz Josef Glacier and saw snow-capped mountains with their lower slopes covered in subtropical forest. At the end of November she at last reached Milford Sound and the scene of previous family visits. When the Guthries voyaged there the sound could only be reached by sea. Marion recorded the stories of three family visits in her memoirs:

> They [Adam Guthrie and his daughter Isabella] approached the head of Milford Sound by sail, later my father also approached the sound by steamship, and in 1954, I was the first to approach it overland, through the Homer Tunnel which had been opened 11 days previously. There was a considerable waterfall in the middle of it. The bridges on the descent to Milford looked very rickety and had no parapets.
>
> In grandmother's day [during William and Isabella's visit, about 1887], there was of course no hotel, and the only accommodation was with the shepherd, one Sutherland. When I told them at the hotel of the two previous visits of my family they got very excited and looked up their register which unfortunately didn't go back further than 1928.

In the South Island wilderness known as Fiordland the great inlet created by Milford Sound extends like a trailing mirror for a distance of 22 kilometres The 'shepherd' whom the

Burrells met was Donald Sutherland, a Scottish Highlander who had lived there in isolation, receiving stores four times a year from Dunedin. People called him 'The Hermit of Milford Sound'. In middle age he acquired a wife who began to take in guests and welcome the first tourists. Over the years Sutherland blazed a trail through dense forest to open a land route to the sound and discovered the gigantic waterfalls which now bear his name.

To the young Isabella her first sight of Milford Sound would have been electrifying and afterwards she cherished the memory of snow-capped peaks reflected in the glassy water and giant cascades plunging through forests tangled with creepers and ferns. A hundred years later her granddaughter marvelled as she had done as the rosy glow from the setting sun tinted the slopes of Mount Pembroke.

It was mid December when Marion reached Dunedin at the end of her tour. The surrounding hills brought thoughts of Scotland because many of her countrymen had settled there to farm sheep. The city awoke memories of Edinburgh when she discovered not only a 'Princes Street' but 'Castle', 'Frederick' and 'Hanover' Streets as well. There was a 'Water of Leith' and a statue of Robert Burns. Marion found it a friendly place to say farewell to fellow travellers and begin her journey back to Scotland. After two nights in Dunedin she tried a new method of transport and travelled to Wellington by plane.

In the 1950s, when Marion flew in a Dakota with seating for 24 passengers, air travel was still a novel adventure. Things were different then. Instructions to passengers requested punctuality with such politeness they implied that that the plane might be delayed rather that leave a traveller stranded. Nervous passengers were assured that the pilot was extremely competent and that take-off was 'one of the most exhilarating experiences in the world'. Marion enjoyed the flight to Wellington and continued by sleeper train to Auckland. There was little time to spare before she finally boarded the RMS *Rangitata* and sailed for home on 18 December 1954.

The ship had been built for the New Zealand Shipping Company by John Brown's of Clydebank and refitted after serving as a troop ship during World War II. The voyage to Southampton had been scheduled via the Panama Canal. Marion travelled Tourist Class, having reserved a single berth cabin at a cost of NZ£135 (about £1,400 today). Her time in the Antipodes had inspired her to read the voyages of Captain Cook and on her journey across the Pacific Marion's attention turned to another naval hero who had served under him. Captain Bligh of the *Bounty* had been cast adrift by mutineers and sailed 4,000 miles in an open boat to reach Timor with 18 loyal members of his crew. On returning to Britain Bligh had faced court-martial, but been exonerated. The *Rangitata* called at Pitcairn Island which had been populated by the mutineers and the Tahitian ladies who had sailed with them on the *Bounty*. Marion would have been agog to meet descendants of Fletcher Christian and his rebellious followers, but it is doubtful whether passengers on the *Rangitata* had an opportunity to go ashore.

It was typical of Marion Burrell that, after more than two years spent forging her way far from home, she followed in the wake of her seafaring heroes and completed her travels by circumnavigating the world. When she finally reached Southampton she returned to Scotland to begin another life.

CHAPTER 12

Silvia

There was no welcoming reception when Marion once more set foot on Scottish soil, as hardly anyone knew when she slipped quietly back to her homeland. It was a difficult time, because she was extremely hard up and without transport. She lay low at first and little is known of how she got by on her meagre resources. Without the help of additional funds only a full time job could support her. Marion had proved herself no shirker, but with her humble qualifications it would have been hard to be a working woman and retain the social standing to which she had been born. In the 1950s it was not usual for mature ladies of her class to undertake paid employment.

Though many friends were concerned about her, the contacts she maintained remain unknown. Financial help was proffered when she was in extremis and family members are known to have given support but the process was both embarrassing and problematic. Aunt Mary Mitchell suffered for befriending her niece because every act antagonized her brother Willie. When Marion struggled to obtain funds by breaking a Trust that her father had set up, her aunt was involved, and this created a conflict with Merrick who felt obliged to protect his mother's interests. Years of anxiety followed while Marion consulted lawyers and made thwarted attempts to achieve financial independence.

During this time she made herself at home in low-priced lodgings in South Queensferry, by the Firth of Forth. The old ferry town was on a hillside, intersected by winding, cobbled streets. Marion liked to claim that she had lived next to the local tart, which may not have been an empty jest because there was a naval base at Rosyth, just across the Forth. Gradually word of her return got round, though it took time for her family and friends to discover where she was living. When they realized her predicament they wanted to help because she was entirely reliant on public transport. Eventually Marion's parents learned where she was and her mother telephoned, inviting her to lunch at Hutton Castle. When Marion used lack of transport as an excuse Constance offered to send her chauffeur, but she still refused. Like her father, she too could be intransigent.

Living in reduced circumstances made it hard for her to be sociable, but she managed to meet up with friends who lived nearby, such as Jane Stewart-Clark who welcomed her to Dundas Castle. Sholto Douglas was in his eighties and nearing the end of his life, but the loving bond created by their clandestine affair still existed between them. Their secret had remained hidden from public scrutiny so, playing the part of an old family friend, Marion used to visit him and try to return a little of the comfort he had given her when she had come to him, broken-hearted, more than 20 years before. Major Douglas died in 1959 and included a bequest for Marion in his will. After the recipient had also died his photograph was discovered in her sitting room concealed behind a framed picture of her Grandma Mitchell.

But there were also highlights during this period of Marion's life. It must have been through the kindness of a benefactor that she eventually acquired a small second-hand car. Her Aunt Mary welcomed her in Ayrshire, and Perceton once more became her home base. At St Ninian's Church in Troon, on the Ayrshire coast, there was a happy reunion with the Rev. Jim McGill and his wife Rosemary. Marion was able to catch up with her godson Gavin and meet his teenage cousin Richard Sprackling, with whom she made an immediate hit. As the rector's birthday fell on St Ninian's Day, a small pilgrimage was arranged to the coast in Wigtownshire to celebrate Holy Communion in St Ninian's cave on the edge of the Irish Sea. It was said that the saint had gone there to seek solitude and pray. Richard carried a card table and candlesticks which were used to improvise an altar. The youngster said he enjoyed the occasion even though his uncle denied him a share of the Communion wine.

In London, Marion took Richard out from school and met him off the train with a box of false moustaches and spectacles from Hamleys as he had suggested that their rendezvous might call for a disguise. When treated to a slap-up meal at Simpson's in the Strand he declined the famous roast beef, and asked instead for fish and chips which Marion gleefully ordered for them both. One day she turned up in her tiny car at Richard's home and invited him and his parents to pile in and join her on a tour of the Oxford colleges. After an entertaining, if not entirely comfortable outing, the Spracklings said it had been like 'spending an afternoon with Joyce Grenfell'.

But there was no jollity at Hutton Castle, where Marion's parents continued to decline. In March 1958, as squalls buffeted the battlements and jackdaws garrisoned the tower, the world became aware that Sir William Burrell had finally died. His long and remarkable life had lasted for 96 years, and nearly eight of them had passed since his daughter fled from their family home. That painful rift had prevailed and, when her father's funeral was being planned, Marion was filled with such horror at the prospect of meeting her mother again she almost refused to attend. Eventually she was persuaded, after her cousins Merrick and Alan Mitchell promised to stand guard on either side of her throughout the entire proceedings till William Burrell was laid to rest at Largs in the sunny hillside cemetery which overlooks the Firth of Clyde.

Constance had continued to take first place and influence her husband's thinking with infusions of vitriol guaranteeing the condemnation of their daughter. Before he died Burrell had done everything within his power to avoid leaving either money or property to Marion, although she was his only child and should have been his rightful heir. He did, however, provide an annuity to benefit one of his nieces. Prior to decreeing innumerable complicated instructions regarding the future of the Burrell Collection, his will had been set up to provide every conceivable care for his wife. William Burrell's heart seems to have been permanently turned against his daughter – his pride had been incurably injured when his ambitious plans for her failed him again and again. Marion was blamed for the monumental failure of her parents' schemes, and therefore she could never be forgiven. As the infirmities of old age slowly set in, their attitude towards her had hardened beyond all hope of redemption.

Paradoxically, the stupendous generosity of William Burrell had been displayed to the world when he presented the

Burrell Collection to the City of Glasgow in 1944. It is significant that this priceless gift to Burrell's native city was bestowed by both 'Sir William and Lady Burrell'. By including his wife's name with his own Burrell had paid her the greatest compliment of which he was capable. With Constance always close at hand, the strains of their private life may have increased the intensity of Burrell's collecting for he remained a dedicated enthusiast, fired by his consuming interest and the overwhelming desire to share his wealth. In response, Sir William was honoured with the Freedom of the City of Glasgow in 1944. He donated £10,000 (£358,000 today) to purchase radium for the Glasgow Cancer Hospital and in 1946 received Glasgow's prestigious St Mungo Prize which is awarded triennially to the person who has made the greatest contribution to the city. For years since then he had been increasing the collection and supervising plans for its final home, although a site for the museum had continued to elude him. His requirements for the Burrell Collection raised problems which would remain unsolved for 40 years, and William Burrell died a sadly disappointed man.

Her father's death was infinitely painful for Marion. In spite of the conflicts which had driven them apart she never ceased to respect and admire him and for all the anguish she had suffered, there were countless interests which both had yearned to share. From the depths of her soul she still worshipped her father and for the rest of her life she would grieve for him. His daughter would always revere William Burrell as a great man who was fallible, just like the rest of mankind. While over the years his mind had focused with increasing intent on each chosen goal, the relentless application which brought him success had brought misery to his child.

Constance Burrell had devoted her life to her husband and now she was bereft. While he made allowance for her deficiencies her public image had endured, and in the eyes of the world she had fulfilled her role as consort to Sir William Burrell. Though Constance did not possess the vibrant intellect of her husband or daughter, she had continued to take first place in William's life and influence his thinking, even though, for many years her mind had often been deranged by mental illness. Condemned to survive in loveless isolation, the widowed Lady Burrell lived on at Hutton Castle where echoing rooms now lay stripped of her husband's treasures. With few friends left to support her, she compensated for the inconvenience, the reduction in staff and the lack of a daughter to tend her by enlisting the service of a lady companion.

After her father's death Marion found some consolation because she was no longer short of funds. Though Burrell had done his best to leave his only child without a penny, under Scots law Marion was entitled to receive one third of his estate and in due course the money she so badly needed was at last available. At the age of 58 Burrell's daughter was for the first time in a position to buy property of her own. Having decided to make her home in Edinburgh, she chose the south side of the city to avoid the North Sea haar from the Firth of Forth, and purchased a sunny, west-facing flat at 92 Findhorn Place. The flat cost £3,000 (£54,000 today) and occupied the two upper floors of a terraced house which had small gardens to the front and back. Having said it was absurd to pay £7,000 for a house in a new development, she soon increased her outlay by employing the best decorator in town. Her colour scheme was deceptively simple because everything was painted white and set off by natural hair cord carpets. The curtains and chair covers were off-white and the kitchen looked like an operating theatre, but against this background of porridge and cream, her skilled distribution of objets d'art was stunning. She moved in triumphantly on 15 November 1960.

'Matthew' wrote from London wishing her well in her new home, regretting that he had not been there to help her move in. He had come up in the restaurant world and now it was his turn to have staff problems. Then a book arrived at Findhorn Place from José Plaza. Knowing Marion's love of art he had sent her *Italian Painters of the Renaissance* by Bernard Berenson. In her 'Grave and Gay' album she recorded lines from José's letters:

Why are there so many 'ifs' in life?
To a large degree we are slaves of our past.
The peace of one's own company. ...

Within months of finally achieving her own address Marion appeared in public at the Smith Art Gallery in Stirling when in May 1961 she had been invited to open an exhibition of items from the Burrell Collection as part of the Stirling Festival. Grasping her opportunity she praised her father's 'fabulous collection' and told of his early experiences in collecting, but she chose not to speak about art because 'It is rather like the Victorian child who should be seen and not heard'. She then proceeded to upbraid the Glasgow Corporation for failing to find a site where the Burrell Collection would be permanently on view. As Sir William Burrell had provided half a million pounds (about nine million today) for this building Marion denounced the Corporation, saying that, having accepted the gift of the Burrell Collection, they had for 17 years failed to honour their part of the contract. Her accusations caused a stir, adding weight to complaints which were being raised in Glasgow. Mugdock Castle had been offered by Sir Hugh Fraser and after Marion's outburst more discussions followed, but the ruined castle was considered too near Glasgow and conversion too costly. Once again the project foundered.

In 1961, three years after the death of her husband, Lady Burrell died at Hutton Castle. Despite years of failing health she had lived to 85. Her mental problems had gradually increased, and having learned to use ill health as a tool when situations troubled her, she had withdrawn into a shadowy world where her mind became lost in a web of duplicity. Because Marion had made her jealous there had been no loving bond between mother and daughter. Resentment had blighted Constance's life, and she became confused and suffered from delusions. When nearing the end of her days, Lady Burrell had confided an outlandish claim that she had once conducted an illicit affair with the Earl of Glasgow. Though the charming 8th Earl was known to have enamored more than one lady, Constance Burrell was never a contender, and her fantasy could have sprung from a latent desire to emulate the conquests of her daughter. Modern psychiatry will treat paranoia, but then mental illness was taboo and often misunderstood, so many cases were disregarded and never diagnosed.

In Constance Burrell's will Marion received nothing but the household linen and her mother's personal effects. The latter consisted only of Lady Burrell's discarded clothes, her jewels and furs having been deliberately excluded. When Marion fell from favour back in the 1930s, her father resolved that she should never inherit any of his properties. This decision caused him endless trouble while he considered other ways to dispose of his Hutton Castle estate and additional land which included the farms of Blackburn and Whiterig. Towards the end of his life he dreamed up a fantastic scheme, decreeing in his will that after both he and his wife had died, his Hutton estate should become a kind of corporate vacation resort to be offered in turn to banks and insurance companies and finally to the National Trust. Predictably, there were no takers, and Burrell's properties were ultimately sold. Major George Houston, who lived nearby at Hutton Castle Mains, became the owner of Hutton Castle; he was descended from the family of Janet Houston who married Burrell's grandfather in 1831. For many years after Lady Burrell's death the dismantled castle lay neglected and unoccupied, but in 1984 it was resold and began to revive in the skilled hands of Anthony Gray who has dedicated himself to a total restoration.

When Hutton Castle was finally dismantled, some household items and furniture did come Marion's way. Merrick Mitchell was a Burrell Trustee and kindly ensured that his cousin was provided with sufficient for her needs. Among her acquisitions were two fine oak dressers and a Queen Anne bureau which had been in her bedroom at Hutton Castle. The bureau was topped by a glass-fronted cabinet in which she displayed small objets d'art which pleased her. Like her father, Marion's taste was unerring and restrained. Also like him, she was protective of her possessions. Distrusting anyone who might damage, pry or interfere, she preferred to clean and care for them herself.

There were no paintings at Findhorn Place. Since all hope of inheriting some had come to naught, she refrained from buying any of her own, and instead enhanced her flat with well-framed reproduction prints. Just inside her front door a peacock's feather stood erect in a tall green vase while a parade of Tudor portraits, drawn by Holbein, invited visitors to come upstairs. Crawhall's *Spangled Cock* splashed vibrant colour from the landing and a print of Boudin's *Empress Eugenie at Trouville* hung above Marion's bed. In her sitting room, red and green Ming vases were flanked by a pair of Chinese 'Foo' dogs which guarded her George II mantelpiece. On arriving at her flat guests would relax by the fireside to enjoy Marion's treasures as her sherry decanter offered welcoming libations accompanied by her time-honoured toast 'To absent friends!'

Being free at last to spend money of her own was an unfamiliar experience and Marion took time to get used to it. She continued to preserve a low profile and was careful not to throw her money about. Adapting to so many changes made her feel insecure, and sometimes she sought health cures and religious retreats. In 1962 she joined St Aidan's Church in Edinburgh, having been introduced to the rector by her friend, the Rev. Jim McGill. When she attended his church in Troon, McGill had been struck by the warmth with which she had approached residents in a council scheme and invited them to join St Ninian's congregation. One of them became a friend, and came to visit her at Findhorn Place. Although Marion had moved in high society she was never a snob and, like her father who had lived among working class people, she could be at ease with men and women from every walk of life.

The congregation of St Aidan's had been dwindling when the Rev. Rodney Grant became 'Curate in charge'. When Marion joined his flock he always called her 'Miss Burrell'. It may have been a desire for expiation which made her ask him to conduct a special requiem in memory of her mother. Grant saw at once that she needed fellowship and an opportunity to serve a cause. Marion became Church Treasurer and threw in her lot wholeheartedly. The congregation began to build up, and the living increased. Marion took pleasure in donating a gift of £2,000 (£36,000 today) to refurbish the church.

St Aidan's had taken on a new life and Grant was allocated an Assistant Curate. Both men were single, and one evening in 1965 Miss Burrell joined them for an outing to the cinema. While they were all enjoying *The Happiest Days of Your Life* a terrible disaster occurred. During the rector's absence the rectory went up in flames and when the clergymen returned from their jolly evening out they were greeted by a scene of devastation. Although the cause of the blaze is not known, the damage which followed rendered their residence uninhabitable. The rector was forced to move to alternative accommodation while the curate, who had lodged with him, was given refuge at 92 Findhorn Place. Marion was glad to come to the rescue and it made a pleasant change for her to have a man about the house. In the meantime she did her best to support the reverend gentlemen by taking the pair of them out for meals, for which she always paid. But from time to time she got carried away and insisted on giving them presents. Marion's generosity could sometimes be embarrassing and, in spite of her kindness, the curate was probably relieved when he received another appointment.

When Marion gave the rector a picture she possessed, her insecurity became evident. It was just a printed reproduction of an Old Master painting, and probably of less value than its heavy wooden frame, but almost at once she said that she missed it, and asked to have it back. Although Grant readily agreed, she became filled with remorse and finally told him to keep it. Mary Mitchell had recently died at Perceton and Grant knew that Miss Burrell was grieving for her much loved aunt, so he suggested a change of scene might help to restore her spirits. A Mediterranean cruise was recommended and the seasoned traveller boldly went off to tour ancient sites and once again revelled in new discoveries. The highlight of Marion's adventure was a visit to the Vatican in Rome where she was granted an audience with Pope Paul VI – it would seem that an influential friend had arranged for her to receive this honour. Her vacation was a great success and she came home exultant.

But, by the end of the year, there was trouble at St Aidan's when Marion fell out with another lady member of the congregation. When a conflict of ideas arose she insisted that her antagonist should be denied admission to the vestry. As a benefactor of the church she expected to have her way, so when Grant refused to comply she exploded. In a towering rage she gathered up the money from the church treasury, stormed into the bank and scattered it on the counter, while loudly denouncing the unfortunate rector of St Aidan's. On hearing what had happened, he hastily wrote her a card and sent it with a bouquet of flowers, but Marion took them back to the shop and flung them on the floor. When the florist reported this to Grant he wrote again, but received no reply. Miss Burrell had severed her connections with the Anglican Church forever.

This extraordinary episode could be taken as another of Marion's eccentricities, but the cause went deeper than that. Her violent outbursts bore the signs of a breakdown. Though no one had been aware of her anguish Marion was a soul in torment. In her 'Grave and Gay' album she wrote:

> Suffering does not last. But having suffered lasts forever.
> It is not what we suffer but how we suffer that matters.
> Man was made to love and love must be free.

Marion's keenness to press gifts on her friends came from her thwarted need to love and be loved. Believing the rector of St Aidan's had rejected her and let her down, she could not forgive him for her own outrageous folly. Neither could she forgive herself for the pain she continued to suffer from a father she admired and still longed to love.

With brave determination Marion managed to master her grief and make the most of her life. There were more Continental travels which she undertook alone, but she was rarely short of entertaining company. Her little car had been replaced by a Rover which gave her endless trouble so she drove to Solihull and demanded satisfaction from the Managing Director of the company. In London she bought herself an expensive emerald ring. She already possessed several gemstone rings and the massive emerald weighed 6.87 carats, but she did not flash it about. It may have been chosen to go with the large diamond and emerald cluster ear studs she loved to wear. She had no inhibitions about wearing them although a policeman warned that a criminal might be taking note. Marion loved jewellery and one day she spied a pair of 'garnet' earrings in a Bond Street window. On asking to inspect them, she was told that the stones were rubies! After some scrutiny she commented dismissively 'Not a good colour. Are they?'

Buying presents delighted her and I still treasure her gifts. In Edinburgh, a frilly party frock caught her eye in Jenners.

She wanted me to try it on and hoped to buy it for me. As I would never have worn it I did not want her to waste her money, but having gratefully declined I regretted disappointing her. She liked to see the latest fashions but when browsing in Miss Selfridge the security tags puzzled her. I explained that an alarm would go off if a shoplifter tried to leave without paying and at once her face lit up. 'Oh what fun!' she squealed, 'Do let's try!' It was all I could do to stop her.

At home she dressed quietly in well-worn tweeds so that no one could guess she was the daughter of a multimillionaire, let alone one of Scotland's celebrated benefactors. Like her father when he skulked around sale rooms, she didn't mind being seen in old clothes. But when she needed to smarten up she liked to be dashing, even when her clothes were home made. Being an experienced dressmaker and embroiderer Marion created with panache. Her knowledge of haute couture was immense, as well as her understanding of style, fabrics and colour. She had learned every trick when it came to cutting costs – 'Always check the garments on a bargain rail' she advised, 'because some may be better finished.' In restaurants she entertained in style, and her welcomes will never be forgotten. She loved to make introductions and bring people together.

Her father's influence was seldom far away. When my mother enthused about a gate-leg table she intended to buy from an antique shop they both frequented, she was not amused when Marion nipped in first and bought it for herself. William Burrell had behaved in exactly the same way. When a fellow collector told him of a Jacobean bed that he hoped to acquire at auction, Burrell promptly outbid him and could not understand why the man never spoke to him again. Marion was more considerate, and assigned the table to my mother in her will. There was a chilly response to the suggestion that Eva should reciprocate with a brass alms dish of hers which Marion happened to covet. When a neighbour planted a shared flowerbed with roses which were not to Marion's taste she dug them up, and when a florist seemed incapable of wrapping a bouquet of flowers she insisted on doing it herself. Should it seem that Marion did not suffer fools gladly that would be untrue – she refused to suffer them at all.

At Findhorn Place her voracious thirst for knowledge was fuelled by her library of books. Significant passages were marked in pencil and observations listed in notebooks. The entire contents of Marion's flat were recorded and valued in an inventory she meticulously compiled herself. Press cuttings and pictures of the Collection were pasted into a large portfolio because every association with her father's success seemed to be cathartic, though when I admired Degas' *Jockeys in the Rain* she rejoined, 'But don't you think their heads are too small?'. In 1970 Miss Burrell performed the opening ceremony at Burrell House in Glasgow where, thanks to her father's generosity, No. 8 Great Western Terrace became a care home, since converted into flats.

After the Smoke Abatement Act had released Glasgow from invasive pollution, there was jubilation when the Cambridge architect Barry Gasson produced with his colleagues the winning design for a new museum to house the Burrell Collection in Pollok Park. Lord Muirshiel was Chairman of the Burrell Trustees, having begun his career in Parliament as Jack Maclay, before becoming Secretary of State for Scotland and Lord Lieutenant of Renfrewshire. Sir William's nephews, Merrick and Alan Mitchell, were also Trustees and they strove loyally to uphold Burrell's wishes while Merrick bombarded Glasgow Council with complicated letters which proved trying for everyone concerned. Over the years, the Trustees have shown their worth by protecting and promoting the Collection while purchasing well-considered additions in accordance with the donor's stipulations. Had Marion been invited to do so she might gladly have served. Her name had come up when Trustees were first appointed, but the Trust lawyer advised against her involvement. Marion was so passionate about her father's collection she might have raised even more problems than he did.

The Burrell Trustees were not as stuffy as they seemed. Lord Muirshiel confessed that when he was asked to serve a second five-year term as Chairman, he protested, 'But I know nothing about Art!' and was firmly told 'That's why we need you, stupid!' The remark was probably made by one of the Mitchells, as they had long been friends. In spite of Merrick's sober demeanour, he was happy to join in a snowball fight, and when their niece said 'Uncle Alan, I do hope you'll come to my wedding' he replied, 'Of course I'd love to, Mary dear, but I think it's Merrick's turn for the suit'.

As work on the new building to house the Burrell Collection was about to begin, Princess Margaret was invited to cut the first sod at Pollok Park. But when the day drew near, Her Royal Highness was struck down with gastric flu. There was panic among the Burrell Trustees. Though Marion was the obvious candidate to assume the task, no one dared to ask her because Merrick and Alan feared she would resent the approach and almost certainly refuse. But Trevor Walden, Director of Glasgow Art Galleries and Museums, encouraged them to grasp the nettle, and to everyone's surprise, Marion rose to the occasion with obvious delight. On 3 May 1978 she delivered her speech with verve and made everyone smile when she proudly proclaimed 'I was brought up in the Burrell Collection'. Then she gave the signal for an enormous bulldozer to cut a swathe through the grass and the sod was well and truly cut.

One reason for the Trustees' diffidence was due to a public announcement Marion had made that year. Without warning, at the age of 75 she changed her Christian name by deed poll so that the 'Marion' Burrell everyone knew would now to be known as 'Silvia'. 'Why?' everyone asked, and 'Why Silvia?' 'I have personal reasons' she replied. Was this her final declaration of independence? Nobody knew what made her do it and she had no intention of telling them. The aura of mystery clearly appealed to her. Most of her contemporaries continued to call her Marion, but the younger generation admired her eccentricity, gladly accepting the change, and even though some cheekily referred to her as 'Cousin Saliva', my family addressed her as 'Aunt Silvia'.

Burrell's daughter suffered from a lifelong identity problem. On her birth certificate she was named 'Marion Miller Mitchell Burrell', but her school books were inscribed 'Constance Marion Lockart Burrell'. Then her father gave her a writing case initialled 'C.M.B.', but in adult years she just wanted to be plain Marion Burrell. She had numerous nicknames, 'Burr' at Heathfield, then 'Mary Ann' to Rosemary Craven. Miss Stewart of Broadmeadows was said to call her 'Miriam', though it might have been 'Mirren', the old Scots version of her name. Sholto inscribed the books he gave her 'From S to Darling O' and to 'Matthew' she was 'Darling Marchen'. To Rosemary Watt, who became the Keeper of the Burrell Collection in 1986, she said, 'Marion is such a stolid kind of name but Silvia makes one think of woodland, nature and freedom'. But the wood nymph in Greek mythology was 'Sylvia', spelt with a 'y'. My godmother pointed out to me that her name was spelt with an 'i', like the heroine in Shakespeare's comedy *The Two Gentlemen of Verona*. The play contains these famous lines:

> Who is Silvia? What is she,
> That all our swains commend her?
> Holy, fair, and wise is she;
> The heaven such grace did lend her,
> That she might admired be.

Sholto Douglas's 'Darling O' presents another mystery. Although his own name began with 'S', his 'S and O' could have been Sebastian and Olivia from Shakespeare's *Twelfth Night*. Then there are numerous possible damsels such as Odette, Odile, Ophelia and Oriana, many of whom seemed to fall out with their fathers – the reader may have more ideas. Silvia certainly knew how to put up a hare and let others enjoy the chase.

By the 1980s Silvia was becoming blind like her father before her. She gave up driving and the Rover had to go. Like her father, she began to walk with a white stick and when a Chinese gentleman helped her cross the street and kindly tipped her a shilling she was delighted. A 'reader' was employed to deal with her mail and, when writing became a problem, she bought a large marker pen and wrote in letters which grew until they were nearly two inches high. When her visiting had to be done by train, she remained undaunted and assured her hosts, 'I had a very good journey, thank you. I sat next to such a charming drunk!' In 1983 a railway locomotive was named 'Sir William Burrell', and Miss Silvia Burrell basked in reflected glory when she attended the ceremony performed by Princess Anne.

Having transferred her allegiance to the Church of Scotland, Silvia became a member of Mayfield Parish Church where the minister and congregation took her to their hearts and cherished her for the rest of her life. The Rev. JS Ritchie became a regular visitor and she was never short of friends. When one of them made her a birthday cake she was almost overcome, saying she had never been given one before.

I was driving in Glasgow one day when my car was stuck in a traffic jam next to Anthony Weld-Forester, now Senior Director of Sotheby's. Anthony wound down his window and said 'Why don't you bring Silvia Burrell to our auction preview at Gleneagles so that we can invite her to dine there as Sotheby's guest?' Silvia accepted with pleasure and dazzled us all with her shimmering kaftan and sparkling jewels. Scottish artists were featured in the preview, and that evening Silvia regaled the people she met with anecdotes about members of their families she had known over the years.

The following day was spent in Stirlingshire where I took my godmother on a boat trip to visit the Isle of Inchmahome on the Lake of Menteith. Aunt Silvia wished to pay homage at the grave of Robert Bontine Cunninghame Graham, a hero she had admired from a distance but never actually met. During his life this eccentric Graham of Gartmore became a gaucho in South America as well as a writer and poet, a Socialist Member of Parliament and eventually the first President of the Scottish National Party. Amid the quiet ruins of Inchmahome Priory Silvia laid roses on the gravestone which bears Don Roberto's name, and also his cattle brand mark. Some of his sayings were recorded in her scrap book.

Property: The true primeval curse.

To be a god is to be quite detached from all around.

The Scots: A fine free fornicating pious folk are we.

Silvia made several visits to Pollok Park in Glasgow while the new museum was under construction. Then the great day came on 21 October 1983 when the Burrell Collection would be opened by Her Majesty Queen Elizabeth II. Sir William Burrell's gift to the City of Glasgow was finally complete and a major celebration was arranged. Seven hundred guests were invited to attend the ceremony and civic dignitaries turned out in full force. The Burrell Trustees were also present, but Merrick Mitchell had recently died and, in the absence of his elder brother, Alan had invited Helen Mitchell, who was a friend and no relation, to accompany him. When Helen arrived to collect him Alan was unwell and upset but insisted 'I must not let Merrick down', and so they both set off to Pollok Park.

On the way, Alan explained his distress because there was concern that the Glasgow councillors had monopolized the tickets for the ceremony with little thought for others who had much closer connections with Sir William Burrell and his collection. When invitations were being distributed Lord Muirshiel had been horrified to learn that Sir William's daughter had not been invited. As Chairman of the Burrell Trustees he at once announced that he would not attend the opening ceremony if Miss Burrell were excluded. Belatedly, Silvia received an invitation, plus an offer to include some of her own friends.

When the two Mitchells arrived at the Burrell Collection, Helen was surprised to discover that, unlike Alan and herself, who had been given tickets for the formal luncheon, his sister Ruth had to make do with a picnic in her car. It then transpired that John Maxwell Macdonald of Pollok and his wife had been treated likewise and, to Lord Muirshiel's fury, John's mother had received no recognition although Dame Anne Maxwell Macdonald had donated Pollok House and Estate to the City of Glasgow in 1967, and thereby provided the site for the Burrell Collection.

When the VIPs were lined up to proceed to the platform for the opening ceremony, Alan and Helen were among the elite who were to sit in the front row. Silvia's godson Gavin McGill had been allocated a seat of lower rank when a neighbouring Councillor enquired suspiciously, 'How did you get in here, sonny?' It was planned that Silvia should join the important guests and meet the Queen before the ceremony, so Lord Muirshiel had taken it upon himself to look after Miss Burrell and insisted that she should sit beside him. As the procession was moving off he advised her to follow closely behind him, but when he looked round she was nowhere in sight. Silvia's presentation to the Queen had to be abandoned – nobody knew where she had gone. Just before the ceremony, she reappeared and managed to find a seat next to George Younger, then Secretary of State for Scotland, although it was said that Alastair Auld, Director of the Glasgow Art Galleries and Museums, was left without one and found himself having to kneel on the platform floor. Though octogenarians sometimes get confused Silvia still got about with remarkable ease and was not, as Helen Mitchell later remarked, 'the kind of old lady to get locked in a lavatory!' Nevertheless, the splendid new ladies' loo at the Burrell was so dark and filled with state-of-the-art appliances even normal-sighted people were having trouble, myself included. This might account for my godmother's unexpected absence.

After the ceremony another opportunity was found for Miss Burrell to meet the Queen. This time everything went without a hitch, and Silvia responded with indefatigable charm. When the formalities were safely over she stopped by a painting by Cranach the Elder and exclaimed, 'I remember that one when I was in my nursery!'

Silvia was overjoyed to see her father's ambition finally realized. After all his years of worry over creating a museum to display more than 8,000 precious items, the new building at Pollok Park would surely have pleased him. The Burrell Collection is set amid pastoral surroundings where the clean lined two-storey building rests happily within the scale of Pollok's ancient trees. Its entrance is approached across a wide green sward and inside, galleries with walls of glass seem to merge with the woodland beyond. Following Burrell's wishes, rooms from Hutton Castle have been reconstructed with their original contents so that visitors may see the setting in which his family lived. Both inside and out, Burrell's genius has added distinction through the medieval stonework which he purchased from property of the late William Randolph Hearst. Modern construction in stone and glass has been enhanced by Gothic and Romanesque windows and arches. The museum entrance is formed by a massive portal from Hornby Castle in Yorkshire. To arrive early and watch the great doors draw slowly apart was for me an unforgettable experience.

The opening of the Burrell Collection received a tumultuous accolade as the museum became one of Scotland's most popular tourist attractions. That year Dr Richard Marks, Keeper of the Burrell Collection, paid Sir William a handsome tribute with his excellent biography entitled *Burrell: Portrait of a Collector.* The Burrell Collection soon became a national treasure while causing a stir throughout the art world. Lord Muirshiel took pleasure in the public response but a few years later he became concerned when the museum came under the collective management of Glasgow Museums and ceased to have a Keeper of its own. He feared that Sir William's creation had been downgraded, and predicted that the change could damage prestige and reduce the Burrell Collection's international status.

Sir William was at heart an immensely generous man who longed to share his magnificent collection and strove to benefit mankind by endowing his life's work to the City of Glasgow. With this amazing gift to crown his labours he saw no need to be portrayed by an artist or have his name carved in stone, because the Burrell Collection would be his epitaph. Although he was a retiring man whose family problems furthered his retreat from public scrutiny, Burrell will always rank among Scotland's great men. He is part of our national heritage and, like his collection, Burrell's remarkable story should belong to future generations with the exhibits pertaining to his life and family history kept permanently on view. With all his eccentricities he was a brilliant and intensely human being whose bountiful collection has been given to us all.

The Burrell Collection enjoys the rarity of having been assembled by one man. The astonishing range of the collector's interest is reflected by the items he acquired, from heavy Tudor furniture and relics from Egyptian tombs, to strands of delicate needlepoint lace and tiny Chinese creatures carved in jade. His passion for history and pageantry is displayed by suits of armour, medieval heraldry, tapestry and stained glass. Burrell's interests drew him into ever-widening fields, penetrating other continents and civilizations. Whether exotic or earthly every aspect of humanity seeks to be revealed. Both humour and pathos are found among the saints and sinners, the beggars and the ballet dancers, the mounted jockeys and the artful gypsies who offer us a gateway to the mind of William Burrell. The collector is always there among his treasures, and a day may come when a perceptive visitor will suddenly glimpse two tall shadowy figures and briefly recognize the silver-haired gentleman with his enraptured daughter, browsing happily together among the exhibits.

Epilogue

News of the Burrell Collection spread round the world and soon reached New Zealand. Silvia was delighted when her cousins from Canterbury on South Island arrived in Scotland – at last she was able to meet Jean Wightman and Peg Oldfield. The sisters were granddaughters of her uncle Adam Burrell, and it was a joy to welcome and share with them her father's great achievement. The New Zealand members of her family have helped to confirm that among Adam's descendants, as well as those of William and George, 'Burrell' males have ceased to exist, so nobody who bears that name is closely related to the collector.

As years went by Silvia's strength began to fail, but her spirit never did. After she fell in the street and broke her arm suggestions of sheltered care were dismissed with disdain, although some part-time help was accepted. Alone at home, aged 89, she fell in her bath and was injured. It was two days before she was rescued and taken to hospital.

Once she was sufficiently recovered, Silvia returned to Findhorn Place, but when a van arrived with 'Aids for the Disabled' they were instantly rejected. 'Those contraptions are for invalids', she declared, 'How can you expect me to recover if I start to rely on those things?'

When the end came a few months later the newspapers announced that Silvia Miller Mitchell Burrell had died at Findhorn Place on 4 January 1992. She had suffered a heart attack, though to the last her sparkle never ceased. On the previous day I had phoned to thank her for a handsome Christmas cheque. Then we enjoyed a lively discussion on how many geans, wild cherry trees, could be bought to enhance the avenue at Ballindalloch. Our conversation ended on a merry note with Silvia's anecdote about an African lady who was laundering clothes in a river when a crocodile tried to bite off her arm. But the victim artfully escaped by stuffing the monster's mouth with her washing so that it couldn't shut! While we both laughed I pictured Silvia rocking with glee as she threw back her head and chuckled.

Like her father's collection, Silvia Burrell was unique. With a well-tuned brain, a capacious memory and wit like a rapier, she was interesting because she was interested, and her mind seemed to overflow with fascinating information. Blessed with an endearing sense of fun, she was consistently entertaining, passionate and sympathetic. From her youth she possessed that effervescent magnetism which made William Burrell perceive his daughter's potential and embark on a strategy destined to wreck her life. A lesser mortal could have been destroyed, but Silvia was made of stronger stuff. Her warmth enfolded the people she met because she had learned that the secret of happiness lies in creating it, and throughout her life she was rewarded with the endless joy that she found in the happiness of others.

Canon Rodney Grant was among many friends who attended her funeral, and after hearing the address by the Rev. JS Ritchie, the Canon conducted a requiem in Silvia's memory at St Aidan's Church, just as he had done for her mother.

I had once suggested to Aunt Silvia that her story should be recorded and she replied, 'I did try to do it, but my father would have said it was just tittle-tattle'. Nevertheless, her dear friend Caird Wilson, whose family had supported her escape, persuaded her to write down some of her stories. Recording happy memories proved to be therapeutic. Not a word was directed against her parents, and her mother was mentioned only four times. The fuller story could then be pieced together from clues at Findhorn Place where Silvia had carefully preserved all her documents and the records concerning her desperate escape. It was not easy to draw her out, but sometimes she would talk of the past. A chink in her armour appeared when I asked, 'Aunt Silvia, after all you have suffered, how is it that you never seem embittered?' and she replied, 'Oh, but I am!' Though the ghosts of the past continued to haunt her she would not give way, for hers is a tale of triumph over adversity and, in spite of her troubles, Silvia Burrell ensured that her story would have a happy ending.

When bequests were granted to relations and friends Silvia also remembered the kind policeman at Hutton who had befriended her. Sadly Frank Whyte died too soon to receive her grateful gift but others benefited from her generosity. During her years at Findhorn Place she continued to live frugally, so nobody could have guessed that she was going to endow a lifeboat. The news came as a complete surprise, just as she had intended. Because her father's success was owed to the wealth he derived from the Burrell fleet, she had always admired the men who go to sea in ships. Silvia paid tribute to their gallantry by leaving her considerable estate to the Royal National Lifeboat Institution. She felt particular concern for lifeboat crews in remote and inhospitable outposts where deeds of heroism often escape the public eye, so for many years she had knitted warm Aran wool mittens and, whenever a set was complete, she would send them off to a deserving lifeboat crew. Before her sight failed Silvia had knitted almost 500 pairs, and grateful letters from the coxswains of many lifeboat stations gave her boundless pleasure.

When she could no longer see to knit, Aunt Silvia came to stay with us and brought with her a small ball of Aran wool. While she was entertaining us as usual, our family nearly went mad as we watched her systematically rewinding her wool over and over again. At the end of her visit she warmly wished us farewell and as she was departing, quietly dropped her ball of wool into a wastepaper bin.

With £680,000 of Silvia's legacy the RNLI was able to build one of their new Mersey Class Lifeboats which was allocated to the Lifeboat Station at Girvan in Ayrshire, a county she knew well. She had asked for her lifeboat to be named just *Silvia*, but in the end everyone agreed that her full name should be used. On 16 October 1993 hundreds gathered at Girvan harbour for the naming of the RNLB *Silvia Burrell*. I was deeply touched to be invited to perform the ceremony. As a shipbuilder's wife I had attended many launches, but never launched a ship. To celebrate my godmother in this way was, for me, the greatest honour. That day I proudly wore the turtle brooch that William Burrell had given his small daughter to commemorate the launching of the *Strathlorne* more than 80 years before. Though Girvan's day of celebration was all too quickly over, the spirit of Burrell's daughter lives on.

Bibliography

An asterisk indicates material which belonged to Marion Burrell.

Anson, Clodagh, 1957. *Victorian Days*,* The Richards Press, London.

Arthur, Liz, 1995. *Embroidery at the Burrell Collection 1600–1700*, John Murray in association with Glasgow Museums, London.

Barrie, JM, 1922. *Courage*,* Hodder and Stoughton, London.

Barrow, John 1906. *Captain Cook's Voyages of Discovery*,* JM Dent, London.

Best, Elsdon, 1924. *The Maori as He Was*,* R.E.Owen, Wellington, New Zealand.

Bolotho, Hector, 1936. *James Lyle Mackay, 1st Earl of Inchcape*, John Murray, London.

Burrell, David, 1975. 'Burrell's *Straths*'*, *Sea Breezes: The magazine of ships and the sea*, 49: 352, 353, 354,355.

Cartland, Barbara, 1970. *We Danced all Night*, Hutchinson and Co., London.

Charteris, Leslie, 1937. translation of *Juan Belmonte Killer of Bulls*,* Heinemann, London.

Cronin, AJ, 1931. *Hatter's Castle*,* Victor Gollancz Ltd, London.

Cunninghame Graham, RB, 1936. *Rodeo*, Windmill Press, London.

Cunninghame Graham, RB, 1937. *Don Roberto*,* Windmill Press, London.

Drummond Gauld H, 1935. *Brave Borderland*,* Thomas Nelson & Sons, Edinburgh.

Edgar, Madalen, 1907. *Stories from Scottish History*,* Harrap, London.

Fowle, Frances, 2010. *Van Gogh's Twin*, National Galleries of Scotland, Edinburgh.

Grimble, Arthur, 1952. *A Pattern of Islands*,* John Murray, London.

Hamilton, Vivien, 1990. *Joseph Crawhall*, John Murray in association with Glasgow Museums, London.

Hamilton, Vivien, 1992. *Boudin at Trouville*, Glasgow Museums, Glasgow.

Hart Davis, Rupert and Holland, Merlin, 1988. *The Complete Letters of Oscar Wilde*, Fourth Estate, London.

Hodgson JC, 1922. 'The Township of Bassington', *Archaeologia Aeliana*.

Jolly, Cyril, 1958. *Henry Blogg of Cromer*,* Harrap, London.

Johnston, Ian, 2000. *Ships for a Nation*, West Dunbartonshire Libraries & Museums, Dumbarton.

Kinross, Lord Patrick Balfour, 1977. *The Ottoman Centuries*,* Morrow Quill Paperbacks, New York.

Lycett Green, Candida, 1994 & 1995. *John Betjeman Letters* vol. 1 1926–1951, vol. 2 1951–1984, Methuen Publishing Ltd, London.

MacDonald, Hugh, 1880. *Rambles Round Glasgow*, Dunn and Wright, Glasgow.

Mackaness, George, 1938. *A Book of the 'Bounty'*,* a selection from Bligh's writings, Everyman, London.

Marks, Richard, 1983. *Burrell, Portrait of a Collector*,* Richard Drew Publishing Ltd, Glasgow.

MacLeod, John, 2011. *River of Fire: The Clydebank Blitz*, Birlinn, Edinburgh.

Miller, Alice Duer, 1941. *The White Cliffs*,* Methuen, London.

Munthe, Axel, 1929. *The Story of San Michele*,* John Murray, London.

Oakley, CA, 1946. *The Second City,* Blackie, Glasgow.

O'Neill, Eugene, 1923. *The Moon of the Caribbees*,* Jonathan Cape, London.

Owen, DDR, 1994. *The Romance of Reynard the Fox*, Oxford University Press, Oxford.

Pigot's *Directory of Northumberland*.

Seymour, Miranda, 1992. *Ottoline Morrell*, Sceptre Books, London.

Van der Post, Laurens, 1958. *The World of the Kalahari*,* Penguin, London.

Varian, HF, 1952. *Some African Milestones*,* George Ronald, Oxford.

Webster, Jack, 1997. *From Dali to Burrell*, B&W Publishing, Glasgow.

Whipple, ABC, 1980. *The Clipper Ships*, Time-Life Books, Chicago.

Wordsdall, Frank, 1979. *The Tenement Way of Life,* Chambers, Edinburgh.

Photographic Credits

Plate 1 is reproduced courtesy of the Scottish Maritime Museum.

Plate 2 is from the Mitchell Library's collection and is © CSG CIC Glasgow Libraries Collection.

Plates 3, 4–7, 10, 12–14, 46–48, 54, 65, 70–73, 75, 77–90, 97–112, 117, are all from the Burrell Collection and are © CSG CIC Glasgow Museums Collection.

Plate 8 is reproduced courtesy of Alan Mitchell.

Plate 11: John Henry Lorimer, Sir Robert Stodart Lorimer, 1864–1929, architect. Courtesy of the Scottish National Portrait Gallery.

Plates 76 and 91–96 are reproduced courtesy of private collections.

Plates 113 and 114 are reproduced courtesy of Sotheby's.

All other photographs are from the author's collection.

Index

Compiled by AMM Stephen

Lightning Source UK Ltd.
Milton Keynes UK
UKOW06f2244280415

250518UK00011B/44/P